MW01157073

THE NEW COLLEGEVILLE
BIBLE COMMENTARY

FIRST AND SECOND SAMUEL

Feidhlimidh T. Magennis

SERIES EDITOR

Daniel Durken, O.S.B.

LITURGICAL PRESS
Collegeville, Minnesota

www.litpress.org

Nihil Obstat: Reverend Robert C. Harren, J.C.L., *Censor deputatus.*
Imprimatur: ✠ Most Reverend John F. Kinney, J.C.D., D.D., Bishop of St. Cloud, Minnesota, October 14, 2011.

Design by Ann Blattner.

Cover illustration: *David Anthology* by Donald Jackson. Copyright 2010 *The Saint John's Bible*, Order of Saint Benedict, Collegeville, Minnesota USA. Used by permission. Scripture quotations are from the New Revised Standard Version of the Bible, Catholic Edition, copyright 1989, 1993 National Council of the Churches of Christ in the United States of America. Used by permission. All right reserved.

Photos: pages 10, 121, 142, Thinkstock.com; pages 53, 72, 103, 111, Wikimedia Commons.

Maps created by Robert Cronan of Lucidity Information Design, LLC.

Scripture texts used in this work are taken from the *New American Bible, revised edition* © 2010, 1991, 1986, 1970 Confraternity of Christian Doctrine, Inc., Washington, DC. All Rights Reserved. No part of this work may be reproduced or transmitted in any form or by any means, electronic or mechanical, including photocopying, recording, or by any information storage and retrieval system, without permission in writing from the copyright owner.

1   2   3   4   5   6   7   8   9

Library of Congress Cataloging-in-Publication Data

Magennis, Feidhlimidh.
    First and Second Samuel / Feidhlimidh Magennis.
        p.   cm. — (The new Collegeville Bible commentary. Old Testament ; v. 8)
    Includes index.
    ISBN 978-0-8146-2842-3
        1. Bible. O.T. Samuel—Commentaries.   I. Title.

BS1325.53.M34 2011
222'.4077—dc23
                                                        2011037878

CONTENTS

ABBREVIATIONS

Books of the Bible

Acts—Acts of the Apostles
Amos—Amos
Bar—Baruch
1 Chr—1 Chronicles
2 Chr—2 Chronicles
Col—Colossians
1 Cor—1 Corinthians
2 Cor—2 Corinthians
Dan—Daniel
Deut—Deuteronomy
Eccl (or Qoh)—Ecclesiastes
Eph—Ephesians
Esth—Esther
Exod—Exodus
Ezek—Ezekiel
Ezra—Ezra
Gal—Galatians
Gen—Genesis
Hab—Habakkuk
Hag—Haggai
Heb—Hebrews
Hos—Hosea
Isa—Isaiah
Jas—James
Jdt—Judith
Jer—Jeremiah
Job—Job
Joel—Joel
John—John
1 John—1 John
2 John—2 John
3 John—3 John
Jonah—Jonah
Josh—Joshua
Jude—Jude
Judg—Judges
1 Kgs—1 Kings

2 Kgs—2 Kings
Lam—Lamentations
Lev—Leviticus
Luke—Luke
1 Macc—1 Maccabees
2 Macc—2 Maccabees
Mal—Malachi
Mark—Mark
Matt—Matthew
Mic—Micah
Nah—Nahum
Neh—Nehemiah
Num—Numbers
Obad—Obadiah
1 Pet—1 Peter
2 Pet—2 Peter
Phil—Philippians
Phlm—Philemon
Prov—Proverbs
Ps(s)—Psalms
Rev—Revelation
Rom—Romans
Ruth—Ruth
1 Sam—1 Samuel
2 Sam—2 Samuel
Sir—Sirach
Song—Song of Songs
1 Thess—1 Thessalonians
2 Thess—2 Thessalonians
1 Tim—1 Timothy
2 Tim—2 Timothy
Titus—Titus
Tob—Tobit
Wis—Wisdom
Zech—Zechariah
Zeph—Zephaniah

The Books of First and Second Samuel

Composition

The books of Samuel are part of a larger continuous history of the Israelites, from their entrance to Canaan under Joshua to the deportation to Babylon in 587 B.C. This extensive narrative is called the Deuteronomistic History because its editors based their theology on the teachings of the book of Deuteronomy. The Deuteronomists were a reformist movement in seventh century Judah who promoted fidelity to the Mosaic covenant: God had chosen and liberated Israel from slavery and granted them the land where they would live out their relationship with God. Through Moses, God offers the people a choice: if they are faithful to the covenant laws, they will prosper; if they are disobedient, they can expect punishment through disaster, invasion, or exile. The Deuteronomistic History is the story of the people's response. The history was first composed in the time of King Josiah (640–609 B.C.) and underwent expansion and revisions during the Babylonian exile. The History was divided into "books" for ease of handling. In the later Greek translation, known as the Septuagint, such division created 1 and 2 Samuel as we know them.

Sources

The composers of 1–2 Samuel made use of older materials, both oral and written. Two sources probably date back to the time of David and Solomon. Scholars call one of the narratives "The History of David's Rise" (1 Sam 16–2 Sam 5). Although the other has been called "The Succession Narrative" (2 Sam 9–20), the narrative seems to focus more on relations within David's family than on the actual succession. The composers of 1–2 Samuel also incorporated shorter narrative cycles and other traditions to create a complex, yet sustained account of a significant period of Israelite history. These Deuteronomist editors tell a story that illustrates their theological views, but they do not completely suppress the views of older material. Thus a multiplicity of "voices" enriches the presentation of the transition taking place.

Narrative art

The subject matter deals with political, personal, and theological issues. To allow these different aspects to be heard and to interact, the writers make use of artistic storytelling; they create a skillful narrative which presents the events, the personalities, and the issues. A key component of this art is the use of speech. Both in the longer set speeches and in the interplay of dialogue, characters interact to influence and persuade, to express motivation and desire, and to shape the reader's understanding of issues. The conscientious reader will pay attention to what the narrator shows, while keeping the larger picture in sight. In doing so, some key ideas emerge.

A period of transition

A transition is occurring in Israelite society, from a scattered, tribal confederacy to a unified, centralized state. The certainties of the old ways have been giving way to an uncertain future. The old ways were not ideal: change is needed to save the people from injustice and oppression. Yet there are aspects of the old ways that must not be left behind: the fundamental nature of the covenant society must be retrieved and represented in the new order. From Hannah's opening prayer, these agendas of change and conservation compete within the books.

Key to the covenant relationship is the question of leadership. Israel has only one true King, the Lord. God's leadership is manifested through human intermediaries. In the period of the Judges, leaders were chosen individually by God for specific tasks. Under the monarchy, leadership is permanent and dynastic. New circumstances require new leaders, yet God's freedom to choose and de-select leaders must be protected. The resolution of this tension is a key issue of the books of Samuel.

Displacement

The long succession of leaders in 1–2 Samuel—Eli, Samuel, Saul, Jonathan, David, Absalom—serves to illustrate the tension between divine choice and human planning. The narrative tells of several attempts to pass power from father to son that are thwarted by the Lord (Eli, Samuel). As a result, accession to power is by displacement. Even when the old guard seeks to exercise paternal control over the new (cf. Samuel over Saul in chaps. 10–15), the Lord guards his prerogative to cast down the old and raise up new leaders (cf. 1 Sam 2:6). The dynastic principle seems to rule out the Lord's freedom to choose. But displacement creates instability and uncertainty. While various human actors attempt to smooth the dynamics of displacement by transfer of allegiance (Jonathan, Michal, Abner), it is the Lord alone who can change the dynamics of displacement to allow for dynastic succession (cf. 2 Sam 7). But even here, the Lord retains the freedom to choose which son will succeed.

Power and prophecy

The ability to choose a successor is a clear demonstration of power over the future. The books of Samuel are deeply interested in the possession, use, and abuse of power. All power and authority devolves from the Lord, and in a covenant society the use of power must comply with the norms of the covenant. In simple terms, humans must obey the Lord in their dealings with one another. Leaders must also be faithful to the Lord's commands or forfeit their position. A critical issue emerges: how is one to know God's will on specific occasions? As well as the emergence of monarchy, the narrative tells of the development of new forms of divine guidance, whether priestly or prophetic. Kings cannot use power for personal benefit without reference to the divine plan. The prophetic vision supplies reminders of God-given norms. Mistakes will be made, as Saul and David amply demonstrate, but divine guidance is on hand to correct and rectify sin.

By the end of 2 Samuel, the key institutions of a monarchical form of covenant society are in place. The transition has been negotiated and a new future opens for Israel. These books enable the modern reader to grow in hope that the God of the covenant will remain faithful to his people as they struggle to find contemporary forms of community in a changing world.

Outline of the Books of Samuel

1 Sam 1–3	Hannah's Gift
1 Sam 4–6	The Ark Narratives
1 Sam 7–15	The Transition to Monarchy
1 Sam 16–2 Sam 5	The Rise of David
2 Sam 5–8	The Reign of David
2 Sam 9–20	The Family of David
2 Sam 21–24	Appendices

The Books of
First and Second Samuel

I. The Last Judges, Eli and Samuel

1 **Elkanah and His Family at Shiloh.** ¹There was a certain man from Ramathaim, a Zuphite from the hill country of Ephraim. His name was Elkanah, the son of Jeroham, son of Elihu, son of Tohu, son of Zuph, an Ephraimite. ²He had two wives, one named Hannah, the other Peninnah; Peninnah had children, but Hannah had no children. ³Each year this man went up from his city to worship and offer sacrifice to the Lord of hosts at Shiloh, where the two sons of Eli, Hophni and Phinehas, were ministering

HANNAH'S GIFT

1 Samuel 1–3

The opening chapters of 1 Samuel are dominated by Hannah and her prayer. In a situation where "everyone did what was right in their own sight" (Judg 21:25), she does what she thinks best for herself and for Israel: the provision of a new leader attuned to the Lord's will who shall replace uninformed priestly corruption. To understand her predicament, and Israel's, the reader should review Judges 17–21.

1:1-28 Hannah's prayer

As in Judges 17:1 and 19:1, this story begins with a man from the hill country of Ephraim (1:1). The anarchy of the closing chapters of Judges is not far away. That chaos is attributed by the narrator to the absence of a king (Judg 17:6; 18:1; 19:1; 21:25). While Elkinah's background is foreboding, the echoes of Judges 13:2 are hopeful: there, a barren wife became the mother of a savior. Will the same happen to Hannah, despite the fraught

▶ This symbol indicates a cross reference number in the *Catechism of the Catholic Church*. See page 165 for number citations.

as priests of the LORD. ⁴When the day came for Elkanah to offer sacrifice, he used to give portions to his wife Peninnah and to all her sons and daughters, ⁵but he would give a double portion to Hannah because he loved her, though the LORD had closed her womb. ⁶Her rival, to upset her, would torment her constantly, since the LORD had closed her womb. ⁷Year after year, when she went up to the house of the LORD, Peninnah would provoke her, and Hannah would weep and refuse to eat. ⁸Elkanah, her husband, would say to her: "Hannah, why are you weeping? Why are you not eating? Why are you so miserable? Am I not better for you than ten sons?"

Hannah's Prayer. ⁹Hannah rose after one such meal at Shiloh, and presented herself before the LORD; at the time Eli the priest was sitting on a chair near the doorpost of the LORD's temple. ¹⁰In her bitterness she prayed to the LORD, weeping freely, ¹¹and made this vow: "O LORD of hosts, if you look with pity on the hardship of your servant, if you remember me and do not forget me, if you give your handmaid a male child, I will give him to the LORD all the days of his life. No razor shall ever touch his head." ¹²As

familial relationships? The family travels regularly to worship in Shiloh, a place most recently associated with the abuse of women (Judg 21:19-21). While Elkinah favors Hannah with a double portion, his action seems self-centered: "Am I not better for you than ten sons?" (1:8). This triggers Peninah's vindictive treatment of her co-wife. Hannah's situation is distressing, but the narrator suggests a deeper conflict. The Lord has made Hannah barren (1:5). Hannah's problems with Elkinah and Peninah are due to the Lord (1:6). It is with the Lord that she must take issue. In verses 1-8, the narrator has sketched out a family crisis which is both theological in nature and national in scope. Hannah's problems reflect Israel's crisis of relationship with the Lord. What will Hannah do?

1:9-19 Hannah's case

Hannah takes up her case with the Lord. Her prayer leads to a resolution of sorts. Hannah passes from fasting and weeping (1:8) to eating and being no longer downhearted (1:18). But appearances are misleading. When Eli learns that she is not drunk but pouring out her troubles to the Lord, he assures her that the request will be granted without knowing its content. As a solution to her affliction she had asked for a male child and then vowed to dedicate the child to the Lord (1:11). The terms of the dedication echo the angel's description of Samson (Judg 13:4-5). Hannah's concern may appear personal, but her vow has national implications. She wants a judge! The child who will save her from torment will also save Israel. As the official representative of the Lord, Eli accepts and blesses a plan at odds with

11

"A son of Jesse of Bethlehem [David] is a skillful harpist. He is also a brave warrior, an able speaker, and a handsome young man. The LORD is certainly with him" (1 Samuel 16:18). A Roman sculpture of David.

she continued praying before the LORD, Eli watched her mouth, [13]for Hannah was praying silently; though her lips were moving, her voice could not be heard. Eli, thinking she was drunk, [14]said to her, "How long will you make a drunken spectacle of yourself? Sober up from your wine!" [15]"No, my lord!" Hannah answered. "I am an unhappy woman. I have had neither wine nor liquor; I was only pouring out my heart to the LORD. [16]Do not think your servant a worthless woman; my prayer has been prompted by my deep sorrow and misery." [17]Eli said, "Go in peace, and may the God of Israel grant you what you have requested." [18]She replied, "Let your servant find favor in your eyes," and left. She went to her quarters, ate and drank with her husband, and no longer appeared downhearted. [19]Early the next morning they worshiped before the LORD, and then returned to their home in Ramah. When they returned Elkanah had intercourse with his wife Hannah, and the LORD remembered her.

Hannah Bears a Son. [20]She conceived and, at the end of her pregnancy, bore a son whom she named Samuel. "Because I asked the LORD for him." [21]The next time her husband Elkanah was going up with the rest of his household to offer the customary sacrifice to the LORD and to fulfill his vows, [22]Hannah did not go, explaining to her husband, "Once the child is weaned, I will take him to appear before the LORD and leave him there forever." [23]Her husband Elkanah answered her: "Do what you think best; wait until you have weaned him. Only may the LORD fulfill his word!" And so she remained at home and nursed her son until she had weaned him.

Hannah Presents Samuel to the Lord. [24]Once he was weaned, she brought him up with her, along with a three-year-old

---

the Lord's usual manner of appointing a judge. His reply in verse 17 plays on the consonants of the Hebrew verb "to ask" which also spell out the name, Saul. Is there a gap between what Hannah asks for and what the Lord plans?

1:20-23 Samuel's birth

The action moves quickly to the birth of the child. But while this is the child "asked for" (Saul), Hannah calls him Samuel. The confusion over the name may indicate a tension between divine and human intentions. Furthermore, when Elkinah asserts his role as dominant parent, Hannah refuses to release the child (1:21-22). This is a strange assertion of female rights, not only against the husband but against the Lord. Hannah will fulfill the vow on her terms. Elkinah's acquiescence introduces another note of foreboding: "Do what you think best" (1:23; cf. Judg 21:2).

1:24-28 Samuel's dedication

At last Hannah brings the child to Shiloh and hands him over to Eli (1:24-25). Her comments acknowledge that the child is the answer to her

bull, an ephah of flour, and a skin of wine, and presented him at the house of the LORD in Shiloh. ²⁵After they had slaughtered the bull, they brought the child to Eli. ²⁶Then Hannah spoke up: "Excuse me, my lord! As you live, my lord, I am the woman who stood here near you, praying to the LORD. ²⁷I prayed for this child, and the LORD granted my request. ²⁸Now I, in turn, give him to the LORD; as long as he lives, he shall be dedicated to the LORD." Then they worshiped there before the LORD.

2 ¹And Hannah prayed:

"My heart exults in the LORD,
    my horn is exalted by my God.
I have swallowed up my enemies;
    I rejoice in your victory.
²There is no Holy One like the LORD;
    there is no Rock like our God.
³Speak boastfully no longer,
    Do not let arrogance issue from
        your mouths.
For an all-knowing God is the LORD,
    a God who weighs actions.

prayer, as Eli promised (1:17). Hannah will now fulfill her vow to the Lord. The verbs of verse 28 ("give," "dedicate") are various forms of the verb "to ask." Samuel is the child asked for; he is now given to the Lord. Samuel is dedicated to the Lord by his mother to save her from affliction (and Israel from anarchy). Hannah's intentions complicate the birth of a savior. The child is given by the Lord, but is also given to the Lord. There is a double origin and claim on the child which could lead to confusion. This very personal problem foreshadows some confusing national solutions to Israel's crisis.

2:1-10 Hannah's song

Hannah closes her conflict with the Lord, the cause of her barrenness, by praising the God who grants her a child. Her song expands beyond her personal situation to include the Lord's dealings with his people. That double focus is suitable for a story which has personal and national dimensions.

The opening six lines (2:1-2) express praise and exaltation in the God who grants victory. The descriptions of God are similar to Psalm 113: this is a God who saves those who call on him. The song then addresses the audience and establishes its theme; a contrast is outlined between boasting and silence (2:3). The haughty will be deposed in favor of the humble by the God who knows and judges all actions.

The core section (2:4-8b) outlines a series of reversals in which the proud are humbled and the lowly raised up. In verses 4-6a there is a downward movement as the established are deposed. At the lowest point, death, an upward movement towards life begins (2:6).

13

4"The bows of the mighty are broken,
  while the tottering gird on
    strength.
5The well-fed hire themselves out
    for bread,
  while the hungry no longer
    have to toil.
The barren wife bears seven sons,
  while the mother of many lan-
    guishes.

6"The LORD puts to death and gives
    life,
  casts down to Sheol and brings
    up again.
7The LORD makes poor and makes
    rich,
  humbles, and also exalts.
8He raises the needy from the dust;
  from the ash heap lifts up the
    poor,
To seat them with nobles

and make a glorious throne
  their heritage.

"For the pillars of the earth are the
    LORD's,
  and he has set the world upon
    them.
9He guards the footsteps of his
    faithful ones,
  but the wicked shall perish in
    the darkness;
  for not by strength does one
    prevail.
10The LORD's foes shall be shattered;
  the Most High in heaven
    thunders;
  the LORD judges the ends of the
    earth.
May he give strength to his king,
  and exalt the horn of his
    anointed!"

The reason for reversal is outlined, beginning with "For" in verse 8c. The celebration of reversal and exaltation is a celebration of the power of God who establishes life and death. Such power is rooted in God's creative activity (2:8c-9a). The Lord creates and establishes order. God sets all things in place and supervises their unfolding. The song ends with a prayer that God will include the king in this manifestation of his saving care (2:10c). The saving help experienced by the poet ("my horn," 2:1) is to be experienced by all in the action of the king ("horn of his anointed," 2:10). This is the first explicit mention of a king. It does not seem to flow from the story. But, following on from Judges 17–21, Hannah's problem occurs in the absence of a king. Hannah took the initiative and forced the hand of the Lord to produce a savior. The song put in her mouth gives a positive understanding of God's salvation as liberation from the mighty. Still, such salvation requires an agent. Hannah looks for a judge, while the book's compilers look for a king. There is a divergence between the expectations of the traditional materials and of the book's editors. At best, God's anointed will be one who implements God's defeat of the haughty and exaltation of the humble. But will Samuel, Hannah's child, achieve that ideal?

The song resembles the Magnificat of Luke's gospel (Luke 1:46-55) at various points: a song of a virgin mother who is gifted with a child, a cele-

[11]When Elkanah returned home to Ramah, the child remained in the service of the LORD under the priest Eli.

Wickedness of Eli's Sons. [12]Now the sons of Eli were wicked; they had respect neither for the LORD [13]nor for the priests' duties toward the people. When someone offered a sacrifice, the priest's servant would come with a three-pronged fork, while the meat was still boiling, [14]and would thrust it into the basin, kettle, caldron, or pot. Whatever the fork brought up, the priest would take for himself. They treated all the Israelites who came to the sanctuary at Shiloh in this way. [15]In fact, even before the fat was burned, the priest's servant would come and say to the one offering the sacrifice, "Give me some meat to roast for the priest. He will not accept boiled meat from you, only raw meat." [16]And if this one protested, "Let the fat be burned first, then take whatever you wish," he would reply, "No, give it to me now, or else I will take it by force." [17]Thus the young men sinned grievously in the presence of the LORD, treating the offerings to the LORD with disdain.

bration of reversals, praise of the saving God who grants a king. Yet that child-king is different. He is God's gift and initiative and so can fully implement God's will for his people.

2:11-36 The haughty fall; the humble rise

The remainder of chapter 2 contrasts the rise of Samuel with the fall of the house of Eli. Thus the reversal proclaimed in Hannah's song begins to take place. The unit is punctuated by references to Samuel in the service of the Lord (2:11, 18; 3:1), a role in which he grows in stature and estimation (2:21, 26; 3:19). Between these framing references are two passages about Eli's sons and a further report about Hannah, contrasting the fortunes of the two families. This sets the scene for the announcement of doom for Eli's family in 2:27-36.

2:12-17 The sons of Eli

The sons of Eli were introduced in 1:3 as ministers at the Shiloh sanctuary. This passage tells how they abuse their position. Contrary to customary practice (outlined in vv. 11-14), their servant would take sacrificial portions that still have fat on them (2:15-16). As this practice is not described in the Pentateuch, the details are uncertain, but it would seem that the fat of the sacrificial animal was reserved to the Lord and so burnt in sacrifice: boiling the meat removes the fat to prepare it for human consumption. The sons of Eli claim the fatty portions and display a lack of reverence for the Lord (2:17). They are the haughty whom Hannah seeks to overthrow.

The Lord Rewards Hannah. [18]Meanwhile the boy Samuel, wearing a linen ephod, was serving in the presence of the LORD. [19]His mother used to make a little garment for him, which she would bring him each time she went up with her husband to offer the customary sacrifice. [20]And Eli would bless Elkanah and his wife, as they were leaving for home. He would say, "May the LORD repay you with children from this woman for the gift she has made to the LORD!" [21]The LORD favored Hannah so that she conceived and gave birth to three more sons and two daughters, while young Samuel grew up in the service of the LORD.

Eli's Futile Rebuke. [22]When Eli was very old, he kept hearing how his sons were treating all Israel, and that they were behaving promiscuously with the women serving at the entry of the meeting tent. [23]So he said to them: "Why are you doing such things? I hear from everyone that your behavior is depraved. [24]Stop this, my sons! The report that I hear the LORD's people spreading is not good. [25]If someone sins against another, anyone can intercede for the sinner with the LORD; but if anyone sins against the LORD, who can intercede for the sinner?" But they disregarded their father's warning, since the LORD wanted them dead. [26]Meanwhile, young Samuel was growing in stature and in worth in the estimation of the LORD and the people.

The Fate of Eli's House. [27]A man of God came to Eli and said to him: "Thus says the LORD: I went so far as to reveal

2:18-21 Eli blesses Elkinah and Hannah

In contrast, Samuel's parents visit regularly to offer sacrifice and to bring Samuel garments appropriate for a servant of the Lord. Eli blesses Elkinah and his wife with words that recall Samuel's status as "dedicated to the LORD" (1:28; 2:20), implicitly contrasting Samuel with his own sons. Hannah is clearly blessed as she bears five more children, almost reaching the total listed in her song (2:5b).

2:22-26 Reversing positions

The narrative returns to the crisis of Eli's sons. Verse 22b makes the crime explicit and contrasts it with the zeal of another Phinehas (Num 25:6-15) who saved the people by killing the sinners. Eli's sons are doomed to die for their sins. The words of Eli (2:24-25) spell out the warning while the narrator supports Eli's concern by noting that the Lord has already decided on their death. They have grown great in sin while Samuel continues to grow in the presence of the Lord (2:26). The reversal of positions is almost completed.

2:27-36 A prophetic oracle

A mysterious man of God delivers an oracle of doom to Eli concerning the displacement of his family, descendants of Moses, from the priesthood,

myself to your father's house when they were in Egypt as slaves to the house of Pharaoh. ²⁸I chose them out of all the tribes of Israel to be my priests, to go up to my altar, to burn incense, and to wear the ephod in my presence; and I assigned all the fire offerings of the Israelites to your father's house. ²⁹Why do you stare greedily at my sacrifices and at the offerings that I have prescribed? Why do you honor your sons more than you honor me, fattening yourselves with the choicest part of every offering of my people Israel? ³⁰This, therefore, is the oracle of the LORD, the God of Israel: I said in the past that your family and your father's house should minister in my presence forever. But now—oracle of the LORD: Far be it from me! I will honor those who honor me, but those who despise me shall be cursed. ³¹Yes, the days are coming when I will break your strength and the strength of your father's house, so that no one in your family lives to old age. ³²You shall witness, like a disappointed rival, all the benefits enjoyed by Israel, but no member of your household shall ever grow old. ³³I will leave you one man at my altar to wear out his eyes and waste his strength, but the rest of your family shall die by the sword. ³⁴This is a sign for you—what happens to your two sons, Hophni and Phinehas. Both of them will die on the same day. ³⁵I will choose a faithful priest who shall do what I have

and its replacement by descendents of Aaron in the person of Zadok. In common with other prophetic oracles, the passage recalls past gracious action and present sins and pronounces judgment. The description of past graces (2:27b-28) climaxes in permission to offer fire offerings; the actions of 2:12-17 are transgressions of this privilege. The accusation goes beyond 2:22-26 to implicate Eli in the sin: "fattening yourselves with the choicest part" (2:29).

It is a key characteristic of the prophetic strands of these books to show that God's word is fulfilled. This oracle looks forward to the deaths of Phinehas and Hophni (2:34) in chapter 4; the slaughter of Eli's house (2:33) in 22:18-19; and the survival of one priest, Abiathar (2:33) in 22:20-23 and 1 Kings 2:27. This pattern of prophecy and fulfillment demonstrates that history unfolds under God's direction. The prophecy ends by looking forward to the establishment of a "faithful" priest and a "lasting" house (2:35); both adjectives translate the same Hebrew term. Such language will also be used in Nathan's oracle (2 Sam 7:16) to describe David's house. The narrator is providing hints of the outcome of national change, the establishment of a royal Davidic dynasty and a priestly dynasty of Zadok. At the same time, the oracle contains ominous warnings that promises made "forever" can be annulled if the recipients do not give full obedience to the

in heart and mind. I will establish a lasting house for him and he shall serve in the presence of my anointed forever. [36]Then whoever is left of your family will grovel before him for a piece of silver or a loaf of bread, saying: Please assign me a priestly function, that I may have a crust of bread to eat."

3 Revelation to Samuel. [1]During the time young Samuel was minister to the LORD under Eli, the word of the LORD was scarce and vision infrequent. [2]One day Eli was asleep in his usual place. His eyes had lately grown so weak that he could not see. [3]The lamp of God was not yet extinguished, and Samuel

was sleeping in the temple of the LORD where the ark of God was. [4]The LORD called to Samuel, who answered, "Here I am." [5]He ran to Eli and said, "Here I am. You called me." "I did not call you," Eli answered. "Go back to sleep." So he went back to sleep. [6]Again the LORD called Samuel, who rose and went to Eli. "Here I am," he said. "You called me." But he answered, "I did not call you, my son. Go back to sleep."

[7]Samuel did not yet recognize the LORD, since the word of the LORD had not yet been revealed to him. [8]The LORD called Samuel again, for the third time. Getting up and going to Eli, he said,

Lord (2:30). Through his prophetic word, God can both promise and punish. The theme of reversal celebrated in Hannah's song is not far away.

3:1–21 Samuel encounters the Lord

The well-known story of Samuel's first encounter with the Lord is the fulfillment of Hannah's plan to provide a replacement for Israel's failed leadership. Replacement implies reversal. Samuel begins "under Eli" (3:1), dependent on the old man for guidance, but ends by revealing God's word to the dependent Eli (3:18). Replacement is needed because divine guidance is missing; verse 1 notes the rarity of divine word and vision. Eli's condition symbolizes the problem for Israel which Samuel shares (3:7): blindness parallels a lack of knowledge of the Lord. In the end, Samuel will be acknowledged by Israel as a prophet; revelation is once more available.

To reach this outcome the Lord initiates the action by calling Samuel (3:4). Ironically, Samuel needs the guidance of Eli to answer this call (3:4-10). The one to be displaced prepares the way for the Lord. This story takes a nasty turn as the Lord announces his decision (3:11-14). The harsh judgment summarizes what the reader learned in 2:27-36, but without qualifications or exemptions. It is a darker and more complete condemnation. Even Eli's complicity is deepened by the accusation that he did not "reprove" his sons (a better translation of verse 13 would be "he did not restrain them"). Just

"Here I am. You called me." Then Eli understood that the LORD was calling the youth. ⁹So he said to Samuel, "Go to sleep, and if you are called, reply, 'Speak, LORD, for your servant is listening.'" When Samuel went to sleep in his place, ¹⁰the LORD came and stood there, calling out as before: Samuel, Samuel! Samuel answered, "Speak, for your servant is listening." ¹¹The LORD said to Samuel: I am about to do something in Israel that will make the ears of everyone who hears it ring. ¹²On that day I will carry out against Eli everything I have said about his house, beginning to end. ¹³I announce to him that I am condemning his house once and for all, because of this crime: though he knew his sons were blaspheming God, he did not reprove them. ¹⁴Therefore, I swear to Eli's house: No sacrifice or offering will ever expiate its crime. ¹⁵Samuel then slept until morning, when he got up early and opened the doors of the temple of the LORD. He was afraid to tell Eli the vision, ¹⁶but Eli called to him, "Samuel, my son!" He replied, "Here I am." ¹⁷Then Eli asked, "What did he say to you? Hide nothing from me! May God do thus to you, and more, if you hide from me a single thing he told you." ¹⁸So Samuel told him everything, and held nothing back. Eli answered, "It is the LORD. What is pleasing in the LORD's sight, the LORD will do."

Samuel Acknowledged as Prophet. ¹⁹Samuel grew up, and the LORD was with him, not permitting any word of his to go unfulfilled. ²⁰Thus all Israel from Dan to Beer-sheba came to know that Samuel was a trustworthy prophet of the LORD. ²¹The LORD continued to appear

like the man of God, Samuel conveys the Lord's word to Eli, but reluctantly! It requires a threatening oath (3:17) to overcome his fear. Eli's reaction is reminiscent of his willingness to accept God's will in answer to Hannah's prayers (3:18). Samuel's reluctance is reminiscent of his mother's delay in giving him up (cf. 1:22-23).

The final paragraph completes the reversal of roles (3:19-21). Samuel is now the accredited prophet of the Lord (note the same Hebrew word lies behind "trustworthy" and, in 2:35-36, "faithful" and "lasting"). The passage also contains a subtle theology of revelation. It distinguishes between Samuel's words and God's word. They are not identical but the latter inspires and makes firm the former. God's revelations to Samuel authorize him to speak for God. Thus the words of Samuel must be heeded (3:19) as the concrete, historical expression of the divine will, yet they are not that divine will itself. The Bible itself struggles to prevent a fundamentalist identification between the divine will and its temporal expression, and requires the reader to do the same.

at Shiloh, manifesting himself to Samuel at Shiloh through his word. Samuel's word spread throughout Israel.

4 **Defeat of the Israelites.** ¹At that time, the Philistines gathered for an attack on Israel. Israel went out to engage them in battle and camped at Ebenezer, while the Philistines camped at Aphek. ²The Philistines then drew up in battle formation against Israel. After a fierce struggle Israel was defeated by the Philistines, who killed about four thousand men on the battlefield. ³When the troops retired to the camp, the elders of Israel said, "Why has the Lord permitted us to be defeated today by the Philistines? Let us fetch the ark of the Lord from Shiloh that it may go into battle among us and save us from the grasp of our enemies."

Loss of the Ark. ⁴So the people sent to Shiloh and brought from there the ark of the Lord of hosts, who is enthroned upon the cherubim. The two sons of Eli, Hophni and Phinehas, accompanied the ark of God. ⁵When the ark of the Lord arrived in the camp, all Israel shouted so loudly that the earth shook. ⁶The Philistines, hearing the uproar, asked, "What does this loud shouting in the camp of the Hebrews mean?" On learning that the ark of the Lord had come

THE ARK NARRATIVES

I Samuel 4:1–7:1

The stories about the ark form a coherent narrative which may seem primitive in its theology yet is highly developed in its narrative skill. The narrator allows the story to unfold, using the speeches to offer insights. The chief "character" is the ark of the Lord, the gold-plated wooden box made to contain the tablets of the covenant (Exod 19–20). It is the symbol of God's presence and power. The main theme of the narrative is the freedom of the God of the exodus: free to take the initiative, to depart or return, but always to act for his own sake. References to exodus and exile abound. A secondary theme is the destruction of the Elides, the old priestly leadership in Israel, clearing the way for the judgeship of Samuel in chapter 7.

4:1-11 The defeat of Israel

The Philistines were more advanced than the Israelites in culture and technology. They dwelt on the coastal plain and were a continuing menace to Israel's survival. Battle is engaged and lost (4:1-2). No reason is given for the attack or defeat, but the elders ask why the Lord allowed it to happen. At one level this reflects their admirable faith in the reality of God's power. But their call for the ark is, at another level, suspect. Can God be brought to heel, his mere presence assuring victory? (4:3-4). The narrator

into the camp, [7]the Philistines were frightened, crying out, "Gods have come to their camp. Woe to us! This has never happened before. [8]Woe to us! Who can deliver us from the power of these mighty gods? These are the gods who struck the Egyptians with various plagues in the desert. [9]Take courage and act like soldiers, Philistines; otherwise you will become slaves to the Hebrews, as they were your slaves. Fight like soldiers!" [10]The Philistines fought and Israel was defeated; everyone fled to their own tents. It was a disastrous defeat; Israel lost thirty thousand foot soldiers. [11]The ark of God was captured, and Eli's two sons, Hophni and Phinehas, were dead.

Death of Eli. [12]A Benjaminite fled from the battlefield and reached Shiloh that same day, with his clothes torn and his head covered with dirt. [13]When he arrived, Eli was sitting in his chair beside the gate, watching the road, for he was troubled at heart about the ark of God. The man, however, went into the city to announce his news; then the whole city cried out. [14]When Eli heard the uproar, he wondered why there was such commotion. Just then the man rushed up to inform him. [15]Eli was ninety-eight years old, and his eyes would not focus. So he could not see. [16]The man said to Eli: "I have come from the battlefield; today I fled from there." He asked, "What happened, my son?" [17]And the messenger answered: "Israel fled from the Philistines; in fact, the troops suffered heavy losses. Your two sons, Hophni and Phinehas, are dead, and the ark of God has been captured." [18]At this mention of the ark of God, Eli fell backward from his chair into the gateway; he died of a broken neck since he was an old man and heavy. He had judged Israel for forty years.

[19]His daughter-in-law, the wife of Phinehas, was pregnant and about to

notes the presence of Phinehas and Hophni with the ark. After chapters 2 and 3, this is not a good sign.

Faced with the ark, the Philistines' comment expresses surprising knowledge of the Lord (4:7-9). They, not the Israelites, recognize the God of the exodus and the free, sovereign power manifested in those events (4:8). Even more surprisingly, that knowledge emboldens them to a major victory over Israel. Almost in passing, the narrator notes the death of Phinehas and Hophni (4:11b). Such narrative structuring suggests that the key to these battles lies in the different perceptions of God: one manipulative and the other recognizing gracious freedom.

4:12-22 Reactions to defeat

The remainder of the chapter deals with the reactions to the rout. The narrator uses a common device of the report from the battlefront (4:12-18; cf. 2 Sam 1:3-4) to build dramatic suspense. The messenger breaks the news

give birth. When she heard the news about the capture of the ark of God and the deaths of her father-in-law and her husband, she crouched down in labor, and gave birth. ²⁰She was about to die when the women standing around her said to her, "Do not be afraid, you have given birth to a son." Yet she neither answered nor paid any attention. ²¹She named the child Ichabod, saying, "Gone is the glory from Israel," referring to the capture of the ark of God and to her father-in-law and her husband. ²²She said, "Gone is the glory from Israel," because the ark of God had been captured.

5 **The Ark in the Temple of Dagon.** ¹The Philistines, having captured the ark of God, transferred it from Ebenezer to Ashdod. ²They then took the ark of God and brought it into the temple of Dagon, placing it beside Dagon. ³When the people of Ashdod rose early the next morning, Dagon was lying face down

on the ground before the ark of the LORD. So they picked Dagon up and put him back in his place. ⁴But early the next morning, when they arose, Dagon lay face down on the ground before the ark of the LORD, his head and hands broken off and lying on the threshold, his trunk alone intact. ⁵For this reason, neither the priests of Dagon nor any others who enter the temple of Dagon tread on the threshold of Dagon in Ashdod to this very day.

The Ark Is Carried About. ⁶Now the hand of the LORD weighed heavily on the people of Ashdod, ravaging them and afflicting the city and its vicinity with tumors. ⁷On seeing how matters stood, the people of Ashdod decided, "The ark of the God of Israel must not remain with us, for his hand weighs heavily on us and Dagon our god." ⁸So they summoned all the Philistine leaders and inquired of them, "What shall we

to Eli in stages, culminating with the capture of the ark (4:12). The shock of this disaster, not the personal loss of his sons, brings about his collapse and death. Only now does the narrator comment that Eli was a judge (4:18). Perhaps the absence of any prior comment emphasizes his ineffectual judgeship, suggesting Eli is more an anti-judge, the last of a failing system of leadership.

Phinehas' wife goes into labor on hearing the news (4:19). In naming her child, she interprets the reversal of fortunes taking place: "The glory has gone into exile from Israel" (translating vv. 21-22 literally). God has seized the initiative from presumptuous Israel and taken the ark out of the sinful hands of the Elide leadership. As a result, Israel is bereft of God's presence.

5:1-12 The ark among the Philistines

Having broken free from Israelite control, the ark is apparently spoils of war for the Philistines, who lodge this trophy in the temple of Dagon

do with the ark of the God of Israel?" The people of Gath replied, "Let them move the ark of the God of Israel to us." So they moved the ark of the God of Israel to Gath. ⁹But after it had been brought there, the hand of the LORD was against the city, resulting in utter turmoil: the LORD afflicted its inhabitants, young and old, and tumors broke out on them. ¹⁰The ark of God was next sent to Ekron; but as it entered that city, the people there cried out, "Why have they brought the ark of the God of Israel here to kill us and our kindred?" ¹¹Then they, too, sent a summons to all the Philistine leaders and pleaded: "Send away the ark of the God of Israel. Send it back to its place so it does not kill us and our kindred." A deadly panic had seized the whole city, since the hand of God lay heavy upon it. ¹²Those who escaped death were afflicted with tumors. Thus the outcry from the city went up to the heavens.

The Ark Is Returned. ¹The ark of the LORD had been in the land of the Philistines seven months ²when they summoned priests and diviners to ask, "What shall we do with the ark of the LORD? Tell us what we should send back with it." ³They replied: "If you intend to send back the ark of the God of Israel, you must not send it alone, but must, by all means, make amends to God through a reparation offering. Then you will be healed, and will learn why God continues to afflict you." ⁴When asked further, "What reparation offering should be our amends to God?" they replied: "Five golden tumors and five golden mice to correspond to the number of Philistine leaders, since the same plague has struck all of you and your leaders. ⁵Therefore, make images of the tumors and of the mice that are devastating your land and so give glory to the God of Israel. Perhaps then God will lift his hand from you, your gods, and your land. ⁶Why should

(5:1-2). Thus begins an entertaining account of the humiliation of the Philistines. They will learn also that the Lord cannot be manipulated. A key word in this chapter is "hand," meaning power to act. Dagon loses his hands (5:4), but the Lord's hand proves to be heavy upon the Philistine cities (5:6, 7, 9, 11). The plagues, reminiscent of the Lord's actions in Egypt, demonstrate who has the power of life and death. In acknowledging that the Lord's hand is heavy, the Philistines confess God's glory (the same Hebrew root lies behind "heavy" and "glory"). They witness the glory in exile by its exodus-like manifestations. In a sense, they testify to the liberation of God to act freely for God's own sake. Those who sought to tame God by manipulating the ark find themselves crying out in dismay (the people of Shiloh in 4:13-14, and the Philistines in 5:12).

6:1-12 The ark's exodus

Having decided to get rid of the ark (5:11), the Philistines consider what tribute must be sent with it (6:3-6). Just as the Hebrew slaves did not leave

you become stubborn, the way the Egyptians and Pharaoh were stubborn? Was it not after he had dealt ruthlessly with them that the Israelites were released and departed? ⁷So now set to work and make a new cart. Then take two milk cows that have not borne the yoke; hitch them to the cart, but drive their calves indoors away from them. ⁸You shall next take the ark of the Lord and place it on the cart, putting the golden articles that you are offering as reparation for your guilt in a box beside it. Start it on its way, and let it go. ⁹Then watch! If it goes up to Beth-shemesh along the route to the Lord's territory, then it was the Lord who brought this great calamity upon us; if not, we will know that it was not the Lord's hand, but a bad turn, that struck us."

The Ark in Beth-shemesh. ¹⁰They acted upon this advice. Taking two milk cows, they hitched them to the cart but shut up their calves indoors. ¹¹Then they placed the ark of the Lord on the cart, along with the box containing the golden mice and the images of the tumors. ¹²The cows went straight for the route to Beth-shemesh and continued along this road, mooing as they went, turning neither right nor left. The Philistine leaders followed them as far as the border of Beth-shemesh. ¹³The people of Beth-shemesh were harvesting the wheat in the valley. They looked up and rejoiced when they saw the ark. ¹⁴The cart came to the field

---

Egypt empty-handed, so the ark must be accompanied by gifts of value (gold), indicative of the giver (five cities), and of the circumstances (models of the plagues). Once again, the Philistines' comments in verses 5-6 make the exodus analogy explicit. They know Israel's faith-story and they recognize Israel's God. They have learned proper humility and avoid the hardened heart of a Pharaoh. Still, they set up tests for the ark (6:7-9). The new cart, the milk cows separated from their calves, and the lack of a driver are all obstacles to be overcome by a god who takes the initiative. This is the key lesson in these narratives. The Lord is not led but takes the lead. And the Lord brings the ark directly to Israelite territory (6:10-12).

6:13–7:1 The ark's homecoming

The Lord's homecoming from exile is met with an appropriate response by his people. There is rejoicing (6:13), sacrifices and worship (6:14-16), and a memorial stone is erected (6:18). The correct attitude towards the ark is to rejoice in God's presence, rather than attempting to use or abuse that presence. However, some lack that reverence (6:19). Such behavior caused the ark's exile in the first place. The death of these men is a sharp reminder of the need to root out such attitudes. Chastened by this reminder, the people of Beth Shemesh transfer the ark to Kiriath-jearim (6:20–7:1) where it is tended by Eleazer. At this point the ark disappears from the book, its

of Joshua the Beth-shemite and stopped there. At a large stone in the field, the wood of the cart was split up and the cows were offered as a burnt offering to the LORD. ¹⁵The Levites, meanwhile, had taken down the ark of God and the box beside it, with the golden articles, and had placed them on the great stone. The people of Beth-shemesh also offered other burnt offerings and sacrifices to the LORD that day. ¹⁶After witnessing this, the five Philistine leaders returned to Ekron the same day.

¹⁷The golden tumors the Philistines sent back as a reparation offering to the LORD were as follows: one for Ashdod, one for Gaza, one for Ashkelon, one for Gath, and one for Ekron. ¹⁸The golden mice, however, corresponded to the number of all the cities of the Philistines belonging to the five leaders, including fortified cities and open villages. The large stone on which the ark of the LORD was placed is still in the field of Joshua the Beth-shemite at the present time.

Penalty for Irreverence. ¹⁹The descendants of Jeconiah did not join in the celebration with the inhabitants of Beth-shemesh when they saw the ark of the LORD, and seventy of them were struck down. The people mourned over this great calamity which the LORD had inflicted upon them. ²⁰The men of Beth-shemesh asked, "Who can stand in the presence of the LORD, this Holy God? To whom can the ark go so that we are rid of it?" ²¹They then sent messengers to the inhabitants of Kiriath-jearim, saying, "The Philistines have returned the ark of the LORD; come down and get it."

7 ¹So the inhabitants of Kiriath-jearim came for the ark of the LORD and

narrative role complete. Its movements have demonstrated the freedom of God to initiate change in Israel. The Elides have been removed from office. Now God can use the one gifted to the Lord without obligation to the giver's plans. Samuel can step forward as God's agent for leadership in Israel.

THE TRANSITION TO MONARCHY

1 Samuel 7–15

The transition from judgeship to kingship is fraught with uncertainty and conflict, particularly at the level of ideology and theology. This narrative was composed using materials from various sources with different viewpoints on monarchy and is often described as a patchwork of pro- and anti-monarchical accounts. The editors have created a sustained narrative reflecting on the complex changes that took place in Israel, which required an accommodation between covenantal theology and a new political ideology of monarchy. Monarchy had advantages—sustained leadership in times of constant military threat—but it also had disadvantages in the social and

brought it into the house of Abinadab on the hill, appointing his son Eleazar as guardian of the ark of the Lord.

Samuel the Judge. ²From the day the ark came to rest in Kiriath-jearim, a long time, twenty years, elapsed, and the whole house of Israel turned to the Lord. ³Then Samuel addressed the whole house of Israel: "If you would return to the Lord with your whole heart, remove your foreign gods and your Astartes, fix your hearts on the Lord, and serve him alone, then the Lord will deliver you from the hand of the Philistines." ⁴So the Israelites removed their Baals and Astartes, and served the Lord alone.

⁵Samuel then gave orders, "Gather all Israel to Mizpah, that I may pray to the Lord for you." ⁶When they had gathered at Mizpah, they drew water and poured it out on the ground before the Lord, and they fasted that day, saying, "We have sinned against the Lord." It was at Mizpah that Samuel began to judge the Israelites.

Rout of the Philistines. ⁷When the Philistines heard that the Israelites had gathered at Mizpah, their leaders went up against Israel. Hearing this, the Israelites became afraid of the Philistines ⁸and appealed to Samuel, "Do not stop crying out to the Lord our God for us,

---

economic spheres. Israel, however, was created from those who escaped slavery under a king, Pharaoh, to be a new type of society with God as king. How will the organization of a theocratic society accommodate a human king? Fundamentally, the narrative is attempting to answer the key question: can divine freedom of action and the human demand for stable leadership be reconciled? The narrative tells how Saul came to be king, using Samuel to voice the concerns of the old order. By chapter 12, an accommodation is brokered, but will it work? Chapters 13–15 suggest it will not, at least not for Saul.

7:2-17 Samuel the Judge

This passage can be read in several contexts. At one level, it is a reversal of the Israelites' defeat in chapter 4. The location is once again called Ebenezer, but now the Israelites fear the enemy and express faith in God, and the Philistines are routed. The crisis of the recent chapters is over as Samuel mediates the Lord's presence to Israel. However, on a wider horizon, this short passage raises many thoughts about the nature of Israelite society.

There seem to be two paradigms at work. One is the paradigm of judgeship. As sketched in Judges 2:16-19, the people turn from God and experience difficulties; in response to their cries, God sends a judge; the judge saves the people; and the judge leads the people for a period of security. Following the death of the judge and a new apostasy, the cycle begins again.

to save us from the hand of the Philistines." ⁹Samuel therefore took an unweaned lamb and offered it whole as a burnt offering to the LORD. He cried out to the LORD for Israel, and the LORD answered him. ¹⁰While Samuel was sacrificing the burnt offering, the Philistines drew near for battle with Israel. That day, however, the LORD thundered loudly against the Philistines, and threw them into such confusion that they were defeated by Israel. ¹¹Thereupon the Israelites rushed out from Mizpah and pursued the Philistines, striking them down even beyond Beth-car. ¹²Samuel then took a stone and placed it between Mizpah and Jeshanah; he named it Ebenezer, explaining, "As far as this place the LORD has been our help." ¹³Thus were the Philistines subdued, never again to enter the territory of Israel, for the hand of the LORD was against them as long as Samuel lived. ¹⁴The cities from Ekron to Gath which the Philistines had taken from Israel were restored to them. Israel also freed the territory of these cities from Philistine domination. There was also peace between Israel and the Amorites.

¹⁵Samuel judged Israel as long as he lived. ¹⁶He made a yearly circuit, passing through Bethel, Gilgal and Mizpah and judging Israel at each of these places. ¹⁷Then he used to return to Ramah, for that was his home. There, too, he judged Israel and built an altar to the LORD.

This passage fits that pattern. The Philistine threat prompts the people to cry out (7:7-8). Samuel intercedes and God delivers the people (7:9-11). Then Samuel is established as judge for a period of peace (7:15-17). Using this pattern, the narrator presents Samuel as a successful and effective judge, in the line of the great judges of Israel.

But another paradigm is visible in the earlier part of the text. Samuel's call for an undivided heart in verse 3 is reminiscent of Moses in Deuteronomy 6:4-5. There are also echoes of Moses' summons to Israel at Sinai (Exod 19:5-6) and Joshua's at Shechem (Josh 24:14-15). A covenant renewal is taking place in verses 3-6. The people "put away" other gods, and they return to the Lord alone. They constitute themselves as the covenant people in faithful obedience to the Lord, with Samuel as the Moses of their day.

These two paradigms overlap: the Israelites put away Baals and Astartes, gods frequently mentioned in the judgeship cycles (cf. Judg 2); when threatened by the Philistines, their mediated cry is an expression of covenantal faith to which God responds as the faithful Lord. Even more boldly, the narrator links covenant and judgeship in verse 6b; the ceremony at Mizpah is when Samuel begins to judge Israel. Using the two paradigms, the narrator presents a dense, theological declaration about the nature of Israelite society and its governance. Israel is, in essence, a covenantal society obedient to one God who is its Lord and king. This society lives covenantal faith

II. Establishment of the Monarchy

8 Request for a King. ¹In his old age Samuel appointed his sons judges over Israel. ²His firstborn was named Joel, his second son, Abijah; they judged at Beer-sheba. ³His sons did not follow his example, but looked to their own gain, accepting bribes and perverting justice. ⁴Therefore all the elders of Israel assembled and went to Samuel at Ramah ⁵and said to him, "Now that you are old, and your sons do not follow your example, appoint a king over us, like all the nations, to rule us."

⁶Samuel was displeased when they said, "Give us a king to rule us." But he prayed to the LORD. ⁷The LORD said: Listen to whatever the people say. You are not the one they are rejecting. They are rejecting me as their king. ⁸They are acting toward you just as they have acted from the day I brought them up from Egypt to this very day, deserting me to serve other gods. ⁹Now listen to them; but at the same time, give them a solemn warning and inform them of the rights of the king who will rule them.

---

boldly in the face of danger, sure of God's power to save. This power is mediated through human intermediaries. This happens most successfully when the roles of priest, prophet, and judge are aligned in a Moses-like figure who calls the people to covenant, intercedes with God, and judges them regularly.

Hannah's personal request has answered Israel's national crisis. During Samuel's lifetime, Israel need not worry about leadership, supplied fully and extensively by him. But Samuel began to judge in 7:6b, and verse 15 reads like the summation of his career. Will Israel have to undergo another exile experience (cf. chapters 4–6) after Samuel's day? The question hangs in the air.

8:1-22 "Give us a king to rule us."

Like Eli, Samuel appoints his sons as successors, but with similar results. The sons pervert "justice" (v.3) just as Eli's sons disregarded the priests' "duties" (2:13 uses the same term, *mishphat*). Hereditary succession does not work. So, just like Hannah, the elders take the initiative. They sum up the situation correctly and then, in the language of Deuteronomy 17:14 which foresees such an eventuality, demand a king (8:5).

Samuel is displeased (8:6). He finds himself in Eli's place (cf. chapter 1) but reacts very differently. Note that three times he will be told to "listen to them" (8:7, 9, 22). Is this a hint that Samuel is not a reliable intermediary because of his vested interests? God accedes to the people's request but describes it as apostasy (8:8). Such behavior could trigger a new judge cycle

The Governance of the King. [10]Samuel delivered the message of the LORD in full to those who were asking him for a king. [11]He told them: "The governance of the king who will rule you will be as follows: He will take your sons and assign them to his chariots and horses, and they will run before his chariot. [12]He will appoint from among them his commanders of thousands and of hundreds. He will make them do his plowing and harvesting and produce his weapons of war and chariotry. [13]He will use your daughters as perfumers, cooks, and bakers. [14]He will take your best fields, vineyards, and olive groves, and give them to his servants. [15]He will tithe your crops and grape harvests to give to his officials and his servants. [16]He will take your male and female slaves, as well as your best oxen and donkeys, and use them to do his work. [17]He will also tithe your flocks. As for you, you will become his slaves. [18]On that day you will cry out because of the king whom you have chosen, but the LORD will not answer you on that day."

Persistent Demand. [19]The people, however, refused to listen to Samuel's warning and said, "No! There must be a king over us. [20]We too must be like all the nations, with a king to rule us, lead

(cf. 7:3) but times have changed! Note the shift from "judges" (8:1) who pervert "justice" (8:2), to a request for a king "to judge" (8:5-6 where the Hebrew verb "to judge" has been translated "to rule us") and a description of the justice of the king (8:9, translated "rights of the king"). The solution to apostasy will now lie with kingship and not judgeship.

8:10-22 King and covenant God

Samuel's description of the "rights of the king" focuses on the socio-economic demands made by the monarchy on the people. Just how negative this report is can be seen by comparing it to Deuteronomy 17:16-20. Samuel seems strongly opposed to having a king, even if there are provisions within the covenantal relationship for such a post. His onslaught climaxes in a warning that the people will become slaves (reversing the benefits of the exodus experience) without recourse to God's help (8:15). Despite this critique, the people repeat their demand, balancing the internal effects ("a king to rule us") with the external advantages (8:20; "lead us in warfare"). Samuel listens and passes on their words. The Lord tells him to grant the request, but he does not. Samuel sends them home (8:22). An impasse has been reached when God's representative does not carry out God's word.

The arguments about a king's behavior have been made, but the real issue is the relationship of king and covenant God. The echoes of Deuteronomy 17:14-20 suggest that kingship could be accommodated in covenantal

us in warfare, and fight our battles." [21]Samuel listened to all the concerns of the people and then repeated them to the LORD. [22]The LORD said: Listen to them! Appoint a king to rule over them. Then Samuel said to the people of Israel, "Return, each one of you, to your own city."

9 **Saul.** [1]There was a powerful man from Benjamin named Kish, who was the son of Abiel, son of Zeror, son of Becorath, son of Aphiah, a Benjaminite. [2]He had a son named Saul, who was a handsome young man. There was no other Israelite more handsome than Saul; he stood head and shoulders above the people.

The Lost Donkeys. [3]Now the donkeys of Saul's father, Kish, had wandered off. Kish said to his son Saul, "Take one of the servants with you and go out and hunt for the donkeys." [4]So they went through the hill country of Ephraim, and through the land of Shalishah. Not finding them there, they continued through the land of Shaalim without success. They also went through the land of Benjamin, but they failed to find the animals. [5]When they came to the land of Zuph, Saul said to the servant who was with him, "Come, let us turn back, lest my father forget about the donkeys and become anxious about us." [6]The servant replied, "Listen! There is a man of God in this city, a man held in high esteem; everything he says comes true. Let us go there now! Perhaps he can advise us about the journey we have undertaken." [7]But Saul said to his servant, "If we go, what can we offer the man? The food in our bags has run out; we have no present to give the man of God. What else do we have?" [8]Again the

relations. The Lord is willing to accept the people's initiative (though describing it as apostasy) and to work with it, just as God accepted Hannah's prayer, but Samuel stands in the way. If this is personal pique, he is told to forget it (8:7). Samuel's description of the rights of the king suggests that Deuteronomy 17:14-20 is too idealistic. The reality for Israel will be much worse, as later history shows. Perhaps Samuel's report represents the voice of the exilic editors who can look back in regret on the failure of Israelite monarchy to implement the covenant ideals.

9:1–10:16 Saul searches for donkeys and finds a kingdom

A prosperous Benjaminite, Kish, loses some donkeys and sends his son to find them. But the son's quest takes a strange turn when he meets Samuel. He is anointed and transformed in preparation to become king. The son's name is Saul.

9:1-10 A fruitless search

The narrator keeps the reader's attention on the search for the donkeys in the first section of the story. Saul's search is long and fruitless. Obstacles have to be overcome so help is needed. Saul is assisted by his servant, who

servant answered Saul, "I have a quarter shekel of silver. If I give that to the man of God, he will advise us about the journey." ⁹(In former times in Israel, anyone who went to consult God used to say, "Come, let us go to the seer." For the one who is now called prophet was formerly called seer.) ¹⁰Saul then said to his servant, "You are right! Come on, let us go!" So they headed toward the city where the man of God lived.

Meeting the Young Women. ¹¹As they were going up the path to the city, they met some young women coming out to draw water and they asked them, "Is the seer in town?" ¹²The young women answered, "Yes, there—straight ahead. Hurry now; just today he came to the city, because the people have a sac-

rifice today on the high place. ¹³When you enter the city, you may reach him before he goes up to the high place to eat. The people will not eat until he arrives; only after he blesses the sacrifice will the invited guests eat. Go up immediately, for you should find him right now."

Saul Meets Samuel. ¹⁴So they went up to the city. As they entered it—there was Samuel coming toward them on his way to the high place. ¹⁵The day before Saul's arrival, the LORD had revealed to Samuel: ¹⁶At this time tomorrow I will send you a man from the land of Benjamin whom you are to anoint as ruler of my people Israel. He shall save my people from the hand of the Philistines. I have looked upon my people; their cry

suggests that they consult an unnamed man of God (9:6). Saul agrees and the quest moves to the next stage (9:10). The narrator uses various terms for this personage—"man of God" (9:6-8, 10), "seer," and "prophet" (9:9)—so that the attentive reader wonders if this is Samuel whose word is always effective (compare 9:6 with 3:19).

9:11-26 Saul's new role

The two travelers are guided to the seer who is indeed Samuel (9:11-13). Now this becomes a quest for leadership in Israel. Revelation becomes the help, rather than human guides. The narrator reports a prior revelation given to Samuel (9:15-16). The Lord is sending his choice to Samuel to be anointed as "ruler" (an archaic term, *nagid*, meaning "designated one" is used here and in 10:1). He is to "save my people," a very covenantal concept (9:16). The Lord is doing this in response to the people's misery and cry for help. It is not obvious that this refers to the request for a king in 8:5. Instead, the Lord seems to be taking the initiative to supply a covenant savior of his choosing. This chosen one will "govern" (9:17) and "save" (9:16) as God intends.

When Saul appears before Samuel, the Lord confirms his selection. Samuel prepares Saul for the amazing change in his quest: the donkeys

has come to me. ¹⁷When Samuel caught sight of Saul, the Lord assured him: This is the man I told you about; he shall govern my people. ¹⁸Saul met Samuel in the gateway and said, "Please tell me where the seer lives." ¹⁹Samuel answered Saul: "I am the seer. Go up ahead of me to the high place and eat with me today. In the morning, before letting you go, I will tell you everything on your mind. ²⁰As for your donkeys that were lost three days ago, do not worry about them, for they have been found. Whom should Israel want if not you and your father's family?" ²¹Saul replied: "Am I not a Benjaminite, from the smallest of the tribes of Israel, and is not my clan the least among the clans of the tribe of Benjamin? Why say such things to me?"

The Meal. ²²Samuel then took Saul and his servant and brought them into the room. He seated them at the head of the guests, of whom there were about thirty. ²³He said to the cook, "Bring the portion I gave you and told you to put aside." ²⁴So the cook took up the leg and what went with it, and placed it before Saul. Samuel said: "This is a reserved portion that is set before you. Eat, for it was kept for you until this time; I explained that I was inviting some guests." Thus Saul dined with Samuel that day. ²⁵When they came down from the high place into the city, a mattress was spread for Saul on the roof, ²⁶and he slept there.

Saul's Anointing. At daybreak Samuel called to Saul on the roof, "Get up, and I will send you on your way." Saul got up, and he and Samuel went outside the city together. ²⁷As they were approaching the edge of the town, Samuel said to Saul, "Tell the servant to go on ahead of us, but you stay here for a moment, that I may give you a word from God."

10 ¹Then, from a flask he had with him, Samuel poured oil on Saul's head and kissed him, saying: "The Lord anoints you ruler over his people Israel. You are the one who will govern the

---

have been found but something else is missing (9:20). The cryptic comments about Israel's desire in verse 20 suggest that Samuel perceives Saul as the answer to the people's request in chapter 8. But Saul is the Lord's chosen, not Israel's. This will create tension later. Samuel now invites Saul to the sacrifice as guest of honor (9:22-24). Saul's new role has a deeply religious character. He belongs more to God than to Israel.

9:27–10:16 Shifting relationships

Before letting them continue their journey, Samuel takes Saul aside to reveal God's intentions (9:27). This is the signal for the anointing of Saul as *nagid*, the one to govern and save (10:1). Saul now knows the contents of God's revelation (9:15-16), but Samuel goes further. He outlines a series of three signs that will authenticate the message (10:1b-6). Following the signs, Saul will be a new man, able to do whatever comes to hand because God

LORD's people and save them from the power of their enemies all around them.

The Signs Foretold. "This will be the sign for you that the LORD has anointed you ruler over his heritage: ²When you leave me today, you will meet two men near Rachel's tomb at Zelzah in the territory of Benjamin. They will say to you, 'The donkeys you went to look for have been found. Now your father is no longer worried about the donkeys, but is anxious about you and says: What shall I do about my son?' ³Farther on, when you arrive at the oak of Tabor, three men will meet you as they go up to God at Bethel; one will be bringing three young goats, another three loaves of bread, and the third a skin of wine. ⁴They will greet you and offer you two elevated offerings of bread, which you should accept from them. ⁵After that you will come to Gibeath-elohim, where the Philistine garrison is located. As you enter that city, you will meet a band of prophets coming down from the high place. They will be preceded by lyres, tambourines, flutes, and harps, and will be in prophetic ecstasy. ⁶The spirit of the LORD will rush upon you, and you will join them in their prophetic ecstasy and will become a changed man. ⁷When these signs have come to pass, do whatever lies to hand, because God is with you. ⁸Now go down ahead of me to Gilgal, for I shall come down to you, to offer burnt offerings and to sacrifice communion offerings. Wait seven days until I come to you; I shall then tell you what you must do."

The Signs Come to Pass. ⁹As Saul turned to leave Samuel, God changed his heart. That very day all these signs came to pass. . . . ¹⁰From there they arrived at Gibeah, where a band of prophets met Saul, and the spirit of God rushed upon him, so that he joined them in their prophetic ecstasy. ¹¹When all who had known him previously saw him in a prophetic state among the prophets, they said to one another, "What has happened to the son of Kish? Is Saul also among the prophets?" ¹²And

---

is with him (10:7). But will he be his own man? Verse 8 immediately ties down Saul's freedom under Samuel's direction: he is to remain idle at Gilgal until Samuel arrives and conducts a sacrifice; then, he will be given instructions. None of this was mentioned in the Lord's instructions. Is Samuel giving concrete expression to the divine word (cf. 3:19-22), or is he voicing his own desire to subordinate the new leader to the old? There is no clear answer here, but the problem will dominate later chapters.

The narrative moves quickly. Already Saul's transformation has commenced (verse 9 refers to a new heart), so the narrator jumps to the last sign where the transformation is completed. The spirit of God takes hold of Saul and he enters a prophetic state (10:10). The public reaction raises the central question: what has become of Saul? (10:11). The Lord designated him as leader, and Samuel anointed him for that role, but now he acts prophetically.

someone from that district responded, "And who is their father?" Thus the saying arose, "Is Saul also among the prophets?" [13]When he came out of the prophetic ecstasy, he went home.

Silence About the Kingship. [14]Saul's uncle asked him and his servant, "Where have you been?" Saul replied, "Looking for the donkeys. When we could not find them, we went to Samuel." [15]Saul's uncle said, "Tell me, then, what Samuel said to you." [16]Saul said to his uncle, "He assured us that the donkeys had been found." But Saul told him nothing about what Samuel had said about the kingship.

Saul Chosen King. [17]Samuel called the people together to the LORD at Mizpah [18]and addressed the Israelites: "Thus says the LORD, the God of Israel: It was I who brought Israel up from Egypt and delivered you from the power of the Egyptians and from the power of all the kingdoms that oppressed you. [19]But today you have rejected your God, who saves you from all your evils and calamities, by saying, 'No! You must appoint a king over us.' Now, therefore, take your stand before the LORD according to your tribes and families." [20]So Samuel had all the tribes of Israel come forward, and the tribe of Benjamin was

There is confusion. Someone adds the astute question, "who is their father?" (10:12). Is Samuel, the leading prophet in Israel, the superior over Saul? His instructions in verse 8 suggest Samuel wants this to be the case. Saul's natural father disappears from the story: when Saul returns home, he meets his "uncle" (10:14-15). Has Kish been demoted to "uncle" now that Saul is among the prophets under Samuel's jurisdiction? The narrator may be signaling that events place Saul in a very awkward set of relationships. At home, Saul is silent about what has happened. His anointing does not become public knowledge. A similar situation develops after the anointing of David (16:1-13) and of Jehu (2 Kgs 9–10). Divine designation is always distinct from public affirmation.

10:17-27 Saul chosen by lot

This passage is ambiguous in content and in relation to the surrounding texts. It does not follow on from 10:16. Rather, it flows more smoothly from the dismissal at 8:22. In that context, Samuel is gathering the people to continue the previous assembly, this time at Mizpah. Read in this way, one expects Samuel to complete the Lord's instructions and appoint a king. However, he does not. Verses 18-19 take the form of an oracle of judgment. Speaking for the Lord, Samuel reformulates 8:7-9 to describe God's deliverance in the past and to denounce Israel's sin: it has rejected God by asking for a king. Comparing these two texts raises the possibility that Samuel is

chosen. [21]Next he had the tribe of Benjamin come forward by clans, and the clan of Matri was chosen, and finally Saul, son of Kish, was chosen. But when they went to look for him, he was nowhere to be found. [22]Again they consulted the LORD, "Is there still someone else to come forward?" The LORD answered: He is hiding among the baggage. [23]They ran to bring him from there; when he took his place among the people, he stood head and shoulders above all the people. [24]Then Samuel addressed all the people, "Do you see the man whom the LORD has chosen? There is no one like him among all the people!" Then all the people shouted out, "Long live the king!"

[25]Samuel next explained to the people the rules of the monarchy, wrote them in a book, and placed them before the presence of the LORD. Samuel then sent the people back to their own homes. [26]Saul also went home to Gibeah, accompanied by warriors whose hearts the LORD had touched. [27]But some worthless people said, "How can this fellow save us?" They despised him and brought him no tribute.

concretizing the Lord's word in terms of his own evaluation of the request; where the Lord puts stress on granting the request, Samuel stresses the rejection of the Lord. But he cannot ignore God's intention completely and so, in place of the usual declaration of punishment, "Now, therefore . . ." starts a process of lots (10:19b).

What does Samuel intend? The process of "taking one's stand before the Lord" and "choosing" is used elsewhere to identify a guilty party (see Josh 7:11-26; 1 Sam 14:36-43). Used in the context of an oracle of judgment, the candidates take their stand for judgment (10:20-22). When Saul is discovered and brought forward, he takes his stand among the people. This should be for judgment but the Lord has intervened to present Saul (10:22). The people are struck by his appearance (10:23). Samuel focuses their attention on the one "whom the LORD has chosen" (10:24). But, together with his description of the people's sin (10:19 recalling Deut 17:14) and his comments in verse 24 (recalling Deut 17:15), Samuel unwittingly has shifted the focus from judgment to the search for a king. The people react positively to Saul's appearance and acclaim him king.

Whatever his motives for selection by lot, Samuel proceeds to explain the "law of royalty" (10:24; the *misphat* of the kingdom). It is unlikely that this is a repeat of 8:11-18. Since it is written in a book (10:25), this teaching may be in line with Deuteronomy 17:16-20. Samuel, willingly or not, is complying with the divine instruction to grant the people's request. All can go home again.

11 Defeat of the Ammonites.

Defeat of the Ammonites. ¹About a month later, Nahash the Ammonite went up and besieged Jabesh-gilead. All the people of Jabesh begged Nahash, "Make a treaty with us, and we will serve you." ²But Nahash the Ammonite replied, "This is my condition for making a treaty with you: I will gouge out the right eye of every man, and thus bring shame on all Israel." ³The elders of Jabesh said to him: "Give us seven days to send messengers throughout the territory of Israel. If there is no one to save us, we will surrender to you." ⁴When the messengers arrived at Gibeah of Saul and reported the news in the people's hearing, they all wept aloud. ⁵Just then Saul came in from the field, behind his oxen. "Why are the people weeping?" he asked. They repeated the message of the inhabitants of Jabesh for him. ⁶As he listened to this report, the spirit of God rushed upon him and he became very angry. ⁷Taking a yoke of oxen, he cut them into pieces and sent them throughout the territory of Israel by messengers saying, "If anyone does not come out to follow Saul and Samuel, the same thing will be done to his oxen!" The dread of the LORD came upon the people and they went forth as one. ⁸When Saul reviewed them in Bezek, there were three hundred thousand Israelites and seventy thousand Judahites.

Saul has been chosen by lot, a public ritual which, in addition to the private anointing, authenticates his position as the Lord's choice. He has support from some warriors (literally, worthy men) who have been influenced by the Lord as Saul was (compare v. 26 with v. 9). But there are others, worthless men, who are not convinced. Just as Saul's possession by the spirit did not impress, so choice by lot leaves some unmoved. Saul's position is not secure.

11:1-15 Can Saul save?

The key task of God's chosen one is to save the people. And Saul has not yet done so. Hence the last episode ended with the question, "How can this fellow save us?" (10:27). Salvation is the key issue of this episode. The narrative is in three parts: describing a need for salvation, discovering the means, and bringing about salvation.

While Saul is chosen to save Israel from the Philistines, an urgent need develops when Nabash threatens to humiliate the people of Jabesh-gilead. The Ammonites were quarrelsome neighbors on the north-eastern shores of the Dead Sea and a regular threat to Israelite settlements such as Jabesh. The inhabitants play for time as they seek someone to rescue them (11:3).

At first the search is fruitless (11:4). Saul's actions depict him as one of the great saviors of old: called away from farming (11:5; cf. Gideon in Judg

⁹To the messengers who had come he said, "Tell the inhabitants of Jabesh-gilead that tomorrow, when the sun grows hot, they will be saved." The messengers went and reported this to the inhabitants of Jabesh, and they rejoiced. ¹⁰The men of Jabesh said to Nahash, "Tomorrow we will surrender to you, and you may do with us whatever you want." ¹¹The next day, Saul arranged his troops in three companies and invaded the camp during the dawn watch. They slaughtered Ammonites until the day had gotten hot; by then the survivors were so scattered that no two of them were left together.

Saul Accepted as King. ¹²The people then said to Samuel: "Who questioned whether Saul should rule over us? Hand them over and we will put them to death." ¹³But Saul objected, "No one will be put to death this day, for today the LORD has rescued Israel." ¹⁴Samuel said to the people, "Come, let us go to Gilgal to renew the kingship there." ¹⁵So all the people went to Gilgal, and there they made Saul king in the LORD's presence. They also sacrificed communion offer-

---

6:11-12), seized by the spirit of the Lord (11:6; cf. Samson in Judg 14:19), and summoning the people (11:7; cf. Judg 19:29-30). The mobilization of the people brings joy to Jabesh-gilead (11:9).

The resolution of the crisis happens swiftly (11:10-11). Saul emerges as the triumphant hero. This prompts a resolution of the doubts expressed about Saul. The narrator brings Samuel on scene as the people seek to punish the doubters of 10:27 (11:12). Saul intervenes for clemency with a classic declaration of faith in the covenant God, "today the LORD has rescued Israel" (11:13). Such a declaration marks him out not just as a military hero, but also as a faithful servant of the Lord. Can Saul save? Yes, and such a man is suitable to lead Israel. Samuel seizes the opportunity to renew the kingship after the last faltering attempt (11:14). The episode culminates at Gilgal when the people make Saul king (11:15).

This narrative incorporates allusions to previous judges, so is Saul more a judge than a king? Like judges he saves, so one more episode is needed to outline how a king in Israel might act. Furthermore, Saul is marked out as belonging to the Lord—the anointing, the seizures by the spirit, his declaration of faith in the savior God—but it is the people who make him king as the answer to their request. Will there be a struggle for ownership of this king? Finally, Samuel appears suddenly and moves the assembly to Gilgal where he sacrifices peace offerings. Is this the Gilgal event that Samuel announced in 10:8, when Samuel took control of the king? There are several questions of role and loyalty yet to be resolved, and the answers will pull Saul in different directions. His kingship is far from secure.

ings there before the LORD, and Saul and all the Israelites rejoiced greatly.

12 **Samuel's Integrity.** ¹Samuel addressed all Israel: "I have granted your request in every respect," he said. "I have set a king over you ²and now the king will lead you. As for me, I am old and gray, and my sons are among you. I was your leader from my youth to the present day. ³Here I stand! Answer me in the presence of the LORD and the LORD's anointed. Whose ox have I taken? Whose donkey have I taken? Whom have I cheated? Whom have I wronged? From whom have I accepted a bribe and shut my eyes because of it? I will make restitution to you." ⁴They replied, "You have neither cheated us, nor oppressed us, nor accepted anything from anyone." ⁵So he said to them, "The LORD is witness against you this day, and the LORD's anointed is witness, that you have found nothing in my possession." "The LORD is witness," they said.

12:1-25 Samuel sets kingship within the covenant

Chapter 12 completes the transition to monarchy. After several digressions and tentative starts, Samuel has acceded to the people's request for a king, as he notes in verse 1. However, the process has not been straightforward. The Lord chose the candidate, Saul, who had to be authenticated by various means. That process resolved opposition to Saul. Samuel voiced his opposition to kingship (8:11-18; 10:18-19), and once more he moves to subordinate the realities of the new leadership to the old covenantal faith structures. This is a key moment in the emergence of monarchy, and consequently in this history of Israel. The compilers of the history place major speeches at key moments (cf. Josh 24 and 1 Kgs 8) to provide theological reflection on what has happened and what lies ahead. Samuel's speech not only addresses the Israelites at Gilgal, but also conveys the biblical writers' understanding to the reader. For these writers, monarchy was a serious risk from the very beginning.

12:1-5 Facing the people

Samuel seeks to vindicate his leadership as a new leadership emerges (12:2). This is a bipartite process. Samuel faces the people: will they accuse him or vindicate his leadership? The Lord and his anointed (Saul) act as witnesses (12:3, 5), nothing more. Interestingly, Samuel's list of possible crimes parallels the "rights of the king" (8:11-18) with its frequent use of "take." Implicitly he is claiming that the old leadership was good; the new is bad. The people vindicate Samuel (12:5) so a new process can commence in which Samuel acts as arbitrator between the Lord and Israel (a tripartite process). This shift in procedure is important: Samuel is carving out a role for the future.

Samuel Admonishes the People. ⁶Samuel continued: "The Lord is witness, who appointed Moses and Aaron and brought your ancestors up from the land of Egypt. ⁷Now take your stand, that I may judge you in the presence of the Lord according to all the gracious acts that the Lord has done for you and your ancestors. ⁸When Jacob and his sons went to Egypt and the Egyptians oppressed them, your ancestors cried out to the Lord. The Lord then sent Moses and Aaron to bring them out of Egypt and settled them in this place. ⁹But they forgot the Lord their God; and so the Lord sold them into the power of Sisera, the captain of the army of Hazor, the power of the Philistines, and the power of the king of Moab, who made war against them. ¹⁰They cried out to the Lord and said, 'We have sinned because we abandoned the Lord and served the Baals and Astartes. Now deliver us from the power of our enemies, and we will serve you.' ¹¹The Lord sent Jerubbaal, Barak, Jephthah, and Samuel; he delivered you from the power of your enemies on every side, so that you could live in security. ¹²Yet, when you saw Nahash, king of the Ammonites, advancing against you, you said to me, 'No! A king must rule us,' even though the Lord your God is your king.

Warnings for People and King. ¹³"Now here is the king you chose. See! The Lord has given you a king. ¹⁴If you fear and serve the Lord, if you listen to the voice of the Lord and do not rebel against the Lord's command, if both you and the king, who rules over you,

12:6-15 Conditions of the covenant

In the new process, the people take their stand as the accusations are made. The many "acts of mercy" of the Lord are contrasted with his continual rejection by Israel. Yet when they cried out, the Lord delivered them, from Jacob to Joshua (12:8) and throughout the period of the judges (12:9-11). The Lord is faithful, the people fickle, but the Lord always provided a savior, so why change the system? If one listens carefully, this summary applies not only to the judges (some ancient texts read "Samson" instead of "Samuel" in verse 11) but also to the career of Samuel (cf. 1 Sam 7). Even in the present crisis the Lord provided a judge-like savior (verse 12 looks to chapter 11), but the people insist on a king. They now have their king (12:13) but he has been given by the Lord and his role is circumscribed within the Lord's covenant. Verses 14-15 are the heart of the speech. In a two-part conditional statement, reminiscent of the book of Deuteronomy, Samuel offers blessing and curse. The conditions are typical of the covenant relationship: fear of the Lord, exclusive service, obedience. This is a reaffirmation of the covenant. The new element comes in those addressed: the "you" of the people becomes "you and your king." The king is part and

follow the Lord your God—well and good. [15]But if you do not listen to the voice of the Lord and if you rebel against the Lord's command, the hand of the Lord will be against you and your king. [16]Now then, stand ready to witness the great marvel the Lord is about to accomplish before your eyes. [17]Are we not in the harvest time for wheat? Yet I will call upon the Lord, and he will send thunder and rain. Thus you will see and understand how great an evil it is in the eyes of the Lord that you have asked for a king." [18]Samuel called upon the Lord, and the Lord sent thunder and rain that day.

Assistance Promised. Then all the people feared the Lord and Samuel. [19]They said to Samuel, "Pray to the Lord your God for us, your servants, that we may not die for having added to all our other sins the evil of asking for a king." [20]"Do not fear," Samuel answered them. "You have indeed committed all this evil! Yet do not turn from the Lord, but serve him with your whole heart. [21]Do not turn aside to gods who are nothing, who cannot act and deliver. They are nothing. [22]For the sake of his own great name the Lord will not abandon his people, since the Lord has decided to make you his people. [23]As for me, far be ▶

parcel of the people under covenant Torah, subject to the same demands for obedience and sharing the same blessing or curse.

12:16-25 Covenantal kingship

Having made this adjudication, Samuel calls the people forward to witness a sign (12:16-18). The sign not only demonstrates the Lord's displeasure (12:17) but also Samuel's position within the new dispensation: *he* calls, the Lord sends. As a result, Samuel is placed with the Lord (12:18) while the king is placed among the people. The people beg for intercession for their sins (12:19) and Samuel responds with an oracle of salvation ("Do not fear . . ."; 12:20-22). The old pattern of crying out for deliverance still functions in the hands of the old leadership! The Lord recognizes their evil but promises not to "abandon his people" (12:22) who must not "turn from the Lord" (12:20).

Samuel concludes by emphasizing his role in the new dispensation as intercessor and teacher (12:23). But he ends with another two-part condition offering blessing or curse (12: 24-25). While the former would end the discourse on a positive, hopeful note, the latter sounds an alarming note of doom for the future.

The effect of this speech is to locate kingship within covenantal relationships. A new leadership has been inaugurated but heavily circumscribed by the dynamics of the old. The guardian of the old ways, Samuel, has a

it from me to sin against the Lᴏʀᴅ by ceasing to pray for you and to teach you the good and right way. ²⁴But you must fear the Lᴏʀᴅ and serve him faithfully with all your heart, for you have seen the great things the Lᴏʀᴅ has done among you. ²⁵If instead you continue to do evil, both you and your king shall be swept away."

III. Saul and David

13 ¹[Saul was . . . years old when he became king and he reigned . . . -two years over Israel.]

Saul Offers Sacrifice. ²Saul chose three thousand of Israel, of whom two thousand remained with him in Michmash and in the hill country of Bethel,

and one thousand were with Jonathan in Gibeah of Benjamin. He sent the rest of the army back to their tents. ³Now Jonathan struck the Philistine garrison in Gibeah, and the Philistines got word of it. Then Saul sounded the horn throughout the land, saying, "Let the Hebrews hear!" ⁴Then all Israel heard the report, "Saul has struck the garrison of the Philistines! Israel has become odious to the Philistines!" Then the army was called up to Saul in Gilgal. ⁵The Philistines also assembled for battle against Israel, with thirty thousand chariots, six thousand horsemen, and foot soldiers as numerous as the sand on the seashore. They came up and encamped in Michmash, east of Beth-aven. ⁶When the soldiers saw they were in danger because

---

key role to play in arbitrating, teaching, and interceding for the people (and their king). Israel may now live under a monarchy, but that monarchy is under the Torah and its representatives. The initiative taken by Israel in asking for a king has been granted, but in a form which allows God the freedom to act for blessing or curse. The people are given Saul ("the one asked for"), but will he be what they wanted? Or will he perish under the tensions of conflicting demands of ownership?

13:1-22 Saul rejected by Samuel

Chapter 13 begins the account of Saul's reign with a regnal formula (13:1), used throughout the history to mark the start of a reign (cf. 2 Sam 5:4), but Saul's age and length of reign are missing. This verse was perhaps introduced at a late stage in the composition of the book, but its faults are consonant with what follows. Saul's reign lacks something. His exploits in the opening verses (13:2-7) suffer setback after setback. The narrator gives special prominence to the perceptions of the people. The people make the king: now they see what Saul makes of the role.

At Gilgal, Saul waits seven days for Samuel (13:8) as he was told to do (cf. 10:8). When Samuel does not appear, Saul begins the sacrifices. Then Samuel appears and rebukes Saul (13:9-14). Both men agree that an appointment was made and not kept, but what then? Saul's excuse (13:11-12)

the army was hardpressed, they hid themselves in caves, thickets, rocks, caverns, and cisterns. ⁷Other Hebrews crossed the Jordan into the land of Gad and Gilead. Saul, however, held out in Gilgal, all his army trembling in fear behind him. ⁸He waited seven days, until the appointed time Samuel had set, but Samuel did not come, and the army deserted Saul. ⁹He then said, "Bring me the burnt offering and communion offerings!" Then he sacrificed the burnt offering.

King Saul Reproved. ¹⁰As he finished sacrificing the burnt offering, there came Samuel! So Saul went out toward him in order to greet him. ¹¹Samuel asked him, "What have you done?" Saul explained: "When I saw that the army was deserting me and you did not come on the appointed day, and that the Philistines were assembling at Michmash, ¹²I said to myself, 'Now the Philistines will come down against me at Gilgal, and I have not yet sought the LORD's blessing.' So I thought I should sacrifice the burnt offering." ¹³Samuel replied to Saul: "You have acted foolishly! Had you kept the command the LORD your God gave you, the LORD would now establish your kingship in Israel forever; ¹⁴but now your kingship shall not endure. The LORD has sought out a man after his own heart to appoint as ruler over his people because you did not observe what the LORD commanded you."

Philistine Invasion. ¹⁵Then Samuel set out from Gilgal and went his own way; but what was left of the army went up after Saul to meet the soldiers, going from Gilgal to Gibeah of Benjamin. Saul then counted the soldiers he had with him, about six hundred. ¹⁶Saul, his son Jonathan, and the soldiers they had with them were now occupying Geba of Benjamin, and the Philistines were encamped at Michmash. ¹⁷Meanwhile, raiders left the camp of the Philistines in three bands. One band took the Ophrah road toward the district of Shual; ¹⁸another turned in the direction of Bethhoron; and the third took the road for Geba that overlooks the Valley of the Hyenas toward the desert.

---

summarizes his predicament. He has too many masters and is the victim of competing demands: the people's desertion, Samuel's orders, and the need to sacrifice to the Lord. He is not free to trust totally in the Lord. Samuel says that Saul has failed to obey the Lord and so the curse of 12:15 comes into play (13:13-14). But more accurately, Saul has failed to obey the command of Samuel, who planned to maintain control over the new king. In a fit of rage, Samuel abandons his protégé. While Saul had been given a new heart (10:9), it is not pliable enough for Samuel's liking. The Lord will look for a man after his own heart (13:14).

Abandoned by Samuel, Saul and the remnant of his forces take up position (13:15-18) while the Philistines move freely in and out of their base camp. Nothing is done to prevent their advance (13:23). The narrator darkens the prospects with a digression (13:19-22) on the technological gap

Disarmament of Israel. [19]Not a single smith was to be found anywhere in Israel, for the Philistines had said, "Otherwise the Hebrews will make swords or spears." [20]All Israel, therefore, had to go down to the Philistines to sharpen their plowshares, mattocks, axes, and sickles. [21]The price for the plowshares and mattocks was two thirds of a shekel, and a third of a shekel for sharpening the axes and for setting the ox-goads. [22]And so on the day of battle neither sword nor spear could be found in the hand of any of the soldiers with Saul or Jonathan. Only Saul and his son Jonathan had them.

Jonathan's Exploit. [23]An outpost of the Philistines had pushed forward to the pass of Michmash.

14 [1]One day Jonathan, son of Saul, said to his armor-bearer, "Come, let us go over to the Philistine outpost on the other side." But he did not inform his father— [2]Saul was sitting under the pomegranate tree in Migron on the outskirts of Gibeah; with him were about six hundred men. [3]Ahijah, son of Ahitub, brother of Ichabod, the son of Phinehas, son of Eli, the priest of the LORD at Shiloh, was wearing the ephod—nor did the soldiers know that Jonathan had gone. [4]Flanking the ravine through which Jonathan intended to cross to the Philistine outpost were rocky crags on each side, one named Bozez and the other Seneh. [5]One crag was to the north, toward Michmash; the other to the south, toward Geba. [6]Jonathan said to his armor-bearer: "Come, let us go over to that outpost of the uncircumcised. Perhaps the LORD will help us, because it is no more difficult for the LORD to grant victory by means of a few than it is by means of many." [7]His armor-bearer

between the Philistines and the Israelites. In such a situation, victory can only be gained by the Lord. Poor Saul was chosen to be the savior, but everything is going wrong for him.

14:1-23 Jonathan's exploit

In contrast, his son Jonathan moves forward (14:1-6). Jonathan does not inform his father (14:1) nor the troops (14:3). Is he distancing himself from Saul? Jonathan expresses faith in the Lord's power to save, no matter the circumstance (14:6), and his armor-bearer commends him to do all that is in his heart (14:7). Is Jonathan the man after the Lord's heart for whom Samuel yearned? Jonathan's choices and actions are constantly announced in faith-filled terms, and the Lord does help Jonathan to a significant victory (14:8-15). The ensuing earthquake is a clear sign of divine victory over the Philistine garrison (14:15). Meanwhile Saul's posture and entourage send the wrong signals: he sits, and he is accompanied by one of the disgraced Elide priesthood (14:2-3). When action is needed, he turns to ritual once again (14:16-19) and nearly misses the opportunity. Saul seems unable to

replied, "Do whatever you think best; I am with you in whatever you decide." [8]Jonathan continued: "When we cross over to those men, we will be visible to them. [9]If they say to us, 'Stay there until we can come to you,' we will stop where we are; we will not go up to them. [10]But if they say, 'Come up to us,' we will go up, because the LORD has delivered them into our hand. That will be our sign." [11]When the two of them came into the view of the Philistine outpost, the Philistines remarked, "Look, some Hebrews are coming out of the holes where they have been hiding." [12]The men of the outpost called to Jonathan and his armor-bearer. "Come up here," they said, "and we will teach you a lesson." So Jonathan said to his armor-bearer, "Climb up after me, for the LORD has delivered them into the hand of Israel." [13]Jonathan clambered up with his armor-bearer behind him. As the Philistines fell before Jonathan, his armor-bearer, who followed him, would finish them off. [14]In this first attack Jonathan and his armor-bearer killed about twenty men within half a furlong. [15]Then terror spread through the camp and the countryside; all the soldiers in the outpost and in the raiding parties shuddered in terror. The earth shook with an awesome shuddering.

Rout of the Philistines. [16]Saul's sentinels in Gibeah of Benjamin saw that the enemy camp had scattered and were running in all directions. [17]Saul said to those around him, "Count the troops and find out if any of us are missing." When they had taken the count, they found Jonathan and his armor-bearer missing. [18]Saul then said to Ahijah, "Bring the ephod here." (Ahijah was wearing the ephod before the Israelites at that time.) [19]While Saul was speaking to the priest, the uproar in the Philistine camp kept increasing. So he said to the priest, "Withdraw your hand." [20]And Saul and all his men rallied and rushed into the fight, where the Philistines, wholly confused, were thrusting swords at one another. [21]The Hebrews who had previously sided with the Philistines and had gone up with them to their camp turned to join the Israelites under Saul and Jonathan. [22]Likewise, all the Israelites who were hiding in the hill country of Ephraim, hearing that the Philistines were fleeing, kept after them in the battle. [23]Thus the LORD saved Israel that day.

Saul's Oath. The battle continued past Beth-aven. [24]Even though the Israelites were exhausted that day, Saul laid an oath on them, saying, "Cursed be the one who takes food before evening,

read the signs of the Lord's victory which are plainly visible to his troops (14:16). Other Israelites are less obtuse: Jonathan's victory triggers a wholesale uprising (14:21-22). Thus the Lord saves Israel (14:23) despite the overwhelming power of the Philistines and the underwhelming caution of Saul.

14:24-46 Jonathan caught in Saul's oath

With the Lord's victory assured, the narrative can focus on Saul's handling of the situation. At once, he complicates the action with an oath (14:24)

before I am able to avenge myself on my enemies." So none of the people tasted food. [25]Now there was a honeycomb lying on the ground, [26]and when the soldiers came to the comb the honey was flowing; yet no one raised a hand from it to his mouth, because the people feared the oath.

Violation of the Oath. [27]Jonathan, who had not heard that his father had put the people under oath, thrust out the end of the staff he was holding and dipped it into the honeycomb. Then he raised it to his mouth and his eyes brightened. [28]At this, one of the soldiers spoke up: "Your father put the people under a strict oath, saying, 'Cursed be the one who takes food today!' As a re-sult the people are weakened." [29]Jonathan replied: "My father brings trouble to the land. Look how bright my eyes are because I had this little taste of honey. [30]What is more, if the army had eaten freely of the enemy's plunder when they came across it today, surely the slaughter of the Philistines would have been the greater by now!"

Consuming the Blood. [31]After the Philistines were routed that day from Michmash to Aijalon, the people were completely exhausted. [32]So the army pounced upon the plunder and took sheep, oxen, and calves, slaughtering them on the ground and eating the meat with the blood in it. [33]Informed that the army was sinning against the Lord by

---

cursing anyone who eats that day while battle continues. At one level, such fasting is part of a holy war, a means of devoting oneself to the Lord's cause. But victory *has been* granted so such preparations are redundant. The oath hinders progress by weakening the soldiers who hear and keep it (14:25-26) while creating a snare for Jonathan who does not (14:27). A soldier witnesses Jonathan eating honey and reports the negative effects of the oath. This leads Jonathan to voice the pragmatic interpretation: had the people eaten, the victory would be greater (14:30). Further, he describes Saul as one who "brings trouble to the land" (14:29), a serious accusation calling to mind the crimes of Achan (cf. Josh 7).

The oath creates another transgression (14:31-35). In their hunger, the army fails to prepare meat in the ritually correct manner (cf. Lev 3:17). Saul responds in an efficient manner: he can deal with ritual if not with its spirit.

Saul takes the initiative at last to continue the plunder (14:36). The army's response is non-committal and the priest has little difficulty in deflecting Saul into another ritual. But engagement in a ritual does not guarantee communication with the Lord (14:37). Saul assumes a sin has been committed and begins an investigation using the Urim and Thummim, or sacred lots. With another oath he vows that the guilty will die (14:39). The people's silence suggests they are not happy with this turn of events. The process is

eating the meat with blood in it, Saul said: "You have broken faith. Roll a large stone here for me." ³⁴He continued: "Mingle with the people and tell each of them, 'Bring an ox or sheep to me. Slaughter them here and then eat. But you must not sin against the LORD by eating meat with blood in it.'" So that night they all brought whatever oxen they had seized, and they slaughtered them there; ³⁵and Saul built an altar to the LORD—this was the first time he built an altar to the LORD.

Jonathan in Danger of Death. ³⁶Then Saul said, "Let us go down in pursuit of the Philistines by night, to plunder them until daybreak and leave no one alive." They replied, "Do what you think best." But the priest said, "Let us consult God." ³⁷So Saul inquired of God: "Shall I go down in pursuit of the Philistines? Will you deliver them into the hand of Israel?" But he received no answer on this occasion. ³⁸"All officers of the army," Saul announced, "come forward. Find out how this sin was committed today. ³⁹As the LORD lives who has given victory to Israel, even if my son Jonathan has committed it, he shall surely die!" But none of the people answered him.

⁴⁰So he said to all Israel, "Stand on one side, and my son Jonathan and I will stand on the other." The people responded, "Do what you think best." ⁴¹And Saul said to the LORD, the God of Israel: "Why did you not answer your servant this time? If the blame for this resides in me or my son Jonathan, LORD, God of Israel, respond with Urim; but if this guilt is in your people Israel, respond with Thummim." Jonathan and Saul were designated, and the people went free. ⁴²Saul then said, "Cast lots between me and my son Jonathan." And Jonathan was designated. ⁴³Saul said to Jonathan, "Tell me what you have done." Jonathan replied, "I only tasted a little honey from the end of the staff I was holding. Am I to die for this?" ⁴⁴Saul declared, "May God do thus to me, and more, if you do not indeed die, Jonathan!"

Rescue of Jonathan. ⁴⁵But the soldiers protested to Saul: "Is Jonathan to die, the man who won this great victory for Israel? This must not be! As the LORD lives, not a single hair of his head shall fall to the ground, for God was with him in what he did today!" Thus the soldiers rescued Jonathan and he did not die.

carried through until Jonathan is taken and admits that he ate the honey. Saul is consistent in demanding his son's death (14:44). However, the army intervenes to stop this becoming a tragedy (14:45). They declare their evaluation of the day's events: Jonathan is the one who brought victory (not Saul) and shall not die (despite Saul's oaths). Thus, the people end Saul's initiative and close the sorry episode.

Chapters 13 and 14 contrast Jonathan, trusting in the Lord and willing to be the means of victory, with a hesitant, ritual-bound Saul for whom events go very wrong. Bereft of Samuel's guidance, he struggles to uncover the Lord's will without success. He therefore stumbles from one mistake

⁴⁶After that Saul gave up the pursuit of the Philistines, who returned to their own territory.

Saul's Victories. ⁴⁷After taking possession of the kingship over Israel, Saul waged war on its enemies all around—Moab, the Ammonites, Edom, the kings of Zobah, and the Philistines. Wherever he turned, he was successful ⁴⁸and fought bravely. He defeated Amalek and delivered Israel from the hand of those who were plundering them.

Saul's Family. ⁴⁹The sons of Saul were Jonathan, Ishvi, and Malchishua; the name of his firstborn daughter was Merob; the name of the younger was Michal. ⁵⁰The name of Saul's wife was Ahinoam, daughter of Ahimaaz. The name of his general was Abner, son of Ner, Saul's uncle; ⁵¹Kish, Saul's father, and Ner, Abner's father, were sons of Abiel.

⁵²There was heavy fighting with the Philistines during Saul's lifetime. Whenever Saul saw any strong or brave man, he took him into his service.

15 Disobedience of Saul. ¹Samuel said to Saul: "It was I the LORD sent to anoint you king over his people Israel. Now, therefore, listen to the message of the LORD. ²Thus says the LORD of hosts: I will punish what Amalek did to the Israelites when he barred their way as they came up from Egypt. ³Go,

to another in an attempt to appease the Lord. This becomes too much for the people, who block his ritual-driven destruction of the victory. The narrator has shaped the story to share the people's perceptions with the reader: it was the people (and Samuel) who made Saul king, and in these chapters the people come to regret their choice. Saul's kingship cannot be maintained if these key players no longer back him.

14:47-52 Summary of Saul's reign

Despite the negative picture of the last narrative, the reign of Saul did last many years and he achieved some notable successes which the narrator lists in this summary. Also listed are the names of his family. But the summary ends by noting that Saul never brought the Philistine threat to an end.

15:1-35 Saul rejected as king

This chapter opens with a concise statement of the settlement reached in chapter 12: Samuel stands as the voice of the covenant God and the king must listen to that voice (15:1). This narrative sets up a specific case study of the theological settlement: Saul will be judged on his ability to obey. The Lord's will is the extermination of the Amalekites (15:2-3; cf. Deut 25:17-19). Extermination is abhorrent to modern ears, but the ban is actually a consecration of Amalek to the Lord. That nation is set aside for the Lord's use and destruction ensures that it is beyond human interference.

47

now, attack Amalek, and put under the ban everything he has. Do not spare him; kill men and women, children and infants, oxen and sheep, camels and donkeys."

⁴Saul alerted the army, and at Telaim reviewed two hundred thousand foot soldiers and ten thousand men of Judah. ⁵Saul went to the city of Amalek and set up an ambush in the wadi. ⁶He warned the Kenites: "Leave Amalek, turn aside and come down so I will not have to destroy you with them, for you were loyal to the Israelites when they came up from Egypt." After the Kenites left, ⁷Saul routed Amalek from Havilah to the approaches of Shur, on the frontier of Egypt. ⁸He took Agag, king of Amalek, alive, but the rest of the people he destroyed by the sword, putting them under the ban. ⁹He and his troops spared Agag and the best of the fat sheep and oxen, and the lambs. They refused to put under the ban anything that was worthwhile, destroying only what was worthless and of no account.

Samuel Rebukes Saul. ¹⁰Then the word of the LORD came to Samuel: ¹¹I regret having made Saul king, for he has turned from me and has not kept my command. At this Samuel grew angry and cried out to the LORD all night. ¹²Early in the morning he went to meet Saul, but was informed that Saul had gone to Carmel, where he set up a monument in his own honor, and that

---

15:4-9 *Disobedience*

Saul initially obeys the Lord's command and is successful. The narrator then reports what "He and his troops" do. Saul and the people are acting together, as expected when Samuel outlined the conditions of the new settlement (12:14-15). Contrary to instructions (15:9) they spare the best of the booty when the Lord said, "Do not spare . . ." (15:3).

15:10-23 *Punishment*

Verses 10-11 are the heart of the narrative. The Lord reveals his decision: "I regret having made Saul king." The reason is expressed in terms of apostasy and disobedience, two sides of the one coin. After initial opposition to the Lord's willingness to appoint a king (ch. 8), Samuel had invested his hopes in a pliable Saul (ch. 10), but was disappointed by Saul's independence (13:13-14). Saul was Samuel's foothold in the new dispensation. If the Lord rejects Saul, Samuel has nothing either. Perhaps this explains Samuel's anger in verse 11.

Samuel's confrontation with Saul is clinical and penetrating (15:12-23). Saul states his obedience to the Lord's command (15:13), but the evidence contradicts him and Samuel cuts through his subtle distinctions (15:14). Two excuses form Saul's defense: he distinguishes between his actions and those of the people, and he claims that the spared booty was for sacrifice. There is no evidence for the latter excuse. The former is contradicted by the

on his return he had gone down to Gilgal. ¹³When Samuel came to him, Saul greeted him: "The LORD bless you! I have kept the command of the LORD." ¹⁴But Samuel asked, "What, then, is this bleating of sheep that comes to my ears, the lowing of oxen that I hear?" ¹⁵Saul replied: "They were brought from Amalek. The people spared the best sheep and oxen to sacrifice to the LORD, your God; but the rest we destroyed, putting them under the ban." ¹⁶Samuel said to Saul: "Stop! Let me tell you what the LORD said to me last night." "Speak!" he replied. ¹⁷Samuel then said: "Though little in your own eyes, are you not chief of the tribes of Israel? The LORD anointed you king of Israel ¹⁸and sent you on a mission, saying: Go and put the sinful Amalekites under a ban of destruction. Fight against them until you have exterminated them. ¹⁹Why then have you disobeyed the LORD? You have pounced on the spoil, thus doing what was evil in the LORD's sight." ²⁰Saul explained to Samuel: "I did indeed obey the LORD and fulfill the mission on which the LORD sent me. I have brought back Agag, the king of Amalek, and, carrying out the ban, I have destroyed the Amalekites. ²¹But from the spoil the army took sheep and oxen, the best of what had been banned, to sacrifice to the LORD your God in Gilgal." ²²But Samuel said:

"Does the LORD delight in burnt offerings and sacrifices
as much as in obedience to the LORD's command?
Obedience is better than sacrifice, to listen, better than the fat of rams.
²³For a sin of divination is rebellion, and arrogance, the crime of idolatry.
Because you have rejected the word of the LORD,
the LORD in turn has rejected you as king."

Rejection of Saul. ²⁴Saul admitted to Samuel: "I have sinned, for I have transgressed the command of the LORD and

reported facts (15:9) and the theological frame within which monarchy is to function: it is not a valid excuse. Samuel cuts through the excuses to the main accusation: disobedience of the Lord's command (15:19). Samuel's prophetic word of judgment (15:22-23) poetically balances "obedience" against "sin," "rebellion," "arrogance," and "idolatry," in summation, rejection of the Lord's command. The punishment for disobedience is measured: rejection for rejection.

15:24-35 Setting the stage for a new beginning

Saul acknowledges his sin in two stages (15:24-25 and 30) in the hope of reconnecting with Samuel and thus with the Lord. His first request for forgiveness (15:25) is rebuffed by a repetition of judgment. Looking forward to 2 Samuel 12, David will find himself in a similar position and be forgiven. Why Saul is not forgiven is a mystery unresolved in this text. In desperation,

your instructions. I feared the people and obeyed them. ²⁵Now forgive my sin, and return with me, that I may worship the Lord." ²⁶But Samuel said to Saul, "I will not return with you, because you rejected the word of the Lord and the Lord has rejected you as king of Israel." ²⁷As Samuel turned to go, Saul seized a loose end of his garment, and it tore off. ²⁸So Samuel said to him: "The Lord has torn the kingdom of Israel from you this day, and has given it to a neighbor of yours, who is better than you. ²⁹The Glory of Israel neither deceives nor repents, for he is not a mortal who repents." ³⁰But Saul answered: "I have sinned, yet honor me now before the elders of my people and before Israel. Return with me that I may worship the Lord your God." ³¹And so Samuel returned with him, and Saul worshiped the Lord.

Samuel Executes Agag. ³²Afterward Samuel commanded, "Bring Agag, king of Amalek, to me." Agag came to him struggling and saying, "So it is bitter death!" ³³And Samuel said,

"As your sword has made women
    childless,
  so shall your mother be childless
    among women."

Then he cut Agag to pieces before the Lord in Gilgal. ³⁴Samuel departed for Ramah, while Saul went up to his home

---

Saul grasps at Samuel's cloak, and the torn fragment only becomes a prophetic sign to underline the rejection of Saul (15:27-28). Samuel's concluding remark creates more difficulties for the reader (15:29). He claims that the Lord does not repent, yet the Lord said in verse 11 that he does, and in verse 35 the narrator will confirm this repentance. In the story of Saul's rejection, the reader comes face to face with the mystery of the Lord's ability to change.

Once more Saul acknowledges his sin and asks Samuel to maintain the appearance of support (15:30). Without comment, Samuel agrees, and completes the extermination commanded in verses 2-3 (15:31-33).

The narrator offers some parting observations about Samuel. He goes home (15:34), and he never sees Saul again (15:35). Samuel's grief arises from the failure of the arrangements he had established in chapter 12. Saul's disobedience places him under the curse of 12:15 and Samuel's hopes to create a prophet-led monarchy collapse. But the double failure of Saul and Samuel is based in the deeper dynamics of the Lord's plan. Samuel declared, "The Glory of Israel neither deceives nor repents" (15:29). Saul's monarchy was of the people's making, not the Lord's. The Lord's plan for Israel continues to unfold even when complicated or thwarted by human initiatives. Saul was one such initiative: he will always be the king "asked for." Now that his failure is clear, and his rejection declared, the Lord can create a new beginning for a monarchy of his own choosing.

in Gibeah of Saul. [35]Never again, as long as he lived, did Samuel see Saul. Yet he grieved over Saul, because the LORD repented that he had made him king of Israel.

16 **Samuel Is Sent to Bethlehem.** [1]The LORD said to Samuel: How long will you grieve for Saul, whom I have rejected as king of Israel? Fill your horn with oil, and be on your way. I am sending you to Jesse of Bethlehem, for from among his sons I have decided on a king. [2]But Samuel replied: "How can I go? Saul will hear of it and kill me." To this the LORD answered: Take a heifer along and say, "I have come to sacrifice to the LORD." [3]Invite Jesse to the sacrifice, and I myself will tell you what to do; you are to anoint for me the one I point out to you.

Samuel Anoints David. [4]Samuel did as the LORD had commanded him. When he entered Bethlehem, the elders of the city came trembling to meet him and asked, "Is your visit peaceful, O seer?" [5]He replied: "Yes! I have come to sacrifice to the LORD. So purify yourselves and celebrate with me today." He also had Jesse and his sons purify themselves and invited them to the sacrifice. [6]As they came, he looked at Eliab and thought, "Surely the anointed is here

THE RISE OF DAVID

1 Samuel 16:1–2 Samuel 5:12

In chapter 16, David is introduced and begins his long rise to become king of Israel and Judah (2 Sam 5). It is generally accepted that the Deuteronomists incorporated a very old document, possibly put together in the court of David or Solomon, which has been called "The History of David's Rise" (1 Sam 16:14–2 Sam 5:12). The document explains why Saul's monarchy disappears and legitimates David's accession. It affirms that the Lord was with David (16:18; 17:37; 18:12, 14, 28) and had departed from Saul (16:14).

16:1-13 Samuel anoints David

With 16:1, a new initiative begins. This time, the Lord is in charge of the action, prompting and directing each step. The Lord's beginning reverses the ending of Saul's kingship. Verse 1a echoes the content of 15:35b to effect this transition from rejection to selection of a new anointed.

There are close similarities between the anointing of David and of Saul (9:1–10:16). Both are carried out by Samuel under a cloak of secrecy; this time it involves a visit to a city to conduct a sacrifice to which certain people are invited. After each anointing, the spirit of the Lord rushes upon the anointed. Yet there are striking differences. The Lord is much more prominent in directing Samuel and explicit in naming his choice in 16:4-13. And

before the LORD." [7]But the LORD said to Samuel: Do not judge from his appearance or from his lofty stature, because I have rejected him. God does not see as a mortal, who sees the appearance. The LORD looks into the heart. [8]Then Jesse called Abinadab and presented him before Samuel, who said, "The LORD has not chosen him." [9]Next Jesse presented Shammah, but Samuel said, "The LORD has not chosen this one either." [10]In the same way Jesse presented seven sons before Samuel, but Samuel said to Jesse, "The LORD has not chosen any one of these." [11]Then Samuel asked Jesse, "Are these all the sons you have?" Jesse replied, "There is still the youngest, but he is tending the sheep." Samuel said to Jesse, "Send for him; we will not sit down to eat until he arrives here." [12]Jesse had the young man brought to them. He was ruddy, a youth with beautiful eyes, and good looking. The LORD said: There —anoint him, for this is the one! [13]Then Samuel, with the horn of oil in hand, anointed him in the midst of his brothers, and from that day on, the spirit of the LORD rushed upon David. Then Samuel set out for Ramah.

David Wins Saul's Approval. [14]The spirit of the LORD had departed from Saul, and he was tormented by an evil spirit from the LORD. [15]So the servants of Saul said to him: "Look! An evil spirit from God is tormenting you. [16]If your lordship will order it, we, your servants here attending to you, will look for a man skilled in playing the harp. When

there is an interesting exploration of the importance of appearances (16:7). These similarities and differences further support the notion of a new beginning which corrects the previous attempt to choose a king.

Saul's appearance distinguished him and his stature marked him out as a suitable candidate (cf. 9:2 and 10:23-24). Samuel continues to be influenced by appearances (16:6) but the Lord stops him: "God does not see as a mortal" (16:7). Samuel has not fully grasped the essence of divine discernment; he rejected Saul (13:14) for not having a heart attuned to the Lord, but he has not yet abandoned judgments based on appearances. The mystery for humans is to understand the criteria of the Lord and to live accordingly. It is ironic that David will be described as "ruddy, a youth with beautiful eyes, and good looking" (16:12), since all of this is supposedly irrelevant.

Anointing David is Samuel's last prophetic act. He retires to Ramah. The initiative started by Hannah's request is now complete and the Lord's own response to her situation can commence.

16:14-23 Saul appoints David

The spirit links these two accounts of David's selection: where the spirit of the Lord seizes David (16:13), it abandons Saul and is replaced by an evil

"Then Samuel, with the horn of oil in hand, anointed David in the midst of his brothers; and from that day on, the spirit of the Lord rushed upon David" (1 Samuel 16:13). Byzantine silver plate, ca. 29–30.

the evil spirit from God comes upon you, he will play and you will feel better." [17]Saul then told his servants, "Find me a good harpist and bring him to me." [18]One of the servants spoke up: "I have observed that a son of Jesse of Bethlehem is a skillful harpist. He is also a brave warrior, an able speaker, and a handsome young man. The LORD is certainly with him."

David Made Armor-Bearer. [19]Accordingly, Saul dispatched messengers to ask Jesse to send him his son David, who was with the flock. [20]Then Jesse took five loaves of bread, a skin of wine, and a young goat, and sent them to Saul with his son David. [21]Thus David came to Saul and entered his service. Saul became very fond of him and made him his armor-bearer. [22]Saul sent Jesse the message, "Let David stay in my service, for he meets with my approval." [23]Whenever the spirit from God came upon Saul, David would take the harp and play, and Saul would be relieved and feel better, for the evil spirit would leave him.

17 The Challenge of Goliath. [1]The Philistines rallied their forces for battle at Socoh in Judah and camped between Socoh and Azekah at Ephesdammim. [2]Saul and the Israelites rallied

---

spirit (16:14). The replacement of spirits in Saul also signals the start of his replacement by David.

David is summoned to court to deal with Saul's torment (16:15-18). Again, appearance provides part of the reason for David's advancement. More notable is the servant's comment that the Lord is with David, in contrast to Saul from whom the Lord has departed (16:18). This story is setting up conflicts to come. A further complication enters the story in verse 21: Saul loved David greatly (translating literally). In these stories, "love" refers to allegiance and fidelity. In effect, Saul adopts David and becomes his surrogate father (16:22), thus binding their fates very closely indeed (cf. 10:11-12). Will Saul's efforts to repeat Samuel's attempt at paternal control be equally disastrous? Or will David be able to escape and become "son" to the Lord?

17:1–18:30 David in the court of Saul

The text of chapters 17 and 18 has a complex compositional and transmission history. Major portions are missing from the oldest Greek translation, preserved in Codex Vaticanus (17:12-32, 41, 48b, 55-58 and 18:1-5, 10-11, 12b, 17-19, 26b, 29b-30), but are contained in the Hebrew manuscripts. Scholars believe that the Old Greek translation is witness to the original version of these chapters. In the fourth century B.C., the text was expanded to incorporate a second storyline. The older storyline develops from David's arrival at court and appointment as armor-bearer (16:14-23), and tells of his

and camped in the valley of the Elah, drawing up their battle line to meet the Philistines. ³The Philistines were stationed on one hill and the Israelites on an opposite hill, with a valley between them.

⁴A champion named Goliath of Gath came out from the Philistine camp; he was six cubits and a span tall. ⁵He had a bronze helmet on his head and wore a bronze breastplate of scale armor weighing five thousand shekels, ⁶bronze greaves, and had a bronze scimitar slung from his shoulders. ⁷The shaft of his javelin was like a weaver's beam, and its iron head weighed six hundred shekels. His shield-bearer went ahead of him.

⁸He stood and shouted to the ranks of Israel: "Why come out in battle formation? I am a Philistine, and you are Saul's servants. Choose one of your men, and have him come down to me. ⁹If he beats me in combat and kills me, we will be your vassals; but if I beat him and kill him, you shall be our vassals and serve us." ¹⁰The Philistine continued: "I defy the ranks of Israel today. Give me a man and let us fight together." ¹¹When Saul and all Israel heard this challenge of the Philistine, they were stunned and terrified.

David Comes to the Camp. ¹²David was the son of an Ephrathite named Jesse from Bethlehem in Judah who had

willingness to volunteer as champion against the Philistine. This story assumes that Saul knows David throughout. The added storyline grows out of 16:1-13 (David as shepherd, at home with his family), and tells how he arrives at the battle scene, meets Saul for the first time, and volunteers as champion. The editors skillfully merge the two traditions to create one of the most memorable narratives of the Old Testament.

17:1-11 The challenge of Goliath

Saul was anointed to end the Philistine threat but he failed to do so (cf. 14:52). This story opens with a major confrontation between the two peoples (17:1-3). The balance of power is tilted heavily in the Philistines' favor. They have a champion (17:4) who strikes fear into the Israelites (17:11). Three things about Goliath are described. Goliath is very tall, but appearances should not count for people of faith (cf. Eliab in 16:6-7). Secondly, he is well-armored, but this did not deter Jonathan in chapter 13. Finally, he is boastful (17:8-10), but God's people should believe the affirmations of Hannah's song (2:3). Yet Saul and the troops do not express covenant faith, nor do they mention the divine name.

17:12-31 David's faith

Into this reign of terror comes David, exuding curiosity and enthusiasm. Using the second storyline, the narrator recaps David's origins and describes how he is transferred from minding sheep to bringing provisions

eight sons. In the days of Saul Jesse was old and well on in years. ¹³The three oldest sons of Jesse had followed Saul to war; the names of these three sons who had gone off to war were Eliab the first-born; Abinadab the second; and Shammah the third. ¹⁴David was the youngest. While the three oldest had joined Saul, ¹⁵David would come and go from Saul's presence to tend his father's sheep at Bethlehem.

¹⁶Meanwhile the Philistine came forward and took his stand morning and evening for forty days.

¹⁷Now Jesse said to his son David: "Take this ephah of roasted grain and these ten loaves for your brothers, and bring them quickly to your brothers in the camp. ¹⁸Also take these ten cheeses for the field officer. Greet your brothers and bring home some token from them. ¹⁹Saul and your brothers, together with all Israel, are at war with the Philistines in the valley of the Elah." ²⁰Early the next morning, having left the flock with a shepherd, David packed up and set out, as Jesse had commanded him. He reached the barricade of the camp just as the army, on their way to the battle-ground, were shouting their battle cry. ²¹The Israelites and the Philistines drew up opposite each other in battle array.

²²David entrusted what he had brought to the keeper of the baggage and hastened to the battle line, where he greeted his brothers. ²³While he was talking with them, the Philistine champion, by name Goliath of Gath, came up from the ranks of the Philistines and spoke as before, and David listened. ²⁴When the Israelites saw the man, they all retreated before him, terrified. ²⁵The Israelites had been saying: "Do you see this man coming up? He comes up to insult Israel. The king will make whoever kills him a very wealthy man. He will give his daughter to him and declare his father's family exempt from taxes in Israel." ²⁶David now said to the men standing near him: "How will the man who kills this Philistine and frees Israel from disgrace be rewarded? Who is this uncircumcised Philistine that he should insult the armies of the living God?" ²⁷They repeated the same words to him and said, "That is how the man who kills him will be rewarded." ²⁸When Eliab, his oldest brother, heard him speaking with the men, he grew angry with David and said: "Why did you come down? With whom have you left those sheep in the wilderness? I know your arrogance and dishonest heart. You came down to enjoy the battle!" ²⁹David protested,

---

to his older brothers (17:12-19). David arrives in time to hear Goliath's morning challenge to the cowering troops (17:20-24). As in all good adventure stories, there is talk of a reward—wealth and the hand of the king's daughter—for the man who kills Goliath. David is not motivated by reward but by faith. He boldly declares his faith in God's power to save (17:26). David's use of the term "the living God" contrasts the God of Israel with idols such as Dagon, whom God has already knocked down in chapter 5. While not a common term, it is the first declaration of faith in this story.

"What have I done now? I was only talking." ³⁰He turned from him to another and asked the same question; and everyone gave him the same answer as before. ³¹The words that David had spoken were overheard and reported to Saul, who sent for him.

David Challenges Goliath. ³²Then David spoke to Saul: "My lord should not lose heart. Let your servant go and fight this Philistine." ³³But Saul answered David, "You cannot go up against this Philistine and fight with him, for you are only a youth, while he has been a warrior from his youth." ³⁴Then David told Saul: "Your servant used to tend his father's sheep, and whenever a lion or bear came to carry off a sheep from the flock, ³⁵I would chase after it, attack it, and snatch the prey from its mouth. If it attacked me, I would seize it by the

throat, strike it, and kill it. ³⁶Your servant has killed both a lion and a bear. This uncircumcised Philistine will be as one of them, because he has insulted the armies of the living God."

³⁷David continued: "The same LORD who delivered me from the claws of the lion and the bear will deliver me from the hand of this Philistine." Saul answered David, "Go! the LORD will be with you."

Preparation for the Encounter. ³⁸Then Saul dressed David in his own tunic, putting a bronze helmet on his head and arming him with a coat of mail. ³⁹David also fastened Saul's sword over the tunic. He walked with difficulty, however, since he had never worn armor before. He said to Saul, "I cannot go in these, because I am not used to them." So he took them off. ⁴⁰Then, staff in hand,

17:32-40 The Lord's deliverance

David's declaration brings him to Saul's attention and David promptly volunteers to be Israel's champion (17:32). Saul demurs because David is only a "youth." The Hebrew term, *na'ar*, has a range of usages (infant, youth, attendant, soldier, royal official) arising from a root meaning of dependence, either within the family or in service. This flexibility of meaning allows the editor to weave together the two storylines. David responds with another speech expressing faith in God as savior (17:34-37). He describes his own experience as shepherd when he would rescue the prey from wild animals (17:35). He was able to do so then because the Lord "delivered" him, and the Lord will deliver him again. At the center of the speech, David restates his anger at the insult to the living God (17:36) and names the Lord as the one who delivers his people. This faith alone makes the difference in battle. Yet Saul, cautious and not so bold in faith, tries to arm David (17:38-39). This would give him a comparable appearance to Goliath, but is not how God wins victories! Appearances or weapons are immaterial to one with faith; David takes the basic armaments of a shepherd or foot soldier (17:40).

David selected five smooth stones from the wadi and put them in the pocket of his shepherd's bag. With his sling in hand, he approached the Philistine.

David's Victory. ⁴¹With his shield-bearer marching before him, the Philistine advanced closer and closer to David. ⁴²When he sized David up and saw that he was youthful, ruddy, and handsome in appearance, he began to deride him. ⁴³He said to David, "Am I a dog that you come against me with a staff?" Then the Philistine cursed David by his gods ⁴⁴and said to him, "Come here to me, and I will feed your flesh to the birds of the air and the beasts of the field." ⁴⁵David answered him: "You come against me with sword and spear and scimitar, but I come against you in the name of the LORD of hosts, the God of the armies of Israel whom you have insulted. ⁴⁶Today the LORD shall deliver you into my hand; I will strike you down and cut off your head. This very day I will feed your dead body and the dead bodies of the Philistine army to the birds of the air and the beasts of the field; thus the whole land shall learn that Israel has a God. ⁴⁷All this multitude, too, shall learn that it is not by sword or spear that the LORD saves. For the battle belongs to the LORD, who shall deliver you into our hands."

⁴⁸The Philistine then moved to meet David at close quarters, while David ran quickly toward the battle line to meet the Philistine. ⁴⁹David put his hand into the bag and took out a stone, hurled it with the sling, and struck the Philistine on the forehead. The stone embedded itself in his brow, and he fell on his face to the ground. ⁵⁰Thus David triumphed over the Philistine with sling and stone; he struck the Philistine dead, and did it without a sword in his hand. ⁵¹Then David ran and stood over him; with the Philistine's own sword which he drew from its sheath he killed him, and cut off his head.

Flight of the Philistines. When the Philistines saw that their hero was dead, they fled. ⁵²Then the men of Israel and Judah sprang up with a battle cry and pursued them to the approaches of Gath and to the gates of Ekron, and Philistines

---

17:41-54 Victory in battle

The two champions square off (17:40b-41), and each hurls insults and threats (17:43-47). But David's speech is framed with declarations of faith. He names his God in contrast to the anonymous Philistine gods of Goliath's curse: "the LORD of hosts, the God of the armies of Israel" (17:45). The battle shows that "the LORD shall deliver you into my hand" (17:46). David is proclaiming the same good news of salvation for all to hear, as did Jonathan (compare 14:47 with 13:6).

Following the declaration, the account of the battle is swift and decisive (17:48-51). The real issues have been dealt with. Appropriately, the Lord's victory causes panic among his enemies and a rout ensues (17:51-53). Verse 54 is anachronistic; Jerusalem is not yet an Israelite city.

fell wounded along the road from Shaaraim as far as Gath and Ekron. [53]When they returned from their pursuit of the Philistines, the Israelites looted their camp. [54]David took the head of the Philistine and brought it to Jerusalem; but he kept Goliath's armor in his own tent.

David Presented to Saul. [55]As Saul watched David go out to meet the Philistine, he asked his general Abner, "Abner, whose son is that young man?" Abner replied, "On your life, O king, I have no idea." [56]And the king said, "Find out whose son the lad is." [57]So when David returned from slaying the Philistine, Abner escorted him into Saul's presence. David was still holding the Philistine's head. [58]Saul then asked him, "Whose son are you, young man?" David replied, "I am the son of your servant Jesse of Bethlehem."

18 David and Jonathan. [1]By the time David finished speaking with Saul, Jonathan's life became bound up with David's life; he loved him as his very self. [2]Saul retained David on that day and did not allow him to return to his father's house. [3]Jonathan and David made a covenant, because Jonathan loved him as his very self. [4]Jonathan took off the cloak he was wearing and handed it over to David, along with his military dress, even his sword, bow, and belt. [5]David then carried out successfully every mission on which Saul sent him. So Saul put him in charge of his soldiers; this met with the approval of the whole army, even Saul's officers.

Saul's Jealousy. [6]At the approach of Saul and David, on David's return after striking down the Philistine, women came out from all the cities of Israel to meet Saul the king, singing and dancing,

---

17:55-58 A failure of recognition

It is strange that Saul and Abner do not know who David is. This is understandable as part of the second, added storyline, but creates a certain tension in the final text. Is Saul's failure to recognize David a sign of his failure to recognize the Lord's support of this savior of the people?

18:1-30 Relations at Saul's court

This chapter describes the complex relationships between David, Saul and his family, and the public. David's successes win him the "love" of almost all, while Saul grows embittered towards the rising star. "Love" carries tones of personal affection, but the political dimensions of loyalty and allegiance are never far away. The narrative shifts between the reactions of Saul's children and the public. Much of the narrative reports events from Saul's perspective; his thoughts and intentions are revealed by the narrator. This enables the reader to appreciate Saul's ironic intimation of David's goal (18:8) while failing to see the reason until the end: the Lord is with David (cf. 18:12, 14, 28). David's thoughts are hidden. This reticence means he is a blank page for both reader and Saul.

with tambourines, joyful songs, and stringed instruments. ⁷The women played and sang:

"Saul has slain his thousands,
    David his tens of thousands."

⁸Saul was very angry and resentful of the song, for he thought: "They give David tens of thousands, but only thousands to me. All that remains for him is the kingship." ⁹From that day on, Saul kept a jealous eye on David.

¹⁰The next day an evil spirit from God rushed upon Saul, and he raged in his house. David was in attendance, playing the harp as at other times, while Saul was holding his spear. ¹¹Saul poised the spear, thinking, "I will nail David to the wall!" But twice David escaped him. ¹²Saul then began to fear David because the LORD was with him but had turned away from Saul. ¹³Saul sent him out of his presence and appointed him a field officer. So David led the people on their military expeditions ¹⁴and prospered in all his ways, for the LORD was with him. ¹⁵Seeing how he prospered, Saul feared David. ¹⁶But all Israel and Judah loved David, since he led them on their expeditions.

Saul Plots Against David. ¹⁷Saul said to David, "Look, I will give you my older daughter, Merob, in marriage if you become my warrior and fight the battles of the LORD." Saul thought, "I will not lay a hand on him. Let the hand

---

Verses 1-4 emphasize Jonathan's love for David. Jonathan identifies with David and gives him his regalia, treating him as an equal. But the Hebrew verb underlying "to be bound to" (18:1) can also mean "to be in conspiracy with." Where Saul attempted to hold on to Samuel's garment (symbol of the kingdom) in 15:27, Jonathan hands over his cloak. Jonathan's actions may be read as generosity or treachery. The covenant made by Jonathan in verse 3 will prove critical. Saul and David will react differently to his "love."

The song of the women, a public acclamation of both Saul and David, prompts the first indication of Saul's resentment (18:6-9). He interprets the song with faulty literalism, but if his suspicions are poorly based, his intuition is accurate: David is the one who will receive the kingship (cf. 13:14). But Saul fails to see the Lord's hand at work. Tension mounts as David's task of soothing Saul only provokes more rage (18:10-11). Appointing David to the field provides temporary respite but advances David's popularity (18:13-16). Nothing is going right for Saul. No wonder, the narrator comments, since the Lord is with David and has departed from Saul (18:12).

The next two incidents deal with Saul's daughters. Saul uses the ploy of marriage to entice David into dangerous exploits in the hope that he will be killed. The first attempt (18:17-19) involving Merob fizzles out as David declines the king's offer. By contrast, Michal loves David (18:20). David's claim to be unworthy allows Saul to set the trap. For once, the narrator

of the Philistines strike him." [18]But David answered Saul: "Who am I? And who are my kindred or my father's clan in Israel that I should become the king's son-in-law?" [19]But when the time came for Saul's daughter Merob to be given to David, she was given as wife to Adriel the Meholathite instead.

[20]Now Saul's daughter Michal loved David. When this was reported to Saul, he was pleased. [21]He thought, "I will offer her to him as a trap, so that the hand of the Philistines may strike him." So for the second time Saul said to David, "You shall become my son-in-law today." [22]Saul then ordered his servants, "Speak to David privately and say: The king favors you, and all his officers love you. You should become son-in-law to the king." [23]But when Saul's servants mentioned this to David, he said: "Is becoming the king's son-in-law a trivial matter in your eyes? I am poor and insignificant." [24]When his servants reported David's answer to him, [25]Saul commanded them, "Say this to David: The king desires no other price for the bride than the foreskins of one hundred Philistines, that he may thus take vengeance on his enemies." Saul intended to have David fall into the hands of the Philistines. [26]When the servants reported this offer to David, he was pleased with the prospect of becoming the king's son-in-law. Before the year was up, [27]David arose and went with his men and slew two hundred Philistines. He brought back their foreskins and counted them out before the king that he might become the king's son-in-law. So Saul gave him his daughter Michal as wife. [28]Then Saul realized that the LORD was with David and that his own daughter Michal loved David. [29]So Saul feared David all the more and was his enemy ever after.

[30]The Philistine chiefs continued to make forays, but each time they took the field, David was more successful against them than any of Saul's other officers, and his name was held in great esteem.

reports David's reaction: he "was pleased" to become the king's son-in-law (18:26). Perhaps this is a hint that Michal's love is reciprocated. At the least, Michal's love for David suggests she is willing to transfer her loyalty to make him a royal figure. David is more than successful in passing the test (18:27) and Saul realizes that the Lord is with David, as are his children and his people. But still, it is not clear that Saul yet realizes that David is the Lord's chosen one to replace him. Saul continues to oppose David and his unstoppable rise to the throne.

19:1–21:1 Jonathan and David

Jonathan is the key character in chapters 19–20. As Saul moves beyond placing David in harm's way to openly plotting to kill him (19:1), David withdraws from court. Throughout that process, Jonathan acts as intermediary between king and servant in an attempt to resolve their conflict. In terms of the overall narrative, this mediation serves a more profound

19 **Persecution of David.** ¹Saul discussed his intention to kill David with his son Jonathan and with all his servants. But Saul's son Jonathan, who was very fond of David, ²told him: "My father Saul is trying to kill you. Therefore, please be on your guard tomorrow morning; stay out of sight and remain in hiding. ³I, however, will go out and stand beside my father in the countryside where you are, and will speak to him about you. If I learn anything, I will let you know."

⁴Jonathan then spoke well of David to his father Saul, telling him: "The king should not harm his servant David. He has not harmed you, but has helped you very much by his deeds. ⁵When he took his life in his hands and killed the Philistine, and the LORD won a great victory for all Israel, you were glad to see it. Why, then, should you become guilty of shedding innocent blood by killing David without cause?" ⁶Saul heeded Jonathan's plea and swore, "As the LORD lives, he shall not be killed." ⁷So Jonathan summoned David and repeated the whole conversation to him. He then brought David to Saul, and David served him as before.

David Escapes from Saul. ⁸When war broke out again, David went out to fight against the Philistines and inflicted such a great defeat upon them that they fled from him. ⁹Then an evil spirit from the LORD came upon Saul as he was

---

purpose. As Saul's son, Jonathan stands to inherit the throne. But he aligns himself with David and transfers allegiance ("love" and "kindness") to him. Jonathan thus "abdicates" and allows David to replace him. He becomes the human legitimation of David's accession. These chapters play a pivotal role in the justification of David's rise to power.

19:1-7 Jonathan defends David

The narrator emphasizes Jonathan's place at court: he is called "son" twice in verse 1 and he speaks of Saul as "father" (19:2) and "king" (19:4). Jonathan is located firmly on Saul's side of the conflict, yet he is "very fond" of David (19:1). Friendship prompts him to defend David and argue his case before the king (19:4-6) to good effect. Jonathan is an effective mediator (19:7) and restores harmony for a time.

19:8-17 The flight from Saul

But renewed evidence that the Lord is with David reopens the divisions, or, put theologically, the evil spirit comes on Saul again. Verses 9-10 repeat 18:10-11 but with greater intensity. Saul strikes with the spear this time. Saul then sets up an assassination attempt, but Michal saves David (19:11-17). David is passive throughout these incidents. David is gifted by the Lord with protectors and deliverance. In the tradition of strong biblical

sitting in his house with spear in hand while David was playing the harp nearby. ¹⁰Saul tried to pin David to the wall with the spear, but David eluded Saul, and the spear struck only the wall, while David got away safely.

¹¹The same night, Saul sent messengers to David's house to guard it, planning to kill him in the morning. David's wife Michal informed him, "Unless you run for your life tonight, tomorrow you will be killed." ¹²Then Michal let David down through a window, and he made his escape in safety. ¹³Michal took the teraphim and laid it in the bed, putting a tangle of goat's hair at its head and covering it with a blanket. ¹⁴When Saul sent officers to arrest David, she said, "He is sick." ¹⁵Saul, however, sent the officers back to see David and commanded them, "Bring him up to me in his bed, that I may kill him." ¹⁶But when the messengers entered, they found the teraphim in the bed, with the tangle of goat's hair at its head. ¹⁷Saul asked Michal: "Why did you lie to me like this? You have helped my enemy to get away!" Michal explained to Saul: "He threat-ened me, saying 'Let me go or I will kill you.'"

David and Saul in Ramah. ¹⁸When David got safely away, he went to Samuel in Ramah, informing him of all that Saul had done to him. Then he and Samuel went to stay in Naioth. ¹⁹When Saul was told that David was at Naioth in Ramah, ²⁰he sent officers to arrest David. But when they saw the band of prophets presided over by Samuel in a prophetic state, the spirit of God came upon them and they too fell into the prophetic ecstasy. ²¹Informed of this, Saul sent other messengers, who also fell into the prophetic ecstasy. For the third time Saul sent messengers, but they too fell into a prophetic ecstasy.

Saul Among the Prophets. ²²Finally Saul went to Ramah himself. Arriving at the large cistern in Secu, he asked, "Where are Samuel and David?" Someone answered, "At Naioth in Ramah." ²³As he walked from there to Naioth in Ramah, the spirit of God came upon him also, and he continued on, acting like a prophet until he reached Naioth in Ramah. ²⁴Then he, too, stripped himself

women (e.g., Rahab in Josh 2), Michal is successful in her subterfuge and enables David to escape (19:12, 18). His flight from Saul begins.

19:18-24 David meets Samuel

David's first destination is with Samuel. The narrative does not report Samuel's reaction to what has happened, but he sides with David by accompanying him to Naioth. Divine protection is also displayed by the prophetic frenzy which overtakes the sets of messengers. When Saul arrives, he too comes under prophetic influence. Prophetic ecstasy marked Saul's appointment as leader (10:10-12) and now it is the public manifestation that he is stripped of appointment (19:23-24). His fall from grace is complete, though his removal from office will take many more chapters.

of his garments and remained in a prophetic state in the presence of Samuel;
all that day and night he lay naked. That
is why they say, "Is Saul also among the
prophets?"

20 **David Consults with Jonathan.**
¹David fled from Naioth in
Ramah, and went to Jonathan. "What
have I done?" he asked him. "What
crime or what offense does your father
hold against me that he seeks my life?"
²Jonathan answered him: "Heaven forbid that you should die! My father does
nothing, great or small, without telling
me. Why, then, should my father conceal
this from me? It cannot be true!" ³But
David replied: "Your father is well
aware that I am favored with your
friendship, so he has decided, 'Jonathan
must not know about this or he will be
grieved.' Nevertheless, as the LORD lives
and as you live, there is only a step between me and death." ⁴Jonathan then
said to David, "I will do whatever you
say." ⁵David answered: "Tomorrow is

the new moon, when I should in fact
dine with the king. Let me go and hide
in the open country until evening. ⁶If it
turns out that your father misses me, say,
'David urged me to let him go on short
notice to his city Bethlehem, because his
whole clan is holding its seasonal sacrifice there.' ⁷If he says, 'Very well,' your
servant is safe. But if he becomes quite
angry, you can be sure he has planned
some harm. ⁸Do this kindness for your
servant because of the LORD's covenant
into which you brought us: if I am guilty,
kill me yourself! Why should you give
me up to your father?" ⁹But Jonathan
answered: "Not I! If ever I find out that
my father is determined to harm you, I
will certainly let you know." ¹⁰David
then asked Jonathan, "Who will tell me
if your father gives you a harsh answer?"

Mutual Agreement. ¹¹Jonathan replied to David, "Come, let us go out into
the field." When they were out in the
open country together, ¹²Jonathan said

20:1-24 *Testing covenant loyalty*

Next on his flight, David visits Jonathan and speaks for the first time
since 18:24 to protest his innocence (20:1). Jonathan is again characterized
in relation to his father (20:1-3) so that, as one on Saul's side, he can declare
David innocent. David then mentions Jonathan's friendship (20:3), which
he uses to cast doubt on Jonathan's knowledge of Saul's intentions, but he
is also subtly moving Jonathan onto his side of the conflict. Jonathan is
willing to make the move (20:4) and so David outlines a plan to test Saul's
true intentions (20:5-7). David commits Jonathan to his plan by recalling
the covenant between them (20:8; cf. 18:3). This is not a bond between
equals. David calls himself Jonathan's "servant," and it was Jonathan who
made the pact. They may view the relationship differently. For Jonathan it
seems more emotional, but David appeals to covenant loyalty ("kindness,"
hesed).

to David: "As the LORD, the God of Israel, lives, I will sound out my father about this time tomorrow. Whether he is well disposed toward David or not, I will inform you. ¹³Should it please my father to bring any harm upon you, may the LORD do thus to Jonathan and more, if I do not inform you of it and send you on your way in peace. May the LORD be with you even as he was with my father. ¹⁴Only this: if I am still alive, may you show me the kindness of the LORD. But if I die, ¹⁵never cut off your kindness from my house. And when the LORD cuts off all the enemies of David from the face of the land, ¹⁶the name of Jonathan must never be cut off from the family of David, or the LORD will make you answer for it." ¹⁷And in his love for David, Jonathan renewed his oath to him, because he loved him as he loved himself.

¹⁸Jonathan then said to him: "Tomorrow is the new moon; you will be missed, since your place will be vacant. ¹⁹On the third day you will be missed all the more. Go to the spot where you hid on the other occasion and wait near the mound there. ²⁰On the third day of the month I will shoot arrows to the side of it, as though aiming at a target. ²¹I will then send my attendant to recover the arrows. If in fact I say to him, 'Look, the arrow is this side of you; pick it up,' come, for you are safe. As the LORD lives, there will be nothing to fear. ²²But if I say to the boy, 'Look, the arrow is beyond you,' go, for the LORD sends you away. ²³However, in the matter which you and I have discussed, the LORD shall be between you and me forever." ²⁴So David hid in the open country.

David's Absence. On the day of the new moon, when the king sat down at

Jonathan's response comes in two parts. The first (20:11-17) may have been a secondary development during the composition of the book: it does not focus on the immediate context but looks beyond David's rise to his reign, and specifically to 2 Samuel 9. Jonathan replies to the invocation of covenant kindness (cf. vv. 14-15 with v. 8). After piling up oaths to do as David requests (20:12-13), Jonathan prays, "May the LORD be with you even as he was with my father." The heir whom the Lord helped mightily (ch. 14) hands over divine blessing to the future king. In doing so, he can now strike a bargain with that king. Jonathan recognizes that David's accession will involve the destruction of the house of Saul (20:15b), so he binds David to covenant loyalty either to himself (20:14) or to his family (20:15a, 16). The pact of friendship is reformulated to reflect future political realities. (Verse 17 is better translated, "Jonathan made David swear.") Jonathan's "love" for David may be more personal, but he is making political use of it.

The second part of Jonathan's speech (20:18-24) sets up a method for communicating the outcome of David's plan.

the feast to dine, [25]he took his usual place against the wall. Jonathan sat facing him, while Abner sat at the king's side. David's place was vacant. [26]Saul, however, said nothing that day, for he thought, "He must have become unclean by accident." [27]On the next day, the second day of the month, David's place was still vacant. So Saul asked his son Jonathan, "Why has the son of Jesse not come to table yesterday or today?" [28]Jonathan explained to Saul: "David pleaded with me to let him go to Bethlehem. [29]'Please let me go,' he begged, 'for we are having a clan sacrifice in our city, and my brothers insist on my presence. Now then, if you think well of me, give me leave to visit my brothers.' That is why he has not come to the king's table." [30]But Saul grew angry with Jonathan and said to him: "Son of a rebellious woman, do I not know that, to your own disgrace and to the disgrace of your mother's nakedness, you are the companion of Jesse's son? [31]For as long as the son of Jesse lives upon the earth, you cannot make good your claim to the kingship! Now send for him, and bring him to me, for he must die." [32]But Jonathan argued with his father Saul: "Why should he die? What has he done?" [33]At this Saul brandished his spear to strike him, and thus Jonathan learned that his father was determined to kill David. [34]Jonathan sprang up from the table in a rage and ate nothing that second day of the month, because he was grieved on David's account, and because his father had humiliated him.

Jonathan's Farewell. [35]The next morning Jonathan, accompanied by a young boy, went out into the field for his appointment with David. [36]There he said to the boy, "Run and find the arrows."

20:25-34 *The stratagem unfolds*

All the key players are at the feast except David. Saul notes his absence: one day is excusable but not two. Perhaps it was Jonathan's assumption of authority to dismiss David, or his favoritism to the son of Jesse, but Jonathan's explanation triggers a violent response (20:30-31). Saul is abusive of his son and wife, because Jonathan is not acting as *his* son. The breach of father and son is complete when Saul tries to skewer Jonathan, just as he attempted to kill David (cf. v. 33 with 19:10 and 18:11). Jonathan is now fully transferred to David's side and identified with him.

20:35–21:1 *A farewell between friends*

Jonathan informs David by use of the signal with the arrow. It is a nice elongation of the suspense but irrelevant, since the two actually meet for a final farewell. David's prostration before Jonathan is a reminder of the unequal nature of the friendship. But Jonathan summarizes the oaths made as a divinely protected relationship between two equals, and between their posterities (20:42). Jonathan has demonstrated his faithfulness to David,

And as the boy ran, he shot an arrow past him. [37]When the boy made for the spot where Jonathan had shot the arrow, Jonathan called after him, "The arrow is farther on!" [38]Again he called to the boy, "Hurry, be quick, don't delay!" Jonathan's boy picked up the arrow and brought it to his master. [39]The boy suspected nothing; only Jonathan and David knew what was meant. [40]Then Jonathan gave his weapons to his boy and said to him, "Go, take them to the city." [41]When the boy had gone, David rose from beside the mound and fell on his face to the ground three times in homage. They kissed each other and wept aloud together. [42]At length Jonathan said to David, "Go in peace, in keeping with what the two of us have sworn by the name of the Lord: 'The Lord shall be between you and me, and between your offspring and mine forever.'"

21 [1]Then David departed on his way, while Jonathan went back into the city.

The Holy Bread. [2]David went to Ahimelech, the priest of Nob, who came trembling to meet him. He asked, "Why are you alone? Is there no one with you?" [3]David answered the priest: "The king gave me a commission and told me, 'Do not let anyone know anything about the business on which I have sent you or the commission I have given you.' For that reason I have arranged a particular

almost at the cost of his life. David must reciprocate. This final insistence again hints that the relationship was unequally perceived: more a friendship for Jonathan, more a political alliance for David. And if that is so, David's loyalty has yet to be tested. Will he show *hesed* to those who have committed themselves to him: Jonathan, Michal, the Lord?

21:2–22:5 David's flight continues

Since Michal spirited him away (19:12), David has been on the run while others act for him. Now he starts to act on his own, and a new, unflattering portrait emerges, David as deceitful and evasive. Three more stages of his escape are narrated before his flight ends.

His third stop is in Nob to visit Ahimelech the priest (21:2). His solitary arrival frightens Ahimelech and David lies. He needs food and weapons for his escape. His story of a top-secret mission is contrived. Under questioning, the lie is elaborated almost to breaking point. Where are the consecrated men he speaks of (21:3), and can he honestly expect that men would apply holy war strictures (21:6; see Deut 23:10-15) to ordinary forays? Ahimelech accepts the story at face value, even when the so-called secret agent admits he is weaponless (21:9-10). Either he is very trusting or works on a need-to-know basis. It would not matter, but the presence of one of Saul's henchmen will create devastating consequences for David's deceit (21:8).

meeting place with my men. ⁴Now what do you have on hand? Give me five loaves, or whatever you can find." ⁵But the priest replied to David, "I have no ordinary bread on hand, only holy bread; if the men have abstained from women, you may eat some of that." ⁶David answered the priest: "We have indeed stayed away from women. In the past whenever I went out on a campaign, all the young men were consecrated—even for an ordinary campaign. All the more so are they consecrated with their weapons today!" ⁷So the priest gave him holy bread, for no other bread was on hand except the showbread which had been removed from before the LORD and replaced by fresh bread when it was taken away. ⁸One of Saul's servants was there that day, detained before the LORD; his name was Doeg the Edomite, the chief of Saul's shepherds.

The Sword of Goliath. ⁹David then asked Ahimelech: "Do you have a spear or a sword on hand? I brought along neither my sword nor my weapons, because the king's business was urgent." ¹⁰The priest replied: "The sword of Goliath the Philistine, whom you killed in the Valley of Elah, is here wrapped in a garment behind an ephod. If you wish to take it, do so; there is no sword here except that one." "There is none like it," David cried, "give it to me!"

David a Fugitive. ¹¹That same day David fled from Saul, going to Achish, king of Gath. ¹²But the servants of Achish

Next, David flees to a Philistine city, an indication of his desperation to escape Saul's grasp (21:11). David will go so far, even to joining the enemy! The Philistines are well-versed in Israelite affairs and recognize David's potential as king (21:12). This is a very dangerous moment and David shrewdly creates another deceit (21:13-14). Madness cancelled Saul's hold on monarchy (16:14; 18:10; 19:9) and put David in mortal danger. Now David feigns madness to get out of danger by cancelling his royal identity.

Finally, David escapes to the land of Judah (22:1). The empty-handed and deceitful fugitive is home. He has lost everything but now begins to build his own power base. His followers are either fellow Judahites or members of the disaffected. This power base seems to have two aspects. It is a Judean counterbalance to a northern, Benjaminite coalition around Saul. This north-south division will plague Israel throughout the period of monarchy. Secondly, it reflects a division between the haves and the have-nots. This has populist appeal and also taps into covenant consciousness of Israel as slaves granted freedom. David's provision for his parents indicates careful planning for a long rise to power, and this rise is blessed from the start by the unrequested prophetic guidance of Gad.

said to him, "Is this not David, the king of the land? Is it not for him that during their dances they sing out,

'Saul has slain his thousands,
    David his tens of thousands'?"

¹³David took note of these remarks and became very much afraid of Achish, king of Gath. ¹⁴So, he feigned insanity in front of them and acted like a madman in their custody, drumming on the doors of the gate and drooling onto his beard. ¹⁵Finally Achish said to his servants: "You see the man is mad. Why did you bring him to me? ¹⁶Do I not have enough madmen, that you bring this one to rant in my presence? Should this fellow come into my house?"

22 ¹David left Gath and escaped to the cave of Adullam. When his brothers and the rest of his family heard about it, they came down to him there. ²He was joined by all those in difficulties or in debt, or embittered, and became their leader. About four hundred men were with him.

³From there David went to Mizpeh of Moab and said to the king of Moab, "Let my father and mother stay with you, until I learn what God will do for me." ⁴He left them with the king of Moab; they stayed with him as long as David remained in the stronghold.

⁵But Gad the prophet said to David: "Do not remain in the stronghold! Leave! Go to the land of Judah." And so David left and went to the forest of Hereth.

Doeg Betrays Ahimelech. ⁶Now Saul heard that David and his men had been located. At the time he was sitting in Gibeah under a tamarisk tree on the high place, holding his spear, while all his servants stood by him. ⁷So he said to

22:6-23 Slaughter of the priests

Saul begins his pursuit. His spear signals his murderous intent (22:6). He begins to encourage his officers, reminding them of their advantages under his leadership (22:7), but paranoia sets in. Where one may have opposed him, Saul sees all of them as conspirators (22:8). Saul's fellow Benjaminites are silent, suggesting that relations are strained.

Doeg the Edomite, a non-Israelite, reports what he saw at Nob (22:9-10). Now the consequences of his presence unfold (21:8). Two points must be made. Ahimelech is now called the son of Ahitub: so he is the brother of Ahijah who served Saul in chapter 14, and great-grandson of Eli (cf. 14:3). Secondly, Doeg gives pride of place in his report to Ahimelech consulting the Lord for David, something not mentioned previously. Whether Ahimelech did so or not, this act triggers Saul's anger more than any other; it will be the culminating charge in verse 13. Saul was unsuccessful in consulting the Lord in chapter 14; now this family of priests assists David in doing just that. Hence, all the family are summoned (22:11) and condemned (22:17). Ahimelech's defense is an accurate description of affairs from his

them: "Listen, men of Benjamin! Will the son of Jesse give all of you fields and vineyards? Will he appoint any of you an officer over a thousand or a hundred men? ⁸Is that why you have all conspired against me? Why no one told me that my son had made a pact with the son of Jesse? None of you has shown compassion for me by revealing to me that my son has incited my servant to ambush me, as is the case today." ⁹Then Doeg the Edomite, who was standing with Saul's officers, spoke up: "I saw the son of Jesse come to Ahimelech, son of Ahitub, in Nob. ¹⁰He consulted the Lord for him, furnished him with provisions, and gave him the sword of Goliath the Philistine."

Slaughter of the Priests. ¹¹So the king summoned Ahimelech the priest, son of Ahitub, and all his family, the priests in Nob. They all came to the king. ¹²"Listen, son of Ahitub!" Saul declared. "Yes, my lord," he replied. ¹³Saul questioned him, "Why have you conspired against me with the son of Jesse by giving him food and a sword and by consulting God for

him, that he might rise up against me in ambush, as is the case today?" ¹⁴Ahimelech answered the king: "Who among all your servants is as loyal as David, the king's son-in-law, captain of your bodyguard, and honored in your own house? ¹⁵Is this the first time I have consulted God for him? No indeed! Let not the king accuse his servant or anyone in my family of such a thing. Your servant knows nothing at all, great or small, about the whole matter." ¹⁶But the king said, "You shall certainly die, Ahimelech, with all your family." ¹⁷The king then commanded his guards standing by him: "Turn and kill the priests of the Lord, for they gave David a hand. They knew he was a fugitive and yet failed to inform me." But the king's servants refused to raise a hand to strike the priests of the Lord.

¹⁸The king therefore commanded Doeg, "You, turn and kill the priests!" So Doeg the Edomite himself turned and killed the priests that day—eighty-five who wore the linen ephod. ¹⁹Saul also

perspective, but reminding Saul of David's loyalty and position (22:14-15) does not endear him to the paranoid king.

Doeg's treachery does not end there. The Benjaminite servants refuse to execute the king's command. They will not strike fellow Israelites, especially the Lord's priests (22:17). Doeg steps in to do his master's bidding with ruthless efficiency (22:18-19). (The inclusion of Saul's name in verse 19 is incorrect.) The prophecy of 2:31-33 is being fulfilled. The family of Eli is wiped out, but one escapes and flees to that other fugitive from Saul (22:20). When told what happened, David admits partial responsibility (22:21-22), but David does not admit that his deception put Ahimelech in danger to start with! Still, David has started to repay others' loyalty to him. With words that sound like an oracle of salvation ("Stay with me. Fear nothing . . .") he offers his protection to Abiathar (22:23).

put the priestly city of Nob to the sword, including men and women, children and infants, and oxen, donkeys and sheep.

Abiathar Escapes. [20]One son of Ahimelech, son of Ahitub, named Abiathar, escaped and fled to David. [21]When Abiathar told David that Saul had slain the priests of the LORD, [22]David said to him: "I knew that day, when Doeg the Edomite was there, that he would certainly tell Saul. I am responsible for the slaughter of all your family. [23]Stay with me. Do not be afraid; whoever seeks your life must seek my life also. You are under my protection."

23 Keilah Liberated. [1]David was informed that the Philistines were attacking Keilah and plundering the threshing floors. [2]So he consulted the LORD, asking, "Shall I go and attack these Philistines?" The LORD answered, Go, attack them, and free Keilah. [3]But David's men said to him: "Even in Judah we have reason to fear. How much more so if we go to Keilah against the forces of the Philistines!" [4]Again David consulted the LORD, who answered: Go down to Keilah, for I will deliver the Philistines into your power. [5]So David went with his men to Keilah and fought against the Philistines. He drove off their cattle and inflicted a severe defeat on them, and freed the inhabitants of Keilah.

[6]Abiathar, son of Ahimelech, who had fled to David, went down with David to Keilah, taking the ephod with him.

Flight from Keilah. [7]When Saul was told that David had entered Keilah, he thought: "God has put him in my hand, for he has boxed himself in by entering

23:1-28 Saul pursues David

Saul's pursuit of David, begun at 22:6, continues. Both protagonists must abandon their conflict to deal with the continuing Philistine threat. Their responses bracket various incidents of the pursuit. All the time, the key player ensures that the pursuit is futile; the Lord will not give David up to Saul (23:14). Whatever happens in the wilderness, David is the Lord's choice for king.

23:1-13 David saves Keilah

The Philistines attack the Judean town of Keilah (cf. Josh 15:44), which is deep in Philistine territory and of dubious loyalty (cf. 23:11a, 12a). David's rescue is a risky venture, but he reacts in response to divine guidance, asking the Lord twice if he is to save the town (23:2, 4). Saul knows David's location and David can be trapped there (23:7). Once more, David consults the Lord using the ephod. The process involves prayers (23:10-11a) followed by specific questions requiring a yes/no answer (23:11b-12). Like Saul in chapters 13–14, David makes use of a range of consultation methods. Unlike Saul, the Lord answers him clearly. Saul is without prophet or priest, while David has both. More importantly, the Lord is with him.

a city with gates and bars." ⁸Saul then called all the army to war, in order to go down to Keilah and besiege David and his men. ⁹When David found out that Saul was planning to harm him, he said to the priest Abiathar, "Bring the ephod here." ¹⁰"LORD God of Israel," David prayed, "your servant has heard that Saul plans to come to Keilah, to destroy the city on my account. ¹¹Will they hand me over? Will Saul come down as your servant has heard? LORD God of Israel, tell your servant." The LORD answered: He will come down. ¹²David then asked, "Will the citizens of Keilah deliver me and my men into the hand of Saul?" The LORD answered: They will deliver you. ¹³So David and his men, about six hundred in number, left Keilah and wandered from place to place. When Saul was informed that David had fled from Keilah, he did not go forth.

David and Jonathan in Horesh. ¹⁴David now lived in the strongholds in the wilderness, or in the barren hill country near Ziph. Though Saul sought him continually, the LORD did not deliver David into his hand. ¹⁵While David was in the wilderness of Ziph at Horesh he was afraid that Saul had come out to seek his life. ¹⁶Then Saul's son, Jonathan, came down to David at Horesh and encouraged him in the LORD. ¹⁷He said to him: "Have no fear, my father Saul shall not lay a hand to you. You shall be king of Israel and I shall be second to you. Even my father Saul knows this." ¹⁸The two of them made a covenant before the LORD in Horesh, where David remained, while Jonathan returned to his home.

Treachery of the Ziphites. ¹⁹Some of the Ziphites went up to Saul in Gibeah and said, "David is hiding among us in the strongholds at Horesh on the hill of Hachilah, south of Jeshimon. ²⁰Therefore, whenever the king wishes to come down, let him do so. It will be our task to deliver him into the king's hand." ²¹Saul replied: "The LORD bless you for your compassion toward me. ²²Go now

23:14-18 Jonathan's return

Still, David is apprehensive. The narrator reintroduces Jonathan to serve as another means of divine assurance (23:16). His words are an oracle of salvation ("Have no fear"; 23:17). Jonathan renounces his claim to the throne, making explicit what was implied in 20:12-17. However, surprisingly, he claims that Saul knows David will be king. This looks forward to David's encounter with Saul in the next chapter (24:21). Jonathan has been the human mediator of kingship from Saul to David. His task is done now. For the first time, David makes covenant with Jonathan as a partnership between equals (cf. 18:3; 20:8, 14-17).

23:19-28 David's escape

Treachery once more assists Saul to close in. Some Ziphites betray David's location (23:19-20). Saul is grateful but suspicious of any support (23:21-23). Pursuit quickens through the Judean wilderness and David is

"David now lived in the strongholds in the wilderness, or in the barren hill country near Ziph" (1 Samuel 23:14).

and make sure once more! Take note of the place where he sets foot for I am told that he is very cunning. ²³Look around and learn in which of all the various hiding places he is holding out. Then come back to me with reliable information, and I will go with you. If he is in the region, I will track him down out of all the families of Judah." ²⁴So they went off to Ziph ahead of Saul. At this time David and his men were in the wilderness below Maon, in the Arabah south of the wasteland.

Escape from Saul. ²⁵When Saul and his men came looking for him, David got word of it and went down to the gorge in the wilderness below Maon. Saul heard of this and pursued David into the wilderness below Maon. ²⁶As Saul moved along one side of the gorge, David and his men took to the other. David was anxious to escape Saul, while Saul and his men were trying to outflank David and his men in order to capture them. ²⁷Then a messenger came to Saul, saying, "Come quickly, because the Philistines have invaded the land." ²⁸Saul interrupted his pursuit of David and went to meet the Philistines. This is how that place came to be called the Rock of Divisions.

24 David Spares Saul. ¹David then went up from there and stayed in the strongholds of Engedi. ²When Saul returned from the pursuit of the Philistines, he was told that David was in the desert near Engedi. ³So Saul took three thousand of the best men from all Israel and went in search of David and his men in the direction of the wild goat crags.

---

in grave danger of being encircled. (The NABRE translation uses "gorge" in verse 25 for a Hebrew word meaning "crag, rock" [cf. 14:4-5], which completely changes the topography of the chase! In the Hebrew, David is on one flank of a hill with Saul circling around from the far side.) But just as David is about to be trapped, rescue comes in the unlikeliest of forms. A report of a Philistine attack draws Saul away (23:27-28). The Israelite leader's duty to save the people supersedes a personal vendetta. Is this a fortuitous escape or a divine intervention?

24:1-23 David spares Saul

This chapter is parallel to chapter 26. They are possibly alternative traditions of the same event. This version follows from Jonathan's assertion in 23:17 in a dramatic fashion. Saul the pursuer falls into David's hands; David spares him and makes use of the incident to protest he is innocent of harming Saul. The passage plays two apologetic functions: it absolves David of guilt for Saul's death, and it has Saul acknowledge David as his successor.

24:1-9 Loyalty over opportunity

The action is brief: it sets up the two speeches that form a bipartite judicial process or *rib* (24:10-23). Verses 1-3 pick up the action after the Philistine

⁴When he came to the sheepfolds along the way, he found a cave, which he entered to relieve himself. David and his men were occupying the inmost recesses of the cave.

⁵David's servants said to him, "This is the day about which the Lᴏʀᴅ said to you: I will deliver your enemy into your hand; do with him as you see fit." So David moved up and stealthily cut off an end of Saul's robe. ⁶Afterward, however, David regretted that he had cut off an end of Saul's robe. ⁷He said to his men, "The Lᴏʀᴅ forbid that I should do such a thing to my master, the Lᴏʀᴅ's anointed, to lay a hand on him, for he is the Lᴏʀᴅ's anointed." ⁸With these words David restrained his men and would not permit them to attack Saul. Saul then left the cave and went on his way. ⁹David also stepped out of the cave, calling to Saul, "My lord the king!" When Saul looked back, David bowed, his face to the ground in homage, ¹⁰and asked Saul: "Why do you listen to those who say, 'David is trying to harm you'? ¹¹You see for yourself today that the Lᴏʀᴅ just now delivered you into my hand in the cave. I was told to kill you, but I took pity on you instead. I decided, 'I will not raise a hand against my master, for he is the Lᴏʀᴅ's anointed.' ¹²Look here, my father. See the end of your robe which I hold. I cut off an end of your robe and did not kill you. Now see and be convinced that I plan no harm and no rebellion. I have done you no wrong, though you are hunting me down to take my life. ¹³May the Lᴏʀᴅ judge between me and you. May the Lᴏʀᴅ exact justice from you in my case. I shall not lay a hand on you. ¹⁴As the old proverb says, 'From the wicked comes wickedness.' Thus I will not lay a hand on you. ¹⁵What is the king

interruption (23:28). Saul goes to relieve himself in the cave where David is hiding (24:4). David's men urge him to kill Saul but he does not (24:5), nor will he allow the men to do so (24:8). What is God's will? The men cite a divine word, but such freedom does not allow David to strike the Lord's anointed. Loyalty triumphs over opportunism. David does, however, cut off the corner of Saul's mantle (24:5-6). While he regrets the action, he will make use of it later: it is deeply symbolic of snatching the kingdom (cf. 15:27-28 and 1 Kgs 11:26-40).

24:10-23 Saul's response

When Saul leaves, David calls after him and begins the *rib*, a process in which the accuser seeks to have the accused recognize and confess to a crime. David makes his accusation and outlines the evidence proving his innocence (24:10-12). Saul believed David meant to harm him; this day David could have harmed Saul but did not. David invokes God as witness in verses 13 and 16. In between, he again states the issue. This is a powerful declaration of innocence on David's part.

of Israel attacking? What are you pursuing? A dead dog! A single flea! [16]The LORD will be the judge to decide between us. May the LORD see this, defend my cause, and give me justice against you!"

Saul's Remorse. [17]When David finished saying these things to Saul, Saul answered, "Is that your voice, my son David?" And he wept freely. [18]Saul then admitted to David: "You are more in the right than I am. You have treated me graciously, while I have treated you badly. [19]You have declared this day how you treated me graciously: the LORD delivered me into your hand and you did not kill me. [20]For if someone comes upon an enemy, do they send them graciously on their way? So may the LORD reward you graciously for what you have done this day. [21]And now, since I know that you will certainly become king and that the kingship over Israel shall come into your possession, [22]swear to me by the LORD that you will not cut off my descendants and that you will not blot out my name from my father's house." [23]David gave Saul his oath and Saul returned home, while David and his men went up to the stronghold.

25 **Death of Samuel.** [1]Samuel died, and all Israel gathered to mourn him; they buried him at his home in Ramah. Then David went down to the wilderness of Paran.

Saul's response is simple: he has no defense, only an expression of guilt, namely his weeping (24:17). In this context, "voice" probably denotes "speech," the content rather than the tone of what is said. He resolves the case by declaring David to be "in the right" and his actions to be "gracious" (24:18-20). As David invokes God as witness, Saul prays that the Lord will reward David who was wrongly accused. His reply reaches a climax in verses 21-22. Forced to admit he was in the wrong, Saul must now face the realization that David will be king. The corner of the mantle is proof here, recalling Saul's own attempt to snatch Samuel's cloak (15:27-28) and Samuel's words in 13:13-14, which Saul now echoes. Like Jonathan before him, Saul now asks that his family will not be exterminated (cf. 20:14-15). As in the previous episode, when David's kingship has been acknowledged, he gives his oath to Saul.

This is an important moment in the history of David's rise. This *rib* absolves David of the charge of regicide. The Lord will ensure that David gains the throne after Saul dies, but it will be the Lord's doing, not David's grasping.

25:1 Death of Samuel

This report interrupts the story but it may be necessary for the narrator to remove Samuel, who sought control over the king, before David begins entry into that kingship.

Nabal and Abigail. ²There was a man of Maon who had property in Carmel; he was very wealthy, owning three thousand sheep and a thousand goats. At the time, he was present for the shearing of his flock in Carmel. ³The man's name was Nabal and his wife was Abigail. The woman was intelligent and attractive, but Nabal, a Calebite, was harsh and bad-mannered. ⁴While in the wilderness, David heard that Nabal was shearing his flock, ⁵so he sent ten young men, instructing them: "Go up to Carmel. Pay Nabal a visit and greet him in my name. ⁶Say to him, 'Peace be with you, my brother, and with your family, and with all who belong to you. ⁷I have just heard that shearers are with you. Now, when your shepherds were with us, we did them no injury, neither did they miss anything while they were in Carmel.

⁸Ask your servants and they will tell you. Look kindly on these young men, since we come at a festival time. Please give your servants and your son David whatever you can.'"

⁹When David's young men arrived, they delivered the entire message to Nabal in David's name, and then waited. ¹⁰But Nabal answered the servants of David: "Who is David? Who is the son of Jesse? Nowadays there are many servants who run away from their masters. ¹¹Must I take my bread, my wine, my meat that I have slaughtered for my own shearers, and give them to men who come from who knows where?" ¹²So David's young men retraced their steps and on their return reported to him all that had been said. ¹³Thereupon David said to his men, "Let everyone strap on his sword." And everyone did so, and

25:2-44 The story of Abigail

The story of David, Nabal, and Abigail interrupts the wider drama but casts light on the options facing David. Given the inconsistent behavior of Saul, David has two options: do battle with a paranoid Saul, or make peace with a repentant Saul who recognizes David's future. This story illustrates the options: Nabal (meaning "fool") obstructs; Abigail assists. One path involves bloodshed, the other wealth and a wife! Which will David choose? But the story is more than an illustration of options because Abigail is no mere cipher. She is "intelligent and attractive" (25:3). Her husband is defined by possessions (25:2), but she seeks to create relationships. Like Hannah and Michal, this is a powerful woman whose actions shape the ensuing history. This is her story, so what does she want?

25:2-13 A negative portrayal

David is portrayed negatively here. He is a criminal godfather demanding protection money from Nabal. Nabal refuses to pay this leader of malcontents (cf. 22:2), and David vows vengeance (cf. 25:21-22). David is rapacious, ready to kill to grasp his goals.

David put on his own sword. About four hundred men went up after David, while two hundred remained with the baggage.

[14]Abigail, Nabal's wife, was informed of this by one of the servants, who said: "From the wilderness David sent messengers to greet our master, but he screamed at them. [15]Yet these men were very good to us. We were not harmed, neither did we miss anything all the while we were living among them during our stay in the open country. [16]Day and night they were a wall of protection for us, the whole time we were pasturing the sheep near them. [17]Now, see what you can do, for you must realize that otherwise disaster is in store for our master and for his whole house. He is such a scoundrel that no one can talk to him." [18]Abigail quickly got together two hundred loaves, two skins of wine, five dressed sheep, five seahs of roasted grain, a hundred cakes of pressed raisins, and two hundred cakes of pressed figs, and loaded them on donkeys. [19]She then said to her servants, "Go on ahead; I will follow you." But to her husband Nabal she said nothing.

[20]Hidden by the mountain, she came down riding on a donkey, as David and his men were coming down from the opposite direction. When she met them, [21]David had just been saying: "Indeed, it was in vain that I guarded all this man's possessions in the wilderness, so that nothing of his was missing. He has repaid good with evil. [22]May God do thus to David, and more, if by morning I leave a single male alive among all those who belong to him." [23]As soon as Abigail saw David, she dismounted quickly from the donkey and, falling down, bowed low to the ground before David in homage.

[24]As she fell at his feet she said: "My lord, let the blame be mine. Please let your maidservant speak to you; listen to

25:14-23 Nabal's household

Nabal has household problems. His servant (25:14-17) and his wife (25:18-19) do not support his action. Contempt drips from every word. If no servant can talk to Nabal, Abigail does not even try. She acts quickly, decisively, and freely with her husband's possessions to save the household from David's anger. Or so it would seem. She demands full attention from David, but to what end?

25:24-35 Abigail's judgment

She addresses David as "my lord" and calls herself "your maidservant," appropriate terms of address to a social superior, or of a wife to a husband. But Abigail never acknowledges Nabal as her husband, only referring to him as "that scoundrel" (25:25). This attractive woman is making a play for David! Her main task is to divert David from bloodshed, though demurely she attributes this action to the Lord. The shedding of blood could tarnish

the words of your maidservant. ²⁵My lord, do not pay any attention to that scoundrel Nabal, for he is just like his name. His name means fool, and he acts the fool. I, your maidservant, did not see the young men whom my lord sent. ²⁶Now, therefore, my lord, as the Lᴏʀᴅ lives, and as you live, the Lᴏʀᴅ has kept you from shedding blood and from avenging yourself by your own hand. May your enemies and those who seek to harm my lord become as Nabal! ²⁷Accept this gift, then, which your maidservant has brought for my lord, and let it be given to the young men who follow my lord. ²⁸Please forgive the offense of your maidservant, for the Lᴏʀᴅ shall certainly establish a lasting house for my lord, because my lord fights the battles of the Lᴏʀᴅ. Let no evil be found in you your whole life long. ²⁹If any adversary pursues you to seek your life, may the life of my lord be bound in the bundle of the living in the care of the Lᴏʀᴅ your God; may God hurl out the lives of your enemies as from the hollow of a sling. ³⁰And when the Lᴏʀᴅ fulfills for my lord the promise of success he has made concerning you, and appoints you as ruler over Israel, ³¹you shall not have any regrets or burdens on your conscience, my lord, for having shed innocent blood or for having rescued yourself. When the Lᴏʀᴅ bestows good on my lord, remember your maidservant." ³²David said to Abigail: "Blessed is the Lᴏʀᴅ, the God of Israel, who sent you to meet me today. ³³Blessed is your good judgment and blessed are you yourself. Today you have prevented me from shedding blood and rescuing myself with my own hand. ³⁴Otherwise, as the Lᴏʀᴅ, the God of Israel, lives, who has kept me from harming you, if you had not come so promptly

---

David's standing within the covenant community. It is a key concern of the narrative to absolve David from the charge that he was a usurper. David cannot be seen to seize the throne; it is, and must be seen to be, the gift of the Lord. He cannot be seen to "gain victory by your own hand" (the literal translation of "rescuing yourself personally" in verses 26 and 31). Astutely, Abigail presents herself as the Lord's instrument to keep David safe in this venture, but her foresight is greater still. She looks forward to David's victory and predicts a "lasting house" (25:28), something not even the Lord has mentioned! She recognizes David is going to be "ruler over Israel" (25:30). This is the sort of language Samuel would use. Is she making a play to be kingmaker? It takes a woman to build a dynasty: "remember your maidservant" (25:31)!

David blesses her good judgment (25:33). She has averted the danger to her household, but more importantly she has protected David from bloodguilt and vengeance. He is happy to take her wealth (25:35a), but does he acknowledge her request to be remembered? His final comment is very obscure (25:35b).

to meet me, by dawn Nabal would not have had so much as one male left alive." ³⁵David then took from her what she had brought him and said to her: "Go to your home in peace! See, I have listened to your appeal and have granted your request."

Nabal's Death. ³⁶When Abigail came to Nabal, he was hosting a banquet in his house like that of a king, and Nabal was in a festive mood and very drunk. So she said not a word to him until daybreak the next morning. ³⁷But then, when Nabal was sober, his wife told him what had happened. At this his heart died within him, and he became like a stone. ³⁸About ten days later the LORD struck Nabal and he died. ³⁹Hearing that Nabal was dead, David said: "Blessed be the LORD, who has defended my cause against the insult from Nabal, and who restrained his servant from doing evil, but has repaid Nabal for his evil deeds."

David Marries Abigail and Ahinoam. David then sent a proposal of marriage to Abigail. ⁴⁰When David's servants came to Abigail in Carmel, they said to her, "David has sent us to make his proposal of marriage to you." ⁴¹Rising and bowing to the ground, she answered, "Let your maidservant be the slave who washes the feet of my lord's servants." ⁴²She got up immediately, mounted a donkey, and followed David's messengers, with her five maids attending her. She became his wife. ⁴³David also married Ahinoam of Jezreel. Thus both of them were his wives. ⁴⁴But Saul gave David's wife Michal, Saul's own daughter, to Palti, son of Laish, who was from Gallim.

25:36-44 Nabal's death

Abigail leaves the future king and returns to her drunken "king." She says nothing until Nabal is at his most fragile, and then delivers her news. In a society based on honor/shame, her report is devastating. Nabal suffers a stroke (25:37; "his heart died within him"). She has all but killed him, but the Lord intervenes to protect her from bloodguilt (25:38). With Nabal out of the way, David is free to take his wife. Abigail's response sounds bashful (25:41), but she wastes no time and travels to David with a full retinue to signal her status (25:42). She is no coy trophy wife but David's equal in cunning. However David has one final trick. He marries Ahinoam at the same time (25:43), so Abigail does not get her way in full. She has a new rival, even as Saul gives David's first wife, Michal, to another man.

In the emergent, monarchical Israel, sexual relations and power politics intertwine. Royal polygyny is a mark of status and a means to form alliances. By removing Michal, Saul is cutting David off from his house. David builds his own harem in opposition, but perhaps he is preventing Abigail gaining too much influence in that household. In this chapter a pattern begins to emerge, by which David's sexual relationships will constantly affect his monarchy for good and ill.

26 **David Spares Saul Again.** ¹Men from Ziph came to Saul in Gibeah, reporting that David was hiding on the hill of Hachilah at the edge of Jeshimon. ²So Saul went down to the wilderness of Ziph with three thousand of the best warriors of Israel, to search for David in the wilderness of Ziph. ³Saul camped beside the road on the hill of Hachilah, at the edge of Jeshimon. David, who was living in the wilderness, saw that Saul had come into the wilderness after him ⁴and sent out scouts, who confirmed Saul's arrival. ⁵David then went to the place where Saul was encamped and saw the spot where Saul and his general, Abner, son of Ner, had their sleeping quarters. Saul was lying within the camp, and all his soldiers were bivouacked around him. ⁶David asked Ahimelech the Hittite, and Abishai, son of Zeruiah

and brother of Joab, "Who will go down into the camp with me to Saul?" Abishai replied, "I will." ⁷So David and Abishai reached Saul's soldiers by night, and there was Saul lying asleep within the camp, his spear thrust into the ground at his head and Abner and his troops sleeping around him.

⁸Abishai whispered to David: "God has delivered your enemy into your hand today. Let me nail him to the ground with one thrust of the spear; I will not need to strike him twice!" ⁹But David said to Abishai, "Do not harm him, for who can lay a hand on the LORD's anointed and remain innocent? ¹⁰As the LORD lives," David declared, "only the LORD can strike him: either when the time comes for him to die, or when he goes out and perishes in battle. ¹¹But the LORD forbid that I lay a hand

26:1-25 David spares Saul again

Chapter 26 parallels chapter 24. While this important encounter deserves to be reported from several angles, the second account must move the overall narrative forward. Chapter 24 looked back to Jonathan's claim (23:17) and brought that narrative thread to fulfillment. Chapter 26 looks forward; it speaks more clearly of Saul's death (26:9-11), and it prepares for David's exile from the land (26:19-20).

This episode recalls the treachery of the Ziphites (23:19-24) and reactivates Saul's pursuit (26:1-4). This time David is ready for Saul's arrival and takes the initiative to enter the enemy camp (26:5-7). Saul and David have their seconds with them, Abner and Abishai, making the incident more public and preparing for events after Saul's death (2 Sam 3). Once again, David gives a strongly theological argument for not harming Saul (26:9-11), but goes further to state his belief that the Lord will handle Saul's death. It will not be David's doing. David takes Saul's spear, the weapon used in attempts on David's life. The narrator's comment in verse 12 confirms that the Lord is backing David on this occasion.

The dialogue is more complex than in chapter 24. Firstly, David speaks with Abner (26:15-16). It is a clever speech which both praises and condemns

on the Lord's anointed! Now take the spear at his head and the water jug, and let us be on our way." ¹²So David took the spear and the water jug from their place at Saul's head, and they withdrew without anyone seeing or knowing or awakening. All remained asleep, because a deep slumber from the Lord had fallen upon them.

David Taunts Abner. ¹³Crossing over to an opposite slope, David stood on a distant hilltop. With a great distance between them ¹⁴David called to the army and to Abner, son of Ner, "Will you not answer, Abner?" Then Abner shouted back, "Who is it that calls me?" ¹⁵David said to Abner: "Are you not a man? Who in Israel is your equal? Why were you not guarding your lord the king when one of his subjects came to assassinate the king, your lord? ¹⁶What you have done is not right. As the Lord lives, you people deserve death because you have not guarded your lord, the anointed of the Lord. Go, look: where are the king's spear and the water jug that was at his head?"

Saul Admits His Guilt. ¹⁷Saul recognized David's voice and asked, "Is that your voice, David my son?" David answered, "Yes, my lord the king." ¹⁸He continued: "Why does my lord pursue his servant? What have I done? What evil am I planning? ¹⁹Please, now, let my lord the king listen to the words of his servant. If the Lord has incited you against me, may an offering please the Lord. But if it is the people who have done so, may they be cursed before the Lord. They have driven me away so that today I have no share in the Lord's heritage, but am told: 'Go serve other gods!' ²⁰Do not let my blood spill on the ground far from the presence of the Lord. For the king of Israel has come out to seek a single flea as if he were hunting partridge

---

him for dereliction of duty. It acknowledges Saul as king, thus underlining David's loyalty. David then addresses Saul. He complains that Saul's action is driving him from the land (26:19). In exile, he would be cut off from the Lord. Saul admits this is wrong and invites David back (26:21). But David is not willing, and he brandishes the spear to remind Saul of his murderous attempts. David has just spared Saul, so he prays that the Lord will spare his life (26:24) as reward for David's righteousness and faithfulness (26:23). David wants a blessing for protection during exile. Saul confirms this request so David can now go on his way (26:25).

This second encounter attempts to re-establish justice and loyalty between the two protagonists, but the divine plan makes this impossible. David must be king and Saul must go, but they cannot live together. The resolution removes both combatants from the scene of conflict, Israel. David is to leave the land of the covenant under the protection of the Lord. Saul returns home but will also cross boundaries of covenant law. The narrative incorporates strange new twists to the history.

in the mountains." ²¹Then Saul said: "I have done wrong. Come back, David, my son! I will not harm you again, because you considered my life precious today even though I have been a fool and have made a serious mistake." ²²But David answered: "Here is the king's spear. Let an attendant come over to get it. ²³The Lord repays everyone's righteousness and faithfulness. Although the Lord delivered you into my hands today, I could not lay a hand on the Lord's anointed. ²⁴Just as I regarded your life as precious today, so may the Lord regard my life as precious and deliver me from all dangers." ²⁵Then Saul said to David: "Blessed are you, my son David! You

shall certainly succeed in whatever you undertake." David went his way, and Saul returned to his place.

27 David Flees to the Philistines.
¹David said to himself: "I shall perish some day at the hand of Saul. I have no choice but to escape to the land of the Philistines; then Saul will give up his continual search for me throughout the land of Israel, and I will be out of his reach." ²Accordingly, David departed with his six hundred soldiers and went over to Achish, son of Maoch, king of Gath. ³David and his men lived in Gath with Achish; each one had his family, and David had his two wives, Ahinoam from Jezreel and Abigail, the widow of

27:1–28:2 David among the Philistines

The author of the "History of David's Rise" had a major problem. Tradition remembers that David once served the Philistines. Was he a traitor, then? Is he still a vassal of Israel's enemies? The narrative must incorporate this period into David's story and defend him against such charges. On the theological level, chapter 26 has cleared David of the suspicion of "serv[ing] other gods" (26:19)—the Philistine sojourn was blessed by the Lord (26:25). Now the narrator deals with the historical memory. David's move into Philistine territory successfully ends Saul's pursuit (27:1-3). David's exile serves the greater goal of avoiding civil war.

David returns to Achish who dismissed this madman earlier (cf. 20:11-16). Somehow, David is given Ziklag, a Philistine town, which becomes a personal fiefdom of the Davidic family (27:6). There are narrative gaps here which gloss over elements which may reflect badly on David. Why did Achish welcome David? Why did he give David a stronghold?

Instead, the narrator moves swiftly to make use of David's darker characteristic, deception, to celebrate success in the Philistine venture (27:8-12). David raids non-Israelite peoples in the Negev, and while he takes no prisoners, he does take lots of booty. He reports back to Achish and lies (27:10-11). He is pretending to raid Israelite settlements, so he leaves no one alive who may betray this trick. Achish trusts David and the situation lasts for some time.

Nabal from Carmel. [4]When Saul learned that David had fled to Gath, he no longer searched for him.

[5]David said to Achish: "If I meet with your approval, let me have a place to live in one of the country towns. Why should your servant live with you in the royal city?" [6]That same day Achish gave him Ziklag, which has, therefore, belonged to the kings of Judah up to the present time. [7]In all, David lived a year and four months in Philistine territory.

David Raids Israel's Foes. [8]David and his men went out on raids against the Geshurites, Girzites, and Amalekites—peoples living in the land between Telam, on the approach to Shur, and the land of Egypt. [9]In attacking the land David would not leave a man or woman alive, but would carry off sheep, oxen, donkeys, camels, and clothes. Then he would return to Achish, [10]who would ask, "Against whom did you raid this time?" David would reply, "Against the Negeb of Judah," or "Against the Negeb of Jerahmeel," or "Against the Negeb of the Kenites." [11]David never left a man or woman alive to be brought to Gath. He thought, "They will betray us and say, 'This is what David did.'" This was his custom as long as he lived in Philistine territory. [12]Achish trusted David, thinking, "His people Israel must certainly detest him. I shall have him as my vassal forever."

28 [1]In those days the Philistines mustered their military forces to fight against Israel. So Achish said to David, "You realize, of course, that you and your warriors must march out for battle with me." [2]David answered Achish, "Good! Now you shall learn what your servant can do." Then Achish said to David, "I shall appoint you as my permanent bodyguard."

[3]Now, Samuel was dead. All Israel had mourned him and buried him in his city, Ramah. Meanwhile Saul had driven mediums and diviners out of the land.

Saul in Despair. [4]The Philistines rallied and, coming to Shunem, they encamped. Saul, too, mustered all Israel; they camped on Gilboa. [5]When Saul saw the Philistine camp, he grew afraid and

However, a Philistine campaign against Israel begins (28:1) and David must choose. Will he continue as a Philistine vassal and attack Israel, or will he side with his own people? His reply to Achish is a masterful piece of noncommittal ambiguity (28:2). But Achish trusts David and appoints him to his elite troop. The narrator stops the story at this critical moment of decision!

28:3-35 The medium of Endor

The resolution of chapter 26 permitted David to leave the land and enter the domain of other gods. Saul makes a similar journey. Having banished mediums from the land (28:3), he departs to consult one (28:8). She dwells in Endor, behind Philistine lines, so Saul also enters Philistine territory where other gods hold sway! Exile helps the narrator surmount the standoff

lost heart completely. [6]He consulted the LORD; but the LORD gave no answer, neither in dreams nor by Urim nor through prophets. [7]Then Saul said to his servants, "Find me a medium through whom I can seek counsel." His servants answered him, "There is a woman in Endor who is a medium."

The Medium at Endor. [8]So he disguised himself, putting on other clothes, and set out with two companions. They came to the woman at night, and Saul said to her, "Divine for me; conjure up the spirit I tell you." [9]But the woman answered him, "You know what Saul has done, how he expelled the mediums and diviners from the land. Then why are you trying to entrap me and get me killed?" [10]But Saul swore to her by the LORD, "As the LORD lives, you shall incur no blame for this." [11]"Whom do you want me to conjure up?" the woman asked him. "Conjure up Samuel for me," he replied.

Samuel Appears. [12]When the woman saw Samuel, she shrieked at the top of her voice and said to Saul, "Why have you deceived me? You are Saul!" [13]But the king said to her, "Do not be afraid. What do you see?" "I see a god rising from the earth," she replied. [14]"What does he look like?" asked Saul. "An old man is coming up wrapped in a robe," she replied. Saul knew that it was Samuel, and so he bowed his face to the ground in homage.

---

of chapters 24 and 26. Saul will reenter the land as one marked for death in battle (ch. 31). David reenters the land to become king (2 Sam 1-2).

The central character of chapter 28 is a powerful woman who reintroduces the dead Samuel into the story to mediate its final resolution. The medium of Endor plays a complementary role to Hannah: both bring Samuel into the world, both are intent on unblocking the flow of Israelite history, and one stands at either end of the canonical book. To call this woman a witch introduces a negative evaluation which the text does not support. Certainly, Deuteronomy 18:9-22 prohibits occult practices and the woman has been banished, but not even the Deuteronomic editors condemn her. The one evaluation, spoken by Saul, acquits her of blame (28:10).

The Philistines are advancing and Saul is in great fear (28:4-5). He is isolated from the Lord who appointed him for this task (cf. 9:16) but will not answer him (28:6). Saul steps outside his own law to consult the medium at Endor (28:8). He disguises himself as another man (cf. 10:6) in an attempt to get back to the start and reconnect with the Lord through Samuel.

The medium deals with Saul in a mixture of efficiency and caution. Does she recognize Saul despite the disguise? Is she protecting herself from incrimination by having the lawmaker exempt her from blame (28:10)? Her moment of recognition is confusing, suggesting she knows more than she admits (28:11-12).

Saul's Doom. ¹⁵Samuel then said to Saul, "Why do you disturb me by conjuring me up?" Saul replied: "I am in great distress, for the Philistines are waging war against me and God has turned away from me. Since God no longer answers me through prophets or in dreams, I have called upon you to tell me what I should do." ¹⁶To this Samuel said: "But why do you ask me, if the LORD has abandoned you for your neighbor? ¹⁷The LORD has done to you what he declared through me: he has torn the kingdom from your hand and has given it to your neighbor David.

¹⁸"Because you disobeyed the LORD's directive and would not carry out his fierce anger against Amalek, the LORD has done this to you today. ¹⁹Moreover, the LORD will deliver Israel, and you as well, into the hands of the Philistines. By tomorrow you and your sons will be with me, and the LORD will have delivered the army of Israel into the hands of the Philistines."

²⁰Immediately Saul fell full length on the ground, in great fear because of Samuel's message. He had no strength left, since he had eaten nothing all that day and night. ²¹Then the woman came to Saul and, seeing that he was quite terror-stricken, said to him: "Remember, your maidservant obeyed you: I took my life in my hands and carried out the request you made of me. ²²Now you, in turn, please listen to your maidservant. Let me set out a bit of food for you to eat, so that you are strong enough to go on your way." ²³But he refused, saying, "I will not eat." However, when his servants joined the woman in urging him, he listened to their entreaties, got up from the ground, and sat on a couch. ²⁴The woman had a stall-fed calf in the

---

The ghost is recognizable to Saul by its mantle, last seen in 15:27. Samuel is as cantankerous as ever and not in the least impressed by Saul's great distress (28:15). Saul's description of affairs ends with his hope, "I have called upon you to tell me what I should do," a direct echo of 10:8. Samuel failed to fulfill this instruction then, but will he do so now? No, Saul is doomed to be the one who asks—a play on his name—but is never answered (28:16). Instead of recalling chapter 10, Samuel cites 15:28 and specifies who will receive the kingdom: David. Then he announces a terrible doom which subverts the normal saving activity of the Lord to bring death to Saul and his sons (28:19), just as God used the Philistines to destroy Eli and his sons in chapter 4.

The apparition disappears and Saul collapses from a combination of terror and hunger (28:21). He is marked for death. The woman's remarks are measured and reassuring. She cannot deflect his spiritual trauma, but she revives Saul with a kingly meal. As a result, he is able to leave to face his doom. Saul's journey beyond the boundaries brought him into contact with the dead. He returns, but he does not stand among the living. There can be no respite for him. He has begun his journey to the grave.

house, which she now quickly slaughtered. Then taking flour, she kneaded it and baked unleavened bread. ²⁵She set the meal before Saul and his servants, and they ate. Then they got up and left the same night.

29 **David's Aid Rejected.** ¹Now the Philistines had mustered all their forces in Aphek, and the Israelites were encamped at the spring in Jezreel. ²As the Philistine lords were marching their units of a hundred and a thousand, David and his warriors were marching in the rear guard with Achish. ³The Philistine commanders asked, "What are those Hebrews doing here?" Achish answered them: "Why, that is David, the officer of Saul, king of Israel. He has been with me for a year or two, and from the day he came over to me until now I have never found fault in him." ⁴But the Philistine commanders were angered at this and said to him: "Send that man back! Let him return to the place you picked out for him. He must not go down into battle with us; during the battle he might become our enemy. For how else can he win back his master's favor, if not at the expense of our soldiers? ⁵Is this not the David for whom they sing during their dances,

'Saul has slain his thousands,
David his tens of thousands'?"

29:1-11 David rejected

To prolong the tension of the choice facing David (28:1-2), the narrator jumped forward to the eve of battle (28:4). Now, the narrator returns to the Philistine muster (29:1-2) and picks up the story. Ironically, it is the Philistine lords who extricate David from his dilemma by refusing to allow him to march into battle on their side (29:3-5). They are deeply suspicious of his duplicity, and once more the chant of the Israelite women is quoted as evidence of the solidarity between David and Saul (cf. 18:7; 21:11). Achish protests David's innocence (29:3); either he is a fool, or the narrator is trying to suggest loyalty is David's main character trait.

Achish dismisses David with regret and fulsome praise for his loyalty (29:6-7). David protests his innocence (29:8), too much perhaps. He professes loyalty to his king, but which king does he mean, Achish or Saul? Were the Philistine lords correct in guessing that David would switch sides in battle to emerge as the savior of Israel? Do David's protestations arise out of frustration as this plan collapses? The wider narrative would suggest that David is duplicitous but in good cause. However, this text leaves as many gaps as it supplies answers. The narrator struggles to respect the traditional memories of David's absence in Israel's hour of need, while attempting to nudge the reader towards a positive evaluation of his role in the downfall of Saulide Israel.

⁶So Achish summoned David and said to him: "As the LORD lives, you are honest, and I would want you with me in all my battles. To this day I have found nothing wrong with you since you came to me. But in the view of the chiefs you are not welcome. ⁷Leave peacefully, now, and do nothing that might displease the Philistine chiefs." ⁸But David said to Achish: "What have I done? What fault have you found in your servant from the day I entered your service until today, that I cannot go to fight against the enemies of my lord the king?" ⁹"I recognize," Achish answered David, "that you are trustworthy, like an angel of God. But the Philistine commanders are saying, 'He must not go with us into battle.' ¹⁰So the first thing tomorrow, you and your lord's servants who came with you, go to the place I picked out for you. Do not take to heart their worthless remarks; for you have been valuable in my service. But make an early morning start, as soon as it grows light, and be on your way." ¹¹So David and his warriors left early in the morning to return to the land of the Philistines, and the Philistines went on up to Jezreel.

30 **Ziklag in Ruins.** ¹Before David and his men reached Ziklag on the third day, the Amalekites had raided the Negeb and Ziklag. They stormed Ziklag, and set it on fire. ²They took captive the women and all who were in the city, young and old, killing no one, and they herded them off when they left. ³David and his men arrived at the city to find it burned to the ground and their wives, sons, and daughters taken captive. ⁴Then David and those who were with him wept aloud until they could weep no more. ⁵David's two wives, Ahinoam of Jezreel and Abigail, the widow of Nabal from Carmel, had also been carried off. ⁶Now David found himself in great danger, for the soldiers spoke of stoning him, so bitter were they over the

---

30:1-31 Ziklag in ruins

Having removed David from the battlefield, the narrator explains what he was doing in Israel's hour of need. He was engaged with another enemy whom Saul failed to destroy, the Amalekites of chapter 15. David "bring[s] about a rescue" (30:8) through the guidance of the Lord. Where Saul fails to exterminate the Amalekites, a failure which underlies his continued rejection (cf. 28:18), David does destroy the enemy (v. 17). The episode continues the contrast with Saul. Both men find themselves in "great distress" (28:15 and 30:6 use the same verbal construction) because of enemy assault, but David's reaction is one of "courage in the LORD his God" which leads to victory (30:6), and the means to build support among the elders of Judah (30:26-31).

The narrative has various folkloric elements—the captured wives, the obstacles of hunger and exhaustion, the chance find of a slave who acts as guide—and makes a good tale, an encouraging war story before the account

fate of their sons and daughters. David took courage in the Lord his God ⁷and said to Abiathar, the priest, son of Ahimelech, "Bring me the ephod!" When Abiathar brought him the ephod, ⁸David inquired of the Lord, "Shall I pursue these raiders? Can I overtake them?" The Lord answered him: Go in pursuit, for you will certainly overtake them and bring about a rescue.

Raid on the Amalekites. ⁹So David went off with his six hundred as far as the Wadi Besor, where those who were to remain behind halted. ¹⁰David continued the pursuit with four hundred, but two hundred were too exhausted to cross the Wadi Besor and remained behind. ¹¹An Egyptian was found in the open country and brought to David. They gave him food to eat and water to drink; ¹²they also offered a cake of pressed figs and two cakes of pressed raisins. When he had eaten, he revived, for he had not taken food nor drunk water for three days and three nights. ¹³Then David asked him, "To whom do you belong? Where did you come from?"

"I am an Egyptian, the slave of an Amalekite," he replied. "My master abandoned me three days ago because I fell sick. ¹⁴We raided the Negeb of the Cherethites, the territory of Judah, and the Negeb of Caleb; and we set Ziklag on fire." ¹⁵David then asked him, "Will you lead me down to these raiders?" He answered, "Swear to me by God that you will not kill me or hand me over to my master, and I will lead you down to the raiders." ¹⁶So he led them down, and there were the Amalekites lounging all over the ground, eating, drinking, and celebrating because of all the rich plunder they had taken from the land of the Philistines and from the land of Judah.

The Plunder Recovered. ¹⁷From dawn to sundown the next day David attacked them, allowing no one to escape except four hundred young men, who mounted their camels and fled. ¹⁸David recovered everything the Amalekites had taken, and he rescued his two wives. ¹⁹Nothing was missing, small or great, plunder or sons or daughters, of all that the Amalekites had taken. David

of Saul's final defeat. However, some aspects have wider importance. Verse 6 is a rare moment of popular unrest against David. It could be a narrator's flourish to tighten the straits David finds himself in. Or it could prepare for the later dissent over the spoils (30:21-25). The division of forces into an advance party and a rearguard was a regular strategy of David's (cf. 25:13), but there was no previous hint of tension between the two groups. David moves to establish new rules of conduct for dividing the spoils. The rules are egalitarian, but they are rules for a king to make. David is acting as a king, victorious in battle and supported by his God, able to establish "a law and a custom" (*mishpat*) in Israel (30:25). David is establishing that his *mishpat* will not be that described by Samuel (8:10-18); this king will give rather than take.

brought back everything. ²⁰Moreover, David took all the sheep and oxen, and as they drove these before him, they shouted, "This is David's plunder!"

Division of the Plunder. ²¹When David came to the two hundred men who had been too exhausted to follow him, whom he had left behind at the Wadi Besor, they came out to meet David and the men with him. As David approached, he greeted them. ²²But all the greedy and worthless among those who had accompanied David said, "Since they did not accompany us, we will not give them anything from the plunder, except for each man's wife and children." ²³But David said: "You must not do this, my brothers, after what the LORD has given us. The LORD has protected us and delivered into our hands the raiders that came against us. ²⁴Who could agree with this proposal of yours? Rather, the share of the one who goes down to battle shall be the same as that of the one who remains with the baggage—they share alike." ²⁵And from that day forward he made this a law and a custom in Israel, as it still is today.

David's Gifts to Judah. ²⁶When David came to Ziklag, he sent part of the plunder to his friends, the elders of Judah, saying, "This is a gift to you from the plunder of the enemies of the LORD," namely, ²⁷to those in Bethel, Ramoth-negeb, Jattir, ²⁸Aroer, Siphmoth, Eshtemoa, ²⁹Racal, Jerahmeelite cities and Kenite cities, ³⁰Hormah, Borashan, Athach, ³¹Hebron, and to all the places that David and his men had frequented.

31 Death of Saul and His Sons. ¹Now the Philistines went to war against Israel, and the Israelites fled before them, and fell, slain on Mount Gilboa. ²The Philistines pressed hard after Saul and his sons. When the Philistines had struck down Jonathan, Abinadab, and Malchishua, sons of Saul, ³the fury of the battle converged on Saul. Then the

31:1-13 The death of Saul

The narrator returns to the main battle (cf. 28:4) and the outcome of Saul's doom-laden encounter with Samuel (28:15-19). Samuel's declaration of Philistine victory unfolds with unstoppable momentum. They press the attack and the Israelites flee (31:1, 7). They close in on the royal party and slay Saul's sons (31:2). Saul is now alone and mortally wounded (31:3). In the midst of battle, the narrator gives space to Saul's last actions (31:4-5). The narrator marks these deaths in verse 6 with a dignified notice. The whole account of the battle is free from evaluation or editorial touches. It is as if Saul's death is to be accorded the dignity of a faithful record, affording him one last opportunity for an almost heroic end. Samuel has already passed judgment on Saul (28:16-19), yet Saul was the Lord's anointed, the king of Israel. Even in failure that must be honored.

The victory is so complete (31:7) that the Philistines declare it "good news" (31:9). Saul's failure means that the Lord has not saved Israel; it is

archers hit him, and he was severely wounded. [4]Saul said to his armor-bearer, "Draw your sword and run me through; otherwise these uncircumcised will come and abuse me." But the armor-bearer, badly frightened, refused, so Saul took his own sword and fell upon it. [5]When the armor-bearer saw that Saul was dead, he too fell upon his sword and died with him. [6]Thus Saul, his three sons, and his armor-bearer died together on that same day. [7]When the Israelites on the slope of the valley and those along the Jordan saw that the men of Israel had fled and that Saul and his sons were dead, they abandoned their cities and fled. Then the Philistines came and lived in those cities.

[8]On the following day, when the Philistines came to strip the slain, they found Saul and his three sons fallen on Mount Gilboa. [9]They cut off Saul's head and stripped him of his armor; these they sent throughout the land of the Philistines to bring the good news to the temple of their idols and to the people. [10]They put his armor in the temple of Astarte but impaled his body on the wall of Beth-shan.

Burial of Saul. [11]When the inhabitants of Jabesh-gilead heard what the Philistines had done to Saul, [12]all their warriors set out and traveled through the night; they removed the bodies of Saul and his sons from the wall of Beth-shan, and, returning to Jabesh, burned

----

also a failure of the Israelite god before the Philistine idols. As before (cf. 5:1-2), the Philistines place the visible emblems of the Lord's supposed saving power (Saul's armor) in one of their temples. They use his body as a warning to a conquered people (31:10), an act of desecration meant to instill fear in Israel.

Saul has failed to save Israel from the Philistines; but he did save the people of Jabesh-gilead (ch. 11), and they respond in loyalty by rescuing his body and those of his sons (31:11-13). Cremation was not usual Israelite practice. Some suggest that the narrator is mimicking the honor given to heroes in the Greek world, but cremation may have been demanded by the unusual circumstances of Saul's death.

The narrator has brought the history of Saul to a close with a masterful symmetry—one last encounter with Samuel in an attempt to recapture the promise of chapter 10; David tying up the loose ends of the material cause of Saul's rejection in chapter 15; and, finally, burial by those Saul first delivered in chapter 11. The burial of Saul brings 1 Samuel to a close, but this is merely a formal division of the ancient history. Many aspects of the narrative lack resolution: the outcome of the Philistine invasion, the position of David, and, most importantly, the provision of salvation by the Lord for his people.

them. ¹³Then they took their bones and buried them under the tamarisk tree in Jabesh, and fasted for seven days.

The Second Book of Samuel

1 **Report of Saul's Death.** ¹After the death of Saul, David returned from his victory over the Amalekites and stayed in Ziklag two days. ²On the third day a man came from the field of battle, one of Saul's people, with his garments torn and his head covered with dirt. Going to David, he fell to the ground in homage. ³David asked him, "Where have you come from?" He replied, "From the Israelite camp: I have escaped." ⁴"What happened?" David said. "Tell me." He answered that the soldiers had fled the battle and many of them had fallen and were dead; and that Saul and his son Jonathan were dead. ⁵Then David said to the youth who was reporting to him, "How do you know that Saul and his son Jonathan are dead?" ⁶The youth reporting to him replied: "I happened to find myself on Mount Gilboa and saw Saul leaning on his spear, with chariots and horsemen closing in on him. ⁷He turned around and saw me, and called me to him. When I said, 'Here I am,' ⁸he asked me, 'Who are you?' and I replied, 'An Amalekite.' ⁹Then he said to me, 'Stand over me, please, and put me to death, for I am in great suffering, but still alive.' ¹⁰So I stood over him and put him to death, for I knew that he

---

THE RISE OF DAVID (continued)

2 Samuel 1:1–5:12

1:1-16 Report of Saul's death

With the death of Saul, a new and dangerous phase of David's rise begins. The way is clear to the throne, but David's claim must be seen to be legitimate and acceptable to the people. He still must avoid the two dangers Abigail named (cf. 1 Sam 25:30-31): implication in the destruction of the Saulide monarchy, and seizure of the throne. While his presence in Ziklag (1:1) clears him of involvement in Saul's death, the arrival of the messenger focuses attention on David's use of this disaster.

At first, this is a typical report from the battlefront (cf. 1 Sam 4:12, 16-17). There is nothing untoward in the man's appearance, identity, or message. It is only when pushed for details about Saul and Jonathan that a story very different from 1 Samuel 31:1-7 emerges. This man is no mere messenger but an eyewitness and participant in Saul's last moments (1:6-10). He is an Amalekite who killed the king! And he presents the royal insignia as evidence (1:10). Whatever his motivation, he creates a major temptation for David to grasp the royal regalia.

David's response is not what the Amalekite expects. David and his troops grieve deeply for the slain (1:11-12), and then David executes the

could not survive his wound. I removed the crown from his head and the armlet from his arm and brought them here to my lord."

[11]David seized his garments and tore them, and so did all the men who were with him. [12]They mourned and wept and fasted until evening for Saul and his son Jonathan, and for the people of the LORD and the house of Israel, because they had fallen by the sword. [13]David said to the youth who had reported to him, "Where are you from?" He replied, "I am the son of a resident alien, an Amalekite." [14]David said to him, "How is it that you were not afraid to put forth your hand to desecrate the LORD's anointed?" [15]David then called one of the attendants and said to him, "Come, strike him down"; so he struck him and he died. [16]David said to him, "Your blood is on your head, for you testified against yourself when you said, 'I put the LORD's anointed to death.'"

Lament for Saul and Jonathan. [17]Then David chanted this lament for Saul and his son Jonathan [18](he commanded that it be taught to the Judahites; it is recorded in the Book of Jashar):

[19]Alas! the glory of Israel,
    slain upon your heights!
How can the warriors have fallen!
[20]Do not report it in Gath,
    as good news in Ashkelon's
        streets,
Lest Philistine women rejoice,
    lest the women of the uncircum-
        cised exult!

Amalekite (1:15). David is consistent, as he has frequently argued against harming the Lord's anointed (1 Sam 24:7; 26:9). For one last time, David recalls the argument and demonstrates loyalty. The king's death is not a time for grasping but for mourning (1:17).

1:17-27 Elegy for Saul and Jonathan

David's lament is a powerful expression of public grief. Saul may have been rejected by the Lord, but he was still the leader of Israel. His death is a moment of defeat for the people. The warriors have fallen, Israel has been unmanned, and the women are summoned to mourn their fallen heroes. The incomprehension caused by death and defeat act as a refrain, "How can the warriors have fallen!" (1:19, 25, 27). This is a crisis of faith in a god who promises life and salvation. The crisis deepens because the Philistine women rejoice at the "good news" (1:20; cf. 1 Sam 31:9). What should have been a place of blessing has become a place of curse (1:21a). The battle was glorious (1:22) even if it was disastrous (1:21b). Grief is the only response to this crisis, a grief that voices the contradictions and thus opposes them. Only from such remembering can the grief-stricken reclaim the joy of past blessings (1:23-24) as an assurance for future comfort.

This grief is public and personal. All Israel mourns with David for the lost leaders, as he mourns for one he loved. Verse 26b is more precisely

²¹O mountains of Gilboa,
upon you be neither dew nor
rain,
nor surging from the deeps!
Defiled there the warriors' shields,
the shield of Saul—no longer
anointed with oil!
²²From the blood of the slain,
from the bodies of the warriors,
The bow of Jonathan did not turn
back,
nor the sword of Saul return un-
stained.
²³Saul and Jonathan, beloved and
dear,
separated neither in life nor
death,
swifter than eagles, stronger
than lions!
²⁴Women of Israel, weep over Saul,
who clothed you in scarlet and
in finery,
covered your clothing with orna-
ments of gold.
²⁵How can the warriors have fallen
in the thick of battle!
Jonathan—slain upon your
heights!
²⁶I grieve for you, Jonathan my
brother!
Most dear have you been to me;
More wondrous your love to me
than the love of women.
²⁷How can the warriors have fallen,
the weapons of war have per-
ished!

David Is Anointed King. ¹After this, David inquired of the LORD, "Shall I go up into one of the cities of Judah?" The LORD replied to him: Go up. Then David asked, "Where shall I go?" He replied: To Hebron. ²So David went up there, with his two wives, Ahinoam of

---

translated: "More precious have I held your love for me than love of women." Even here, the unequal nature of the relationship cannot be avoided. Jonathan's commitment to David has been consistently noted (1 Sam 18:1, 3; 19:1; 20:3, 17), but there was no such expression of David's feeling for Jonathan. Jonathan's affections motivated him to assist David, protecting him, saving him, and encouraging him. Others have acted simi-larly, particularly the women of 1 Samuel (Michal and Abigail), but none did as much (nor were given as much narrative space) as Jonathan. David is deeply in Jonathan's debt both on a personal and a political level. Only now, when Jonathan is dead, does David acknowledge this (as it was only when Jonathan abdicated his succession rights that David entered a mutual covenant with him in 1 Sam 23:18). David's grief is personal, but one won-ders if the political, public dimension still dominates his reckoning.

2:1-11 Rival kings

This unit contains two accounts of king-making following Saul's death. The narrator draws them together using a Deuteronomistic regnal formula. Such formulae provide a chronological framework for the monarchies of

Jezreel and Abigail, the wife of Nabal of Carmel. ³David also brought up his men with their families, and they dwelt in the towns of Hebron. ⁴Then the men of Judah came there and anointed David king over the house of Judah.

A report reached David that the people of Jabesh-gilead had buried Saul. ⁵So David sent messengers to the people of Jabesh-gilead and said to them: "May you be blessed by the Lᴏʀᴅ for having done this kindness to your lord Saul in burying him. ⁶And now may the Lᴏʀᴅ show you kindness and fidelity. For my part, I will show generosity to you for having done this. ⁷So take courage and prove yourselves valiant, for though your lord Saul is dead, the house of Judah has anointed me king over them."

IV. The Reign of David

Ishbaal King of Israel. ⁸Abner, son of Ner, captain of Saul's army, took Ishbaal, son of Saul, and brought him over to Mahanaim, ⁹where he made him king over Gilead, the Asherites, Jezreel, Ephraim, Benjamin, and the rest of Israel. ¹⁰Ishbaal, son of Saul, was forty years old when he became king over Israel, and he reigned two years; but the house of Judah followed David. ¹¹In all, David was king in Hebron over the

Israel and Judah. In this case, elements of the formula are divided between Ishbaal and David (2:10-11). As in its previous usage (1 Sam 13:1), there is something incomplete and unstable about the formula and the monarchy at this moment.

David's accession results from an inquiry of the Lord (2:1). The Lord clearly moves David into position at Hebron where the men of Judah anoint him king. This public anointing is minimally described (2:4a); there is no religious dimension as in 1 Samuel 16:1-13. It is a sign of public acceptance of the Lord's choice. This acceptance will be a key element in David's efforts to woo the northern tribes. He contacts Jabesh-gilead (2:5-7), a key center of Saulide support, and praises their "kindness" (*hesed*, loyalty) to Saul. Such loyalty calls forth and manifests divine blessing, but how will that blessing be maintained? David presents himself as the partner of Jabesh-gilead in actions which continue loyalty (2:6). This is a bold move to win their support and establish himself as a legitimate successor to Saul.

But David has a rival. Abner takes the Lord's role in moving Saul's surviving son, Ishbaal, into position and establishing him as king (2:8-9). Abner is Saul's general and the power behind the northern throne. There are now two claimants for loyalty, and two powers moving the kings. Hence the regnal formula fragments. A Saulide monarchy continues in the north while David is installed in Hebron. Civil war looms.

house of Judah seven years and six months.

Combat near Gibeon. [12]Now Abner, son of Ner, and the servants of Ishbaal, Saul's son, set out from Mahanaim for Gibeon. [13]Joab, son of Zeruiah, and the servants of David also set out and encountered them at the pool of Gibeon. And they sat down, one group on one side of the pool and the other on the opposite side. [14]Then Abner said to Joab, "Let the young men rise and perform for us." Joab replied, "All right." [15]So they rose and were counted off: twelve of the Benjaminites of Ishbaal, son of Saul, and twelve of David's servants. [16]Then each one grasped his opponent's head and thrust his sword into his opponent's side, and they all fell down together. And so that place was named the Field of the Sides; it is in Gibeon.

Death of Asahel. [17]The battle that day was very fierce, and Abner and the men of Israel were defeated by David's servants. [18]The three sons of Zeruiah were there—Joab, Abishai, and Asahel. Asahel, who was as fleet of foot as a gazelle in the open field, [19]set out after Abner, turning neither right nor left in his pursuit. [20]Abner turned around and said, "Is that you, Asahel?" He replied, "Yes." [21]Abner said to him, "Turn right or left; seize one of the young men and take what you can strip from him." But Asahel would not stop pursuing him. [22]Once more Abner said to Asahel: "Stop pursuing me! Why must I strike you to the ground? How could I show my face to your brother Joab?" [23]Still he refused to stop. So Abner struck him in the abdomen with the heel of his spear, and the weapon protruded from his back. He fell there and died on the spot. All who came to the place where Asahel had fallen and died, halted. [24]But Joab and Abishai continued the pursuit of Abner. The sun had

---

2:12-32 Skirmishes and combat

Civil war places the focus of attention on the generals. Abner and Joab lead out forces which are described in equivalent terms (2:12-13). This balance leads to a standoff. Abner proposes a gladiatorial contest in an attempt to break the deadlock with minimal casualties (2:14), but even here, the sides are evenly matched (2:15-16). Fighting escalates into battle. The three sons of Zeruiah are David's key warriors and constantly enmeshed in violence. On this occasion, the speedy Asahel chases the fleeing Abner (2:19-23). The drama intensifies as Abner tries to avoid killing Asahel for fear of vengeance. His attempts fail; he kills Asahel; bloodshed triggers vengeance (2:24).

The scene is set for a bloody showdown (2:25) when Abner succeeds in parleying a truce (2:26-28). Joab accepts the need to halt the fratricidal bloodshed, but almost too quickly. He is willing to stop the people killing fellow Israelites, but he makes no commitment that his personal vendetta is over. Both sides withdraw to count and bury their dead.

gone down when they came to the hill of Ammah which lies east of the valley toward the wilderness near Geba.

Truce Between Joab and Abner. [25]Here the Benjaminites rallied around Abner, forming a single group, and made a stand on a hilltop. [26]Then Abner called to Joab and said: "Must the sword devour forever? Do you not know that afterward there will be bitterness? How long before you tell the people to stop pursuing their brothers?" [27]Joab replied, "As God lives, if you had not spoken, it would be morning before the people would be stopped from pursuing their brothers." [28]Joab then sounded the horn, and all the people came to a halt, pursuing Israel no farther and fighting no more. [29]Abner and his men marched all night long through the Arabah, crossed the Jordan, marched all through the morning, and came to Mahanaim. [30]Joab, coming from the pursuit of Abner, assembled all the men. Nineteen other servants of David were missing, besides Asahel. [31]But David's servants had struck down and killed three hundred and sixty men of Benjamin, followers of Abner. [32]They took up Asahel and buried him in his father's tomb in Bethlehem. Joab and his men made an all-night march, and dawn found them in Hebron.

[3] [1]There followed a long war between the house of Saul and the house of David, in which David grew ever stronger, but the house of Saul ever weaker.

Sons Born in Hebron. [2]Sons were born to David in Hebron: his firstborn, Amnon, of Ahinoam from Jezreel; [3]the second, Chileab, of Abigail the wife of Nabal of Carmel; the third, Absalom, son of Maacah, who was the daughter of Talmai, king of Geshur; [4]the fourth, Adonijah, son of Haggith; the fifth, Shephatiah, son of Abital; [5]and the sixth, Ithream, by David's wife Eglah. These were born to David in Hebron.

The seeds of this conflict were sown in 1 Samuel 26 when the conflict between Saul and David was widened to include their generals. While the principals refrained from bloodshed, their seconds show little restraint. Violence begets vengeance and threatens to destroy the very thing the kings are quarrelling over, as Abigail warned in chapter 25. Abner emerges in this episode as an honorable man who seeks to limit the bloodshed, but will Joab cooperate? Or will he drag his leader into guilt by association?

3:1-5 Civil war

The civil war is long but unequal. David's "house" is winning and its position becomes more secure: political strength and sexual prowess mirror each other in this culture. This is an appropriate point to list David's sons by his many women. This successful harem will contrast with the competition over Saul's concubine (3:7).

Ishbaal and Abner Quarrel. ⁶During the war between the house of Saul and the house of David, Abner was gaining power in the house of Saul. ⁷Now Saul had had a concubine, Rizpah, the daughter of Aiah. And Ishbaal, son of Saul, said to Abner, "Why have you slept with my father's concubine?" ⁸Enraged at the words of Ishbaal, Abner said, "Am I a dog's head from Judah? As of today, I have been loyal to the house of Saul your father, to his brothers and his friends, and I have kept you out of David's clutches; and today you charge me with a crime involving a woman! ⁹May God do thus to Abner, and more, if I do not carry out for David what the LORD swore to him— ¹⁰that is, take away the kingdom from the house of Saul and establish the throne of David over Israel as well as Judah, from Dan to Beer-sheba." ¹¹Ishbaal was no longer able to say a word to Abner, he feared him so.

Abner and David Reconciled. ¹²Then Abner sent messengers to David in Telam, where he was at the moment, to say, "Make a covenant with me, and you have me on your side, to bring all Israel over to you." ¹³He replied, "Good, I will make a covenant with you. But one thing I require of you. You must not appear before me unless you bring back Michal, Saul's daughter, when you come to present yourself to me." ¹⁴At the same time David sent messengers to Ishbaal, son of Saul, to say, "Give me my wife Michal, whom I betrothed by paying a hundred Philistine foreskins." ¹⁵Ishbaal

3:6-39 Abner, kingmaker betrayed

The quarrel over Rizpah, Saul's concubine, initiates a move by Abner to transfer the allegiance of the north to David. In effect, Abner, who, apart from David, is the only character to cite the Lord, becomes the agent of David's rise to the throne of all Israel, until Joab complicates the plot. The result is an intriguing narrative which illustrates the danger of bloodlust.

3:6-11 Ishbaal's accusation

Women play a crucial, if normally passive, role in Israelite politics. Ishbaal is accusing Abner of usurping the kingdom by taking Saul's concubine (3:6-7). Abner's anger derives from this slight to his loyalty to Saul's house (3:8). Like the people of Jabesh-gilead, his loyalty to the Lord is expressed in concrete terms by loyalty to Saul's family. Ishbaal's accusation pushes Abner to express that loyalty to the Lord in a new political form. He will bring about the Lord's promise to David (3:9-10).

3:12-21 Abner's gift

David is shrewd enough to facilitate Abner. His condition is the return of Michal (3:13). Once he has Saul's daughter (3:14-16), David becomes Saul's son-in-law and legitimate claimant to the loyalty owed to Saul's house, so easing Abner's transfer of allegiance. Abner persuades the elders to make the same transfer by highlighting David's claim to divine approval

sent for her and took her away from her husband Paltiel, son of Laish, [16]who followed her weeping as far as Bahurim. But Abner said to him, "Go back!" So he turned back.

[17]Abner then had a word with the elders of Israel: "For some time you have been wanting David as your king. [18]Now take action, for the LORD has said of David: By David my servant I will save my people Israel from the power of the Philistines and from the power of all their enemies." [19]Abner also spoke with Benjamin, and then went to speak with David in Hebron concerning all that would be agreeable to Israel and to the whole house of Benjamin. [20]When Abner, accompanied by twenty men, came to David in Hebron, David prepared a feast for Abner and for the men who were with him. [21]Then Abner said to David,

"I will now go to assemble all Israel for my lord the king, that they may make a covenant with you; you will then be king over all whom you wish to rule." So David let Abner go on his way in peace.

Death of Abner. [22]Just then David's servants and Joab were coming in from an expedition, bringing much plunder with them. Abner, having been dismissed by David, was no longer with him in Hebron but had gone on his way in peace. [23]When Joab and the whole force he had with him arrived, he was informed, "Abner, son of Ner, came to David, and he let him go on his way in peace." [24]So Joab went to the king and said: "What have you done? Abner came to you! Why did you let him get away? [25]Don't you know Abner? He came to trick you, to learn your comings and goings, to learn everything you do." [26]Joab

---

(3:17-19). In all their dealings Abner acts honorably and David reciprocates (3:20-21). David is the recipient of Abner's gift, but happily plots with him to achieve it. Together they arrange a peaceful transfer of power. David has learned well from Abigail that persuasion and patience outweigh violence as the path to power.

After these negotiations, the narrator begins to refer to David as "the king" (vv. 24, 33, 36, 37, 38) and gives him the title "King David" in verse 31. Abner's negotiations have effectively made David king of all Israel, even if the coronation lies some chapters away.

3:22-39 Joab's crime

However, Joab's actions threaten David's claim to the kingdom. Joab's desire for vengeance colors his reactions to events in his absence (3:22-25). He may be David's chief officer, but he is not under David's control. He acts for his own goals. The narrator stresses the independence (3:26) that results in Abner's murder (3:27). David is shocked and swears his innocence (3:28). He quickly and profusely pins responsibility and punishment on Joab (3:29), while he orders a burial with full honors for Abner. This is a very public show of grief (3:31-35). It is probably heartfelt, but it also serves

then left David and sent messengers after Abner to bring him back from the cistern of Sirah; but David did not know. [27]When Abner returned to Hebron, Joab took him aside within the city gate to speak with him privately. There he stabbed him in the abdomen, and he died for the blood of Asahel, Joab's brother. [28]Later David heard of it and said: "Before the LORD, I and my kingdom are forever innocent. [29]May the blood of Abner, son of Ner, be on the head of Joab and all his family. May Joab's family never be without one suffering from a discharge, or one with a skin disease, or a man who holds the distaff, or one falling by the sword, or one in need of food!" [30]Joab and Abishai his brother had been lying in wait for Abner because he killed Asahel their brother in battle at Gibeon.

David Mourns Abner. [31]Then David said to Joab and to all the people who were with him, "Tear your garments, put on sackcloth, and mourn over Abner." King David himself followed the bier. [32]When they had buried Abner in Hebron, the king wept aloud at the grave of Abner, and all the people wept. [33]And the king sang this lament over Abner:

> Should Abner have died like a fool?
> [34]Your hands were not bound with chains,
> nor your feet placed in fetters;
> As one falls before the wicked, you fell.

And all the people continued to weep for him. [35]Then they went to console David with food while it was still day. But David swore, "May God do thus to me, and more, if before the sun goes down I eat bread or anything else." [36]All the people noted this with approval, just as everything the king did met with their approval. [37]So on that day all the people and all Israel came to know that it was not the king's doing that Abner, son of Ner, was put to death. [38]The king then said to his servants: "Do you not know that a prince, a great man, has fallen today in Israel. [39]Although I am the anointed king, I am weak this day, and these men, the sons of Zeruiah, are too ruthless for me. May the LORD repay the

as a public demonstration of innocence. This crime threatens to wreck the unification of Israel and to besmirch David's kingship. The danger is so great that even the narrator declares David innocent (3:37), as do the people (3:36). Clearly the compilers of the history felt a great need to exonerate David of involvement in the death of an honorable general.

Comparing David's last speech with verse 11 shows that both he and Ishbaal are unable to control their generals. Both are effectively hostage to these men and can be destroyed by their actions. Abner ends Ishbaal's reign by withdrawing support. David's reign is almost destroyed by Joab's crime. The monarchical system threatens to unleash forces which even kings cannot control. The Lord has raised David to the throne, but this will not save the institution from human failings.

evildoer in accordance with his evil deed."

4 **Death of Ishbaal.** ¹When Ishbaal, son of Saul, heard that Abner was dead in Hebron, he lost his resolve and all Israel was alarmed. ²Ishbaal, son of Saul, had two company leaders named Baanah and Rechab, sons of Rimmon the Beerothite, of the tribe of Benjamin—Beeroth, too, was ascribed to Benjamin: ³the Beerothites fled to Gittaim, where they have been resident aliens to this day. ⁴(Jonathan, son of Saul, had a son with crippled feet. He was five years old when the news about Saul and Jonathan came from Jezreel; his nurse took him and fled, but in their hasty flight, he fell and became lame. His name was Meribbaal.) ⁵The sons of Rimmon the Beerothite, Rechab and Baanah, came into the house of Ishbaal during the heat of the day, while he was lying on his bed in the afternoon. ⁶The gatekeeper of the house had dozed off while sifting wheat, and was asleep. So Rechab and his brother Baanah slipped past her ⁷and entered the house while Ishbaal was lying asleep in his bedroom. They struck and killed him, and cut off his head. Then, taking the head, they traveled on the Arabah road all night long.

The Murder Avenged. ⁸They brought the head of Ishbaal to David in Hebron and said to the king: "This is the head of

---

4:1-12 Death of Ishbaal

With Abner dead, the northern kingdom collapses (4:1). Ishbaal is powerless and is assassinated by two officers. Their identity is given in detail (4:2) to state clearly the assassins' family backgrounds and to dissociate them from David's entourage. The murder is swift and brutal, using three verbs: "[they] struck and killed him, and cut off his head" (4:7).

The assassins bring their trophy to David expecting a reward. Their presentation is logical and assured (4:8), but fails to take account of David's loyalty to the family of Saul. His reaction and words recall a similar incident after Saul's death (1:1-16). David has the assassins punished, again using three verbs: "the young men killed them and cut off their hands and feet, hanging them up near the pool in Hebron" (4:12). The punishment fits the crime. As with Abner, David ensures that Ishbaal's remains are buried with dignity. Once again, the narrator demonstrates David's loyalty to the house of Saul and his innocence in planning or benefiting from their deaths. The kingship will come to David, but not by vengeance (contrary to claims in v. 8b).

The narrator inserts one ray of hope for Saul's family. An aside informs the reader of the survival of Jonathan's son, Meribbaal (4:4). The child is crippled and so cannot attain political power, but his existence will provide David with an opportunity to fulfill his oaths to Jonathan (1 Sam 20:14-17) and Saul (1 Sam 24:22-23).

Ishbaal, son of your enemy Saul, who sought your life. Thus has the LORD this day avenged my lord the king on Saul and his posterity." ⁹But David replied to Rechab and his brother Baanah, sons of Rimmon the Beerothite: "As the LORD lives, who rescued me from every distress: ¹⁰the man who reported to me, 'Saul is dead,' and thought he was bringing good news, that man I seized and killed in Ziglag: that was the reward I gave him. ¹¹How much more now, when wicked men have slain an innocent man in bed at home, must I require his blood from you and purge you from the land!" ¹²So at David's command, the young men killed them and cut off their hands and feet, hanging them up near the pool in Hebron. But he took the head of Ishbaal and buried it in Abner's grave in Hebron.

5 David King of Israel. ¹All the tribes of Israel came to David in Hebron, and they said: "Look! We are your bone and your flesh. ²In days past, when Saul was still our king, you were the one who led Israel out in all its battles and brought it back. And the LORD said to you: You shall shepherd my people Israel; you shall be ruler over Israel." ³Then all the elders of Israel came to the king in Hebron, and at Hebron King David made a covenant with them in the presence of the LORD; and they anointed David king over Israel. ⁴David was thirty years old when he became king, and he reigned forty years: ⁵in Hebron he was king over Judah seven years and six months, and in Jerusalem he was king thirty-three years over all Israel and Judah.

5:1-5 David, king of all Israel

The story of David's rise reaches its conclusion. David is crowned king over Israel and establishes his capital. The coronation of David happens in two movements. First, the tribes of Israel meet David and resolve their alarm (5:1-2; cf. 4:1). The tribes stress their solidarity with David as fellow Israelites (5:1), and affirm David's leadership (5:2). They quote a word of the Lord (previously unmentioned) to demonstrate their recognition of his divine appointment to rule ("shepherd") the people. The term, "ruler" (*nagid*), has several echoes: it emphasizes David's role as military leader (cf. Saul's appointment in 1 Sam 9:16), it picks up several predictions of David's rise (1 Sam 13:14; 25:30), and it prepares for anointing (cf. 1 Sam 10:1). It catches the covenantal understanding of the king as leader of God's people, filled with God's spirit and subject to God's word.

Secondly, the scheme of Abner is ratified by the elders (5:3; cf. 3:17-18). David enters a covenant ("agreement") with the elders (cf. Abner's agreement with David in 3:12). Such an action is missing from David's enthronement over Judah: his rule of Israel must recognize and respect the covenant traditions of the whole people. The passage ends with a Deuteronomistic regnal formula. David has begun his reign over all Israel (5:5).

Crumbling ruins of the City of David, Jerusalem.

Capture of Zion. [6]Then the king and his men went to Jerusalem against the Jebusites who inhabited the land. They told David, "You shall not enter here: the blind and the lame will drive you away!" which was their way of saying, "David shall not enter here." [7]David nevertheless captured the fortress of Zion, which is the City of David. [8]On that day David said: "All who wish to strike at the Jebusites must attack through the water shaft. The lame and the blind shall be the personal enemies of David." That is why it is said, "The blind and the lame shall not enter the palace." [9]David took up residence in the fortress which he called the City of David. David built up the city on all sides, from the Millo toward the center. [10]David became ever more powerful, for the LORD of hosts was with him. [11]Hiram, king of Tyre, sent envoys to David along with cedar wood, and carpenters and masons, who built a house for David. [12]David now knew that the LORD had truly established him as king over Israel and had exalted his kingdom for the sake of his people Israel.

5:6-12 Jerusalem's capture

The formula's reference to Jerusalem is quickly sorted out by the account of Jerusalem's capture. Jerusalem lies between the tribal areas of Judah and Benjamin. It was not an Israelite city. David captured it with his own men so that it is truly his city, an autonomous place from which he can rule both Judah and Israel with impartiality. An account of the capture is also given in 1 Chronicles 11:4-9 with less attention to the blind and lame. The comments about the blind and lame stress the city's apparent impregnability, which David overcomes. It is conjectured that his troops broke into the city by climbing up a well shaft linking the city to a spring in the valley below. With David established in Jerusalem, the narrator concludes the story of his rise with two statements of God's support (5:10, 12). The last statement is a fitting summary for this phase in Israel's history.

THE REIGN OF DAVID

2 Samuel 5:13–8:18

Between the major narratives of David's rise (1 Sam 16–2 Sam 5) and of his family (2 Sam 9–20), the compilers of the Deuteronomistic History inserted a collection of stories about David's monarchy. Framed by lists of his family (5:13-16) and his officers (8:15-18), these accounts tell how his monarchy developed. There are stories of his battles and of his dealings with the Lord. Militarily, David moves from defense to expansion. Religiously, attention shifts from the ark to the dynasty of David as the sign of God's continuing presence.

David's Family in Jerusalem. [13]David took more concubines and wives in Jerusalem after he had come from Hebron, and more sons and daughters were born to him. [14]These are the names of those who were born to him in Jerusalem: Shammua, Shobab, Nathan, Solomon, [15]Ibhar, Elishua, Nepheg, Japhia, [16]Elishama, Beeliada, and Eliphelet.

Rout of the Philistines. [17]When the Philistines had heard that David was anointed king over Israel, they marched out in force to come after him. When David heard this, he went down to the refuge. [18]Meanwhile the Philistines had come and deployed themselves in the valley of Rephaim. [19]David inquired of the LORD, "Shall I attack the Philistines, and will you deliver them into my power?" The LORD answered David: Attack, for I will surely deliver the Philistines into your power. [20]So David went to Baal-perazim, and he defeated them there. He said, "The LORD has broken through my enemies before me just as water breaks through a dam." Therefore that place was called Baal-perazim. [21]The Philistines abandoned their gods there, and David and his men carried them away. [22]Once again the Philistines came up and deployed themselves in the valley of Rephaim, [23]and again David inquired of the LORD, who replied: Do not attack the front—circle behind them and come against them near the balsam trees. [24]When you hear the sound of marching

5:13-25 The defeat of the Philistines

David's family is already extensive. Now he adds concubines to his harem. While the later narratives will deal with his children born in Hebron, one son born in Jerusalem should be noted in passing, Solomon.

As David's reign begins, there is unfinished business with the Philistines. It is possible that the Philistines assembled their troops to punish their renegade vassal, so David goes into hiding (5:17). The situation is critical for the new kingdom. The valley of Rephaim gives access from the coast to Jerusalem; controlling it, the Philistines can split the kingdom and dominate its capital. As before, David consults the Lord (5:19; cf. 1 Sam 23:4; 30:7-8; 2 Sam 2:1) and is given clearance to proceed. The first encounter drives the enemy back. The place name means "Lord of the breaking through," signifying the breaking of the Philistine line (5:20). But the Philistines return to the fray and this time the Lord gives quite specific directions (5:23-24). This second battle becomes the occasion of a theophany; the sound of the wind rustling the treetops suggests the footsteps of Israel's divine warrior charging into battle. The rout is complete. The Philistines are driven out of the hill country and confined to the coastal plain. The Lord has marked the beginning of David's reign with a decisive defeat of Israel's greatest enemy as promised (cf. 3:18). The people know for certain that David is the Lord's chosen king.

in the tops of the balsam trees, act decisively, for then the LORD has already gone before you to strike the army of the Philistines. ²⁵David did as the LORD commanded him, and routed the Philistines from Gibeon as far as Gezer.

The Ark Brought to Jerusalem. ¹David again assembled all the picked men of Israel, thirty thousand in number. ²Then David and all the people who were with him set out for Baala of Judah to bring up from there the ark of God, which bears the name "the LORD of hosts enthroned above the cherubim." ³They transported the ark of God on a new cart and took it away from the house of Abinadab on the hill. Uzzah and Ahio, sons of Abinadab, were guiding the cart, ⁴with Ahio walking before it, ⁵while David and all the house of Israel danced before the LORD with all their might, with singing, and with lyres, harps, tambourines, sistrums, and cymbals. ⁶As they reached the threshing floor of Nodan, Uzzah stretched out his hand to the ark of God and steadied it, for the oxen were tipping it. ⁷Then the LORD became angry with Uzzah; God struck him on that spot, and he died there in God's presence. ⁸David was angry because the LORD's wrath had broken out against Uzzah. Therefore that place has been called Perez-uzzah even to this day. ⁹David became frightened of the LORD that day, and he said, "How can the ark of the LORD come to me?" ¹⁰So David was unwilling to take the ark of the LORD with him into the City of David. David deposited it instead at the house of Obed-edom the Gittite.

6:1-23 The ark is brought to Jerusalem

The defeat of the Philistines by the warrior Lord recalls the traditions of holy war. This is a suitable moment to reconnect with the ancient symbol of the Lord of hosts, the ark, which was deposited in Kiriath-jearim (1 Sam 6:21–7:1). By retrieving the ark, David connects his new regime to covenant tradition and thereby gives it further legitimation.

The ark is transported on a new cart and with significant rejoicing (cf. 1 Sam 6), and as before, the narrator highlights the dangers of taking God's presence lightly. Like the descendants of Jeconiah (1 Sam 6:19-20), Uzzah is struck down (6:6-7). David, belatedly, asks "How can the ark of the LORD come to me?" (6:9). Curiously, this is one venture which David initiates without consulting the Lord. His attempt to co-opt the old traditions is checked temporarily by a reminder of the freedom of the Lord of hosts, a key theme of the earlier ark narratives.

The journey resumes with even more religious festivities. Sacrifices (6:13) and communion feasts (6:17-19) are added to the song and dance (6:5, 14-15). David is at the center of worship, dressed in a priest's linen tunic (6:14). He dances with abandon. Is there an echo of Saul's possession by the Spirit (1 Sam 10:5-6) with its combination of music and ecstasy? Is David

¹¹The ark of the LORD remained in the house of Obed-edom the Gittite for three months, and the LORD blessed Obed-edom and all his household. ¹²When it was reported to King David that the LORD had blessed the household of Obed-edom and all that he possessed because of the ark of God, David went to bring up the ark of God from the house of Obed-edom into the City of David with joy. ¹³As soon as the bearers of the ark of the LORD had advanced six steps, he sacrificed an ox and a fatling. ¹⁴Then David came dancing before the LORD with abandon, girt with a linen ephod. ¹⁵David and all the house of Israel were bringing up the ark of the LORD with shouts of joy and sound of horn. ¹⁶As the ark of the LORD was entering the City of David, Michal, daughter of Saul, looked down from her window, and when she saw King David jumping and dancing before the LORD, she despised him in her heart. ¹⁷They brought in the ark of the LORD and set it in its place within the tent which David had pitched for it. Then David sacrificed burnt offerings and communion offerings before the LORD. ¹⁸When David had finished sacrificing burnt offerings and communion offerings, he blessed the people in the name of the LORD of hosts, ¹⁹and distributed among all the people, the entire multitude of Israel, to every man and every woman, one loaf of bread, one piece of meat, and one raisin cake. Then all the people returned to their homes.

²⁰When David went home to bless his own house, Michal, the daughter of Saul, came out to meet him and said, "How well the king of Israel has honored himself today, exposing himself to the view of the slave girls of his followers, as a commoner might expose himself!" ²¹But David replied to Michal: "I was dancing before the LORD. As the LORD lives, who chose me over your father and all his house when he appointed me ruler over the LORD's people, Israel, not only will I make merry before the LORD, ²²but I will demean myself even more. I will be lowly in your eyes, but in the eyes of the slave girls you spoke of I will

caught up in the charismatic exuberance which overpowered Saul? Does Michal despise him for this behavior, reminiscent of her father's darker moments (6:16)?

Following the joyous celebrations, the private encounter picks up this jarring comment. Michal vents her anger about three things: honor, slave girls, and common behavior (6:20). David is reduced in her esteem from king to commoner! David's response ends with her three points in reverse order: lowliness, slave girls, and honor in verse 22. It was for the Lord that he danced (6:21). What right has she to complain? The Lord chose David over Saul. What Michal sees as shame (David exposing himself), David claims as a sign of honor. The theme of reversal of Hannah's song (1 Sam 2) is operating, and it rebounds on Michal, the king's daughter who remains childless and so dishonored in comparison with the slave girls.

be somebody." ²³Saul's daughter Michal was childless to the day she died.

◄ **7** **The Oracle of Nathan.** ¹After the king had taken up residence in his house, and the Lᴏʀᴅ had given him rest from his enemies on every side, ²the king said to Nathan the prophet, "Here I am living in a house of cedar, but the ark of God dwells in a tent!" ³Nathan answered the king, "Whatever is in your heart, go and do, for the Lᴏʀᴅ is with you." ⁴But that same night the word of the Lᴏʀᴅ came to Nathan: ⁵Go and tell David my servant, Thus says the Lᴏʀᴅ: Is it you who would build me a house to dwell in? ⁶I have never dwelt in a house from the day I brought Israel up from Egypt to this day, but I have been going about in a tent or a tabernacle. ⁷As long as I have wandered about among the Israelites, did I ever say a word to any of the judges whom I commanded to shepherd my people Israel: Why have you not built me a house of cedar?

⁸Now then, speak thus to my servant David, Thus says the Lᴏʀᴅ of hosts: I took you from the pasture, from following the flock, to become ruler over my

---

7:1-29 The Lord's promise to David

While 5:17–6:23 show David engaging with the old traditions of Israel to secure his kingdom, chapter 7 marks a new beginning in Israel's relationship with the Lord. David wants to incorporate the ark and its symbolism into the new settlement to ensure the stability of the monarchy. The symbol of the Lord's freedom to move with nomadic tribes and to act independently of the people is to be housed in one location, the royal capital. The Lord resists this imposition but responds with a startling promise which makes the kings the living testimony to God's presence. The oracle of 2 Samuel 7:4-16 is one of the central texts of the Old Testament.

The keyword "house" gives unity to the chapter. Reflecting the tension between freedom and presence, mobility and stability, it has several connotations: dwelling, palace, temple, dynasty. After the introduction (7:1-3) outlining David's plan comes the Lord's oracle through Nathan (7:4-16). A short narrative interlude (7:17-18a) introduces David's prayer as the response to the oracle (7:18b-29).

7:4-16 Nathan's oracle

Scholars suggest that the oracle has been elaborated several times, a sign of constant reflection within the tradition prior to the composition of the book. An original account, possibly dating from David's time, focused on the Lord's rebuttal of David's plan to build a house (temple). Instead the Lord would build David a house (dynasty) and kingdom which would last forever (7:11b, 16). This promise underwent elaboration in prophetic circles to stress David's role as *nagid* (7:8-10) and to focus on Solomon as

people Israel. ⁹I was with you wherever you went, and I cut down all your enemies before you. And I will make your name like that of the greatest on earth. ¹⁰I will assign a place for my people Israel and I will plant them in it to dwell there; they will never again be disturbed, nor shall the wicked ever again oppress them, as they did at the beginning, ¹¹and from the day when I appointed judges over my people Israel. I will give you rest from all your enemies. Moreover, the LORD also declares to you that the LORD will make a house for you: ¹²when your days have been completed and you rest with your ancestors, I will raise up your offspring after you, sprung from your loins, and I will establish his kingdom. ¹³He it is who shall build a house for my name, and I will establish his royal throne forever. ¹⁴I will be a father to him, and he shall be a son to me. If he does wrong, I will reprove him with a human rod and with human punishments; ¹⁵but I will not withdraw my favor from him as I withdrew it from Saul who was before you. ¹⁶Your house and your kingdom are firm forever before me; your throne shall be firmly established forever. ¹⁷In accordance with all these words and this whole vision Nathan spoke to David.

the particular successor (7:14-15). Nathan's role was also enhanced (7:3, 17). The notion of a temple as God's permanent residence generates mixed reactions throughout the Bible, different views which also affect this text. Verses 5-7 were revised to show that such a building compromised God's freedom. Those who saw Solomon's temple as the pinnacle of Israel's relationship with the Lord added verse 13. Such a textual history is complex, but the struggle to understand God's promise today continues a process of interpreting God's will which goes back to its first revelation.

David wishes to build God a house (7:1-2). At best, this gives glory to God (so Nathan interprets David's motive); at worst, it is a domestication of the Lord of Israel. The Lord's intervention rejects such domestication, which runs counter to the fundamental religious experience of Israel, the exodus (7:6-7). In the new dispensation, that experience of the liberating God must be maintained. God's saving presence will not be limited to a place or object, but will be manifest in a people established in security (7:10). To achieve this, the Lord has chosen to raise up an individual as leader (7:8). Just as monarchy is established by divine choice rather than a human one, its stability will be provided by a divine "building" rather than a human "building." The Lord will establish a dynasty for David (7:11b). The present text focuses first on David's immediate successor (7:12-15) before expanding to consider a permanent dynasty (7:16).

The presentation of David's heir is particularly noteworthy. Normally, God's promises are conditional on ethical requirements. While the oracle

David's Thanksgiving. [18]Then King David went in and sat in the LORD's presence and said, "Who am I, Lord GOD, and what is my house, that you should have brought me so far? [19]And yet even this is too little in your sight, Lord GOD! For you have made a promise regarding your servant's house reaching into the future, and giving guidance to the people, Lord GOD! [20]What more can David say to you? You know your servant, Lord GOD! [21]For your servant's sake and as you have had at heart, you have brought about this whole magnificent disclosure to your servant. [22]Therefore, great are you, Lord GOD! There is no one like you, no God but you, as we have always heard. [23]What other nation on earth is there like your people Israel? What god has ever led a nation, redeeming it as his people and making a name by great and awesome deeds, as you drove out the nations and their gods before your people, whom you redeemed for yourself from Egypt? [24]You have established for yourself your people Israel as your people forever, and you, LORD, have become their God. [25]Now, LORD God, confirm the promise that you have spoken concerning your servant and his house forever. Bring about what you have promised [26]so that your name may

does warn of ethical/religious requirements for the members of the dynasty (7:14b), the conditional "if" is not present in the Hebrew text. Instead, the promise is unconditional: "but I will not withdraw my favor from him" (7:15). This is a new departure in Israel's experience of God. In these individuals, the house of David, is invested the hope of Israel. It is the human incarnation of God's promise that is truly messianic: a human being now bears the symbolism of God's presence and power in the world. For Jews and Christians reflecting on this oracle, this human being is the instrument for establishing the reign of justice and peace, covenant fraternity, and integrity.

7:18-29 David's prayer

David's prayer is a fitting response to the oracle. He moves from prostration before the Lord's grace (7:18-21), to praise (7:22-24), and on to petition (7:25-29). The oracle outlined what the Lord will do for David; now David acknowledges the graciousness of God's attention to one who has nothing to recommend him (7:18-21). David locates what the Lord has done for him in the context of God's saving actions for his people (the exodus, 7:22-24). This new revelation is a continuation of that fundamental revelation. This display of humility and praise only emboldens David to petition the Lord to keep his promise! This is a bold faith. Like Jacob (Gen 32:27), David will not let God go until the Lord blesses him and confirms the promise (7:25-29).

"David obeyed the LORD's command and routed the Philistines from Gibeon as far as Gezer" (2 Samuel 5:25). Wall relief of Philistine captives. Mortuary temple of Ramses III, Egypt.

be forever great. People will say: 'The LORD of hosts is God over Israel,' when the house of your servant David is established in your presence. ²⁷Because you, LORD of hosts, God of Israel, have revealed to your servant, 'I will build you a house,' your servant now finds the courage to make this prayer before you. ²⁸Since you, Lord GOD, are truly God and your words are truth and you have made this generous promise to your servant, ²⁹do, then, bless the house of your servant, that it may be in your presence forever—since you, Lord GOD, have promised, and by your blessing the house of your servant shall be blessed forever."

8 **Summary of David's Wars.** ¹After this, David defeated the Philistines and subdued them; and David took . . . from the Philistines. ²He also defeated Moab and measured them with a line. Making them lie down on the ground,

he measured two lengths of line for death, and a full length for life. Thus the Moabites became subject to David, paying tribute. ³David then defeated Hadadezer, son of Rehob, king of Zobah, when he went to re-establish his dominion at the River. ⁴David captured from him one thousand seven hundred horsemen and twenty thousand foot soldiers. David hamstrung all the chariot horses, but left one hundred for his chariots. ⁵The Arameans of Damascus came to help Hadadezer, king of Zobah, but David also defeated twenty-two thousand of them in Aram. ⁶David then placed garrisons in the Damascus region of Aram, and the Arameans became David's subjects, paying tribute. The LORD brought David victory in all his undertakings. ⁷David took the golden shields that were carried by Hadadezer's attendants and brought them to Jerusalem. (These Shishak, king

8:1-14 David's wars

Chapter 8 offers a summary of David's campaigns. Some material looks back to round off stories already told (e.g., v. 1 parallels 5:17-25); other material anticipates and provides context for later stories (e.g., the campaign against Hadadezer in 8:3-6 supports 10:15-19). This unit shows David moving from defense to offense, saving Israel by conquering its neighbors. It is a celebration of his military prowess. It also raises questions about excessive use of power. Moab, an ally during David's rise (1 Sam 22:3-4), is now conquered and most of its fighting men executed (8:2).

War against the Arameans accounts for a significant part of David's campaigns. The campaign against Hadadezer (8:3-6) leads into the gathering of booty and tribute (8:7-12). The focus is on David's accumulation of wealth. Only in verse 11 does the narrator add that the materials were "consecrated to the LORD." The passage as a whole celebrates David's abilities and fame (8:13), but the narrator reminds the reader twice (8:6b and 14b) that the true source of success is the Lord.

of Egypt, took away when he came to Jerusalem in the days of Rehoboam, son of Solomon.) ⁸From Tebah and Berothai, cities of Hadadezer, King David removed a very large quantity of bronze. ⁹When Toi, king of Hamath, heard that David had defeated the entire army of Hadadezer, ¹⁰Toi sent his son Hadoram to wish King David well and to congratulate him on having waged a victorious war against Hadadezer; for Hadadezer had been at war with Toi. Hadoram also brought with him articles of silver, gold, and bronze. ¹¹These also King David consecrated to the LORD along with the silver and gold that he had taken for this purpose from all the nations he had subdued: ¹²from Edom, Moab, the Ammonites, the Philistines, and Amalek, and from the spoils of Hadadezer, son of Rehob, king of Zobah.

¹³On his return, David made a name for himself by defeating eighteen thousand Edomites in the Valley of Salt. ¹⁴He set up garrisons in Edom, and all the Edomites became David's subjects. Thus the LORD brought David victory in all his undertakings.

David's Officials. ¹⁵David was king over all Israel; he dispensed justice and right to all his people. ¹⁶Joab, son of Zeruiah, was in command of the army. Jehoshaphat, son of Ahilud, was chancellor. ¹⁷Zadok, son of Ahitub, and Ahimelech, son of Abiathar, were priests. Shavsha was scribe. ¹⁸Benaiah, son of Jehoiada, was in command of the Cherethites and the Pelethites; and David's sons were priests.

8:15-18 David's government

This section of the book (5:13–8:18) concludes by outlining the key officials in David's government. The government covers all areas of public life: justice, the military, administration, and religion. The list suggests a more complex administration than the family-based government of Saul (cf. 1 Sam 14:49-51). David's administration incorporates the need to establish justice, a key covenantal theme. The success of the king will be measured by his ability to provide justice (cf. Ps 72:1-4; Jer 22:15-16). It is also noteworthy that David's administration includes the Elide priesthood (Abiathar), as well as the Zadokite priesthood which will eventually replace the former (cf. 1 Sam 2:27-36).

THE FAMILY OF DAVID

2 Samuel 9–20

Many scholars identify 2 Samuel 9–20 and 2 Kings 1–2 as a continuous narrative which deals with the question: who will succeed David? It has been called the Succession Narrative. It is suggested that this narrative was composed in court circles soon after the succession was achieved. However, debate still continues about the details of this hypothesis.

9 **David and Meribbaal.** ¹David asked, "Is there any survivor of Saul's house to whom I may show kindness for the sake of Jonathan?" ²Now there was an official of the house of Saul named Ziba. He was summoned to David, and the king asked him, "Are you Ziba?" He replied, "Your servant." ³Then the king asked, "Is there any survivor of Saul's house to whom I may show God's kindness?" Ziba answered the king, "There is still Jonathan's son, the one whose feet are crippled." ⁴The king asked him, "Where is he?" and Ziba answered the king, "He is in the house of Machir, son of Ammiel, in Lodebar." ⁵So King David sent for him and had him brought from the house of Machir, son of Ammiel, from Lodebar. ⁶When Meribbaal, son of Jonathan, son of Saul, came to David, he fell face down in homage. David said, "Meribbaal," and he answered, "Your servant." ⁷"Do not be afraid," David said to him, "I will surely be kind to you for the sake of Jonathan your father. I will restore to you all the lands of Saul your grandfather, and you shall eat at my table always." ⁸Bowing low, he answered, "What am I, your servant, that you should pay attention to a dead dog like me?" ⁹The king then called Ziba, Saul's attendant, and said to him: "All that belonged to Saul and to his entire house, I am giving to your lord's son. ¹⁰You and your sons and servants must till the land for him. You shall bring in

---

2 Samuel 9–20 is a sustained literary masterpiece which skillfully explores the ambiguity of human personality, success and failure, and the tensions that arose in David's household. There is little direct involvement of God, his prophets, or priests. This more secular drama is played out in a strongly religious context. The overall direction of events is set by God's promise to establish this family as a dynasty, but the foibles and faith of human beings complicate yet enrich the unfolding of that plan. It is this aspect that the narrator is particularly keen to explore.

9:1-13 David and Meribbaal

This episode looks back to David's oaths to Jonathan (1 Sam 20:14-17) and Saul (1 Sam 24:21-23). Jonathan made David swear to protect Jonathan's descendants. David now recalls that loyalty ("kindness," *hesed* in vv. 1, 3, 7) and seeks to carry it out. Loyalty is David's key characteristic in chapters 9 and 10. As the narrative opens, David is unaware of any survivor of Saul's house (9:1): the Hebrew text suggests he grows more doubtful (literally in v. 3: "Is there no one still belonging to Saul's house?"). Ziba, however, gives a positive answer (9:3).

The survivor is introduced by description only. The reader can deduce his identity since the description fits 4:4. But the survivor is anonymous and located in a nameless place ("Lodebar" actually means "no word"):

the produce, which shall be food for your lord's household to eat. But Meribbaal, your lord's son, shall always eat at my table." Now Ziba had fifteen sons and twenty servants. [11]Ziba answered the king, "Whatever my lord the king commands his servant, so shall your servant do." And so Meribbaal ate at David's table like one of the king's sons. [12]Meribbaal had a young son whose name was Mica; and all the tenants of Ziba's household worked for Meribbaal. [13]But Meribbaal lived in Jerusalem, because he always ate at the king's table. He was lame in both feet.

10 Campaigns Against Ammon.

[1]After this, the king of the Ammonites died, and Hanun his son succeeded him as king. [2]David said, "I will show kindness to Hanun, the son of Nahash, as his father showed kindness to me." Therefore David sent his servants to Hanun to console him concerning his father. But when David's servants had entered the land of the Ammonites, [3]the Ammonite princes said to their lord Hanun, "Do you think David is doing this—sending you these consolers—to honor your father? Is it not rather to explore the city, to spy on it, and to over-

clearly he is a nonentity! Yet this insignificant person exists in tension with his status as Jonathan's son. Both narrator and David name him (9:6), because he is significant in their eyes.

For David, he is the means to fulfilling oaths. Loyalty is shown by the double gift of restitution and a place of honor at court (9:7). But Meribbaal clings to his nonentity status ("a dead dog"; 9:8). Perhaps he is aware how much safer he is being left alone. David's act of loyalty must be made concrete, and Ziba reenters the drama as the means to carry out David's wishes (9:9-11). A place of honor at the king's table is both a concrete sign of loyalty and a means of watchful control over a potential rallying point for opposition. David is both magnanimous and cautious.

Meribbaal is important in the narrator's eyes. He is named formally as the successor of Saul (9:6), and he has a son (9:12), but he is crippled (9:3, 13). The narrator is teasing the reader to pay attention to Meribbaal, an incapacitated source of danger to David, a test whether David will keep his word, a potential focus for opposition, and an added complication in a crowded royal household.

10:1-19 War with the Ammonites

David not only displays loyalty to individuals, but also in his dealings with surrounding nations. In chapter 10 he intends to maintain "kindness" (*hesed*) with the Ammonites. Saul had defeated Nabash (1 Sam 11), so presumably some form of nonaggression pact had been established. By sending

throw it, that David has sent his servants to you?" ⁴So Hanun seized David's servants, shaved off half their beards, cut away the lower halves of their garments at the buttocks, and sent them away. ⁵David was told of it and he sent word for them to be intercepted, for the men had been greatly disgraced. "Remain at Jericho," the king told them, "until your beards have grown again; then come back here."

⁶When the Ammonites realized that they were in bad odor with David, they sent for and hired twenty thousand Aramean foot soldiers from Beth-rehob and Zobah, as well as the king of Maacah with one thousand men, and twelve thousand men from Tob.

⁷When David heard of this, he sent Joab and his whole army of warriors against them. ⁸The Ammonites marched out and lined up for battle at the entrance of their city gate, while the Arameans of Zobah and Rehob and the men of Tob and Maacah remained apart in the open field. ⁹When Joab saw that there was a battle line both in front of and behind him, he chose some of the best fighters of Israel and lined them up against the Arameans; ¹⁰the rest of the army he placed under the command of his brother Abishai and lined up to oppose the Ammonites. ¹¹And he said, "If the Arameans prove too strong for me, you must come and save me; and if the Ammonites prove too strong for you, I will come to save you. ¹²Hold firm and let us show ourselves courageous for the sake of our people and the cities of our God; and may the LORD do what is good

---

ambassadors to Nabash's son, Hanun, David seeks to continue the pact (10:2). However, Hanun is encouraged to reject David's offer in a particularly shaming fashion (10:3) by unmanning the messengers (10:4) and sending them packing. David's concern for his servants illustrates why he inspires tenacious loyalty (10:5). The Ammonite action, however, is a declaration of war.

The Ammonites hire mercenaries from the Aramean kingdoms in Syria-Lebanon (10:7) so that Joab and the standing army (10:8) must fight on two fronts. Joab emerges as a skilled general (10:9-10) who can also invoke the rhetoric of holy war (10:11). His strategy is successful, but for no reason he withdraws, leaving the Ammonite city intact.

The Arameans rally their forces, and Hadadezer is named as leader (10:16). The outcome is therefore already known (cf. 8:3-6). David takes the field with an all-Israel force. The details of the battle are brief (10:17-18), sufficient to record a major victory which leads to the submission of the Arameans and the isolation of the Ammonites (10:19). The narrator uses this second account of the campaign to provide background for the story to come in chapters 11–12. David's loyalty to his treaty obligations, to his honor, and to his troops also provides an appropriate background to his treatment of Uriah. This man of *hesed* is about to sin spectacularly.

in his sight." [13]Joab therefore advanced with his men for battle with the Arameans, but they fled before him. [14]And when the Ammonites saw that the Arameans had fled, they too fled before Abishai, and reentered their city. Joab then ceased his attack on the Ammonites and came to Jerusalem. [15]Seeing themselves vanquished by Israel, the Arameans held a full muster of troops. [16]Hadadezer sent for and brought Arameans from beyond the River. They came to Helam, with Shobach, the captain of Hadadezer's army, at their head. [17]When this was reported to David, he gathered all Israel together, crossed the Jordan, and went to Helam. The Arameans drew up in formation against David and gave battle. [18]But the Arameans fled before Israel, and David killed seven hundred of their chariot fighters and forty thousand of their foot soldiers. He struck down Shobach, commander of the army, and he died on the field. [19]When Hadadezer's vassal kings saw themselves vanquished by Israel, they made peace with the Israelites and became their subjects. After this, the Arameans were afraid to give further aid to the Ammonites.

David's Sin. [1]At the turn of the year, the time when kings go to war, David sent out Joab along with his officers and all Israel, and they laid waste the Ammonites and besieged Rabbah. David himself remained in Jeru-

11:1-27 David's sin

The narrative of chapter 11 is cleverly composed. While seeming to present all the facts, it refrains from showing the feelings or motives of the characters. The reader sees and hears "from outside," while the inner lives are hidden. The reader unconsciously fills in these gaps with hypotheses to assist evaluation of the action. To fully appreciate the narrative as art, the reader should restrain from guessing, pay attention to what is actually said, and accept that there is room for conflicting interpretations. The full richness of the ambiguity of human action should be allowed to emerge.

11:1-5 Sending for Bathsheba

A good example of the need for restraint occurs in verse 1. The contrast between "when kings go to war" and "David himself remained in Jerusalem" is often read as criticism of David. Perhaps this criticism is warranted, but such arrangements were usual on David's campaigns (cf. 10:7). It is better to pay attention to the verb "to send." This verb occurs masterfully in the narrative to express the sender's control over others. It is a verb of power, even manipulation. David is in control from verse 1. He is the subject of a long series of verbs in verses 2-4a, from rising after a siesta to lying down with the woman. He does what he wants. The flow of David's activity ends with a parenthetical reference to Bathsheba's menstrual cycle.

salem. [2]One evening David rose from his bed and strolled about on the roof of the king's house. From the roof he saw a woman bathing; she was very beautiful. [3]David sent people to inquire about the woman and was told, "She is Bathsheba, daughter of Eliam, and wife of Uriah the Hittite, Joab's armor-bearer." [4]Then David sent messengers and took her. When she came to him, he took her to bed, at a time when she was just purified after her period; and she returned to her house. [5]But the woman had become pregnant; she sent a message to inform David, "I am pregnant."

[6]So David sent a message to Joab, "Send me Uriah the Hittite." Joab sent Uriah to David. [7]And when he came, David asked him how Joab was, how the army was, and how the war was going, and Uriah answered that all was well. [8]David then said to Uriah, "Go down to your house and bathe your feet." Uriah left the king's house, and a portion from the king's table was sent after him. [9]But Uriah slept at the entrance of the king's house with the other officers of his lord, and did not go down to his own house. [10]David was told, "Uriah has not gone down to his house." So he said to Uriah, "Have you not come from a journey? Why, then, did you not go down to your house?" [11]Uriah answered David, "The ark and Israel and Judah are staying in tents, and my lord Joab and my lord's servants are encamped in the open field.

This is beyond David's control, and she now becomes the subject of the verbs (11:4b-5). She is no passive object, but had power over David. She sends him a message that changes everything, "I am pregnant" (11:5).

11:6-14 Sending Uriah

The next scene opens with more sending (11:6). Uriah is the pawn of others' schemes. Usually speech links actions with motives, but here speech does not match action. The suspicion of deception adds new layers of ambiguity. The narrator reports that David asks after the wellbeing of Joab, the troops, and the war (11:7), all in line with previous displays of his loyalty (cf. 10:5). But his speech (11:8) contains two commands, "Go down to your house and bathe your feet" (a euphemism for sexual intercourse). His sole interest is to conceal his paternity of the child. However, Uriah disobeys the king! Throughout verses 9-10, the verb "did not go" keeps repeating. Why did Uriah disobey? Should his speech in verse 11 be read as the words of a pious soldier, or is it an implied criticism of David arising from Uriah's suspicions of the king's motives? The narrator hides the answers. How far can David push Uriah without revealing his hand? How much does Uriah know? The lack of clarity frustrates both David and the reader! Eventually David gives up and sends Uriah with a letter to Joab (11:14), and there is that verb again!

Can I go home to eat and to drink and to sleep with my wife? As the LORD lives and as you live, I will do no such thing." ¹²Then David said to Uriah, "Stay here today also, and tomorrow I will send you back." So Uriah stayed in Jerusalem that day. On the following day, ¹³David summoned him, and he ate and drank with David, who got him drunk. But in the evening he went out to sleep on his bed among his lord's servants, and did not go down to his house. ¹⁴The next morning David wrote a letter to Joab which he sent by Uriah. ¹⁵This is what he wrote in the letter: "Place Uriah up front, where the fighting is fierce. Then pull back and leave him to be struck down dead." ¹⁶So while Joab was besieging the city, he assigned Uriah to a place where he knew the defenders were strong. ¹⁷When the men of the city made a sortie against Joab, some officers of David's army fell, and Uriah the Hittite also died.

¹⁸Then Joab sent David a report of all the details of the battle, ¹⁹instructing the messenger, "When you have finished giving the king all the details of the battle, ²⁰the king may become angry and say to you: 'Why did you go near the city to fight? Did you not know that they would shoot from the wall above? ²¹Who killed Abimelech, son of Jerubbaal? Was it not a woman who threw a millstone down on him from the wall above, so that he died in Thebez? Why did you go near the wall?' Then you in turn are to say, 'Your servant Uriah the Hittite is also dead.'" ²²The messenger set out, and on his arrival he reported to David everything Joab had sent him to tell. ²³He told David: "The men had the advantage

11:15-27 Evaluating David

The narrator allows the reader a clear view of David's plans in the letter (11:15), but texts are no sure guide to events. Joab does not follow David's plan (11:16-17). Joab instructs the messenger on how to report the death of Uriah (11:18-21) but the messenger does not follow Joab's plan, either (11:22-24). Such complications of the plot to kill Uriah implicate more people: Joab, the messenger, and the unfortunate soldiers killed with Uriah. Joab betrays a realization of what is going on in his speculative description of David's outburst (11:20-21) by alluding to the death of Abimelech (Judg 9:50-55), a king whose reign was destroyed by a woman!

In the end, David responds mildly, "Do not let this be a great evil in your sight" (11:25) and is content that the sword devours here and there. Uriah's wife—note the description—grieves for her husband (11:26). But when mourning is over, both she and David carry out two verbs of action (11:27). Is she really a victim of a grasping king? Adultery is concealed. All's well, then? The narrator reports one evaluation completely the opposite of David's (11:25). "But in the sight of the LORD what David had done was evil" (11:27).

over us and came out into the open against us, but we pushed them back to the entrance of the city gate. ²⁴Then the archers shot at your servants from the wall above, and some of the king's servants died; and your servant Uriah the Hittite is also dead." ²⁵David said to the messenger: "This is what you shall say to Joab: 'Do not let this be a great evil in your sight, for the sword devours now here and now there. Strengthen your attack on the city and destroy it.' Encourage him."

²⁶When the wife of Uriah heard that her husband had died, she mourned her lord. ²⁷But once the mourning was over, David sent for her and brought her into his house. She became his wife and bore him a son. But in the sight of the LORD what David had done was evil.

12 **Nathan's Parable.** ¹The LORD sent Nathan to David, and when he came to him, he said: "Tell me how you judge this case: In a certain town there

were two men, one rich, the other poor. ²The rich man had flocks and herds in great numbers. ³But the poor man had nothing at all except one little ewe lamb that he had bought. He nourished her, and she grew up with him and his children. Of what little he had she ate; from his own cup she drank; in his bosom she slept; she was like a daughter to him. ⁴Now, a visitor came to the rich man, but he spared his own flocks and herds to prepare a meal for the traveler who had come to him: he took the poor man's ewe lamb and prepared it for the one who had come to him." ⁵David grew very angry with that man and said to Nathan: "As the LORD lives, the man who has done this deserves death! ⁶He shall make fourfold restitution for the lamb because he has done this and was unsparing."

⁷Then Nathan said to David: "You are the man!

Nathan's Indictment. "Thus says the LORD God of Israel: I anointed you king

12:1-31 The Lord's response

Just as David achieves control, a new sending occurs (12:1). The Lord is in control and delivers judgment. Nathan's parable (12:1a-4) is "the thing wherein I'll catch the conscience of the king" (*Hamlet*, Act 3 Scene 1). The parable contrasts the unfeeling rich man with the doting poor man. The rich man is characterized by the verb "to take," the verb of kings (cf. 1 Sam 8:11-18). David is able to read the parable, but he fails to apply it. Nathan does that for him: "You are the man" (12:7a).

12:7-14 The verdict

Nathan cuts through the ambiguity of chapter 11 and delivers the Lord's verdict. The opening verses sum up the Lord's graciousness towards David (12:7-8) in a way that both echoes the Lord's promise in 7:8-9 and sets the context for David's infidelity. The accusation and condemnation come in two parts. In both, David is accused of spurning or despising the Lord (12:9,

"Then Nathan said to David: 'You are the man!'" (2 Samuel 12:7). The prophet Nathan accuses David of adultery with Bathsheba and the murder of her husband Uriah the Hittite. The child dies. Sculpture located in the Madeleine Church, Paris, France.

over Israel. I delivered you from the hand of Saul. ⁸I gave you your lord's house and your lord's wives for your own. I gave you the house of Israel and of Judah. And if this were not enough, I could count up for you still more. ⁹Why have you despised the Lord and done what is evil in his sight? You have cut down Uriah the Hittite with the sword; his wife you took as your own, and him you killed with the sword of the Ammonites. ¹⁰Now, therefore, the sword shall never depart from your house, because you have despised me and have taken the wife of Uriah the Hittite to be your wife. ¹¹Thus says the Lord: I will bring evil upon you out of your own house. I will take your wives before your very eyes, and will give them to your neighbor: he shall lie with your wives in broad daylight. ¹²You have acted in secret, but I will do this in the presence of all Israel, in the presence of the sun itself."

David's Repentance. ¹³Then David said to Nathan, "I have sinned against the Lord." Nathan answered David: "For his part, the Lord has removed your sin. You shall not die, ¹⁴but since you have utterly spurned the Lord by this deed, the child born to you will surely die." ¹⁵Then Nathan returned to his house.

The Lord struck the child that the wife of Uriah had borne to David, and it became desperately ill. ¹⁶David pleaded with God on behalf of the child. He kept a total fast, and spent the night lying on the ground clothed in sackcloth. ¹⁷The elders of his house stood beside

---

10b). In the first case, infidelity is specified as Uriah's murder; since he died by the sword (which David so casually accepted in 11:25), the sword will hang over David's house (12:9-10a). In the second, the crime is adultery; for taking Uriah's wife, David's wives will be taken from him (12:10b-12). The punishment fits the crimes. The future story of David's family is plotted.

After all the ambiguity of David's actions, his response is a flash of clarity: "I have sinned against the Lord" (12:13). This simple, unelaborated declaration cuts through the web of self-deception and allows God the freedom to create a new future. The Lord responds by "transferring" the consequences of David's sin (the significance of "has removed your sin" in v. 13). The relationship with the Lord remains intact but the implications of the sin must be worked out, starting with the death of the child (12:14).

12:15-25 Repentance

David's actions are reported from the "outside" (12:15-20). Again, this creates confusion about his motives. His explanation ends the opaqueness of the narrative (12:22-23). He has left behind his attempts to manipulate events and people, and now his actions unfold from faith in the Lord as

him to get him to rise from the ground; but he would not, nor would he take food with them. [18]On the seventh day, the child died. David's servants were afraid to tell him that the child was dead, for they said: "When the child was alive, we spoke to him, but he would not listen to what we said. How can we tell him the child is dead? He may do some harm!" [19]But David noticed his servants whispering among themselves and realized that the child was dead. He asked his servants, "Is the child dead?" They said, "Yes." [20]Rising from the ground, David washed and anointed himself, and changed his clothes. Then he went to the house of the LORD and worshiped. He returned to his own house and asked for food; they set it before him, and he ate. [21]His servants said to him: "What is this you are doing? While the child was living, you fasted and wept and kept vigil; now that the child is dead, you rise and take food." [22]He replied: "While the child was living, I fasted and wept, thinking, 'Who knows? The LORD may grant me the child's life.' [23]But now he is dead. Why should I fast? Can I bring him back again? I shall go to him, but he will not return to me." [24]Then David consoled Bathsheba his wife. He went and slept with her; and she conceived and bore him a son, who was named Solomon. The LORD loved him [25]and sent the prophet Nathan to name him Jedidiah, on behalf of the LORD.

End of the Ammonite War. [26]Joab fought against Rabbah of the Ammonites and captured that royal city. [27]He sent messengers to David to say: "I have fought against Rabbah and have taken the water-city. [28]Therefore, assemble the rest of the soldiers, join the siege against the city, and capture it, lest I be the one

---

controller of human affairs. David does not send for Bathsheba but goes to her (12:24). This new series of verbal actions ends with the birth of Solomon. Now it is the Lord who sends (12:25), and the special name denotes the child as a sign of hope in the midst of sin and punishment.

12:26-31 The war and its aftermath

The war has provided the backdrop to these events. Now the narrator can wind it up. As before (10:15-19), David goes forth for the decisive battle when prompted by Joab. David takes the crown of the Ammonite idol (12:30) and much other booty. He also enslaves the population.

David's adultery with Bathsheba triggers the drama of the remainder of 2 Samuel. Nathan's oracle links the turmoil of David's family to that moment of passion, one spring afternoon, as if it were the original sin of the dynasty (cf. Gen 2:8). Clearly, adultery and murder are serious crimes. The narrator refrains from providing motive or extenuating factors, elements which the modern reader seeks in order to make a moral evaluation. Is the narrator suggesting that these are not relevant, or that they offer no diminution of the act? Perhaps. The struggle to interpret and explain the

to capture the city and mine be the name people mention, not yours." [29]So David assembled the rest of the soldiers, went to Rabbah, fought against it, and captured it. [30]He took the crown of Milcom from the idol's head, a talent of gold in weight, with precious stones; this crown David wore on his own head. He also brought out a great amount of spoil from the city. [31]He deported the people of the city and set them to work with saws, iron picks, and iron axes, or put them to work at the brickmold. He dealt thus with all the cities of the Ammonites. Then David and his whole army returned to Jerusalem.

13 Amnon's Rape of Tamar. [1]After this, the following occurred. David's son Absalom had a beautiful sister named Tamar, and David's son Amnon loved her. [2]He was in such anguish over his sister Tamar that he became sick; she was a virgin, and Amnon thought it impossible to do anything to her. [3]Now Amnon had a friend named Jonadab, son of David's brother Shimeah, who was very clever. [4]He asked him, "Prince, why are you so dejected morning after morning? Why not tell me?" So Amnon said to him, "I am in love with Tamar, my brother Absalom's sister." [5]Then Jonadab replied, "Lie down on

---

actions of David is an important struggle, but it does not excuse him of his sin. After the ambiguity of human affairs in chapter 11 comes the all-seeing clarity of judgment in chapter 12. In the former, we strive for clarity of motive; in the latter, faithful receptivity provides guidance.

13:1-22 Amnon rapes Tamar

Chapters 13–14 describe a new family crisis. Absalom's sister is raped by her half-brother and Absalom takes revenge. The sins of David are repeated in the next generation. The narrator provides much more access to the inner lives of the characters, exploring particularly the interplay of action and emotion. In the opening episode (13:1-22), familial ties pepper the narrative. The reader is not allowed to forget such relationships, which set limits on proper behavior and create hierarchies of power and responsibility. Uncontrolled desire confuses proper relations; the language of "brother/sister" can also express passionate love (cf. Song 4:9-10).

Amnon is in love with his half-sister Tamar (13:1, 4), but this is a consuming emotion that renders him irrational (13:2). His wily cousin, Jonadab, concocts a scheme to give Amnon private access to Tamar (13:5). Everyone plays along without a hint of suspicion (13:6-10). Does no one else notice Amnon's dejection, or ask why?

In contrast to Amnon's irrationality, Tamar speaks with cool argument. She names the crime immediately. "Do not force me" (13:12; cf. 13:14, 22, 32) denotes the humiliation of a woman by sexual violence. The action is

your bed and pretend to be sick. When your father comes to visit you, say to him, 'Please let my sister Tamar come and encourage me to take food. If she prepares something in my presence, for me to see, I will eat it from her hand.'" ⁶So Amnon lay down and pretended to be sick. When the king came to visit him, Amnon said to the king, "Please let my sister Tamar come and prepare some fried cakes before my eyes, that I may take food from her hand."

⁷David then sent home a message to Tamar, "Please go to the house of your brother Amnon and prepare some food for him." ⁸Tamar went to the house of her brother Amnon, who was in bed. Taking dough and kneading it, she twisted it into cakes before his eyes and fried the cakes. ⁹Then she took the pan and set out the cakes before him. But Amnon would not eat; he said, "Have everyone leave me." When they had all left him, ¹⁰Amnon said to Tamar, "Bring

the food into the bedroom, that I may have it from your hand." So Tamar picked up the cakes she had prepared and brought them to her brother Amnon in the bedroom. ¹¹But when she brought them close to him so he could eat, he seized her and said to her, "Come! Lie with me, my sister!" ¹²But she answered him, "No, my brother! Do not force me! This is not done in Israel. Do not commit this terrible crime. ¹³Where would I take my shame? And you would be labeled a fool in Israel. So please, speak to the king; he will not keep me from you." ¹⁴But he would not listen to her; he was too strong for her: he forced her down and raped her. ¹⁵Then Amnon felt intense hatred for her; the hatred he felt for her far surpassed the love he had had for her. Amnon said to her, "Get up, leave." ¹⁶She replied, "No, brother, because sending me away would be far worse than this evil thing you have done to me." He would not listen to her,

---

both wrong and unwise, she argues. Committing this "terrible crime," Amnon will be classed as a "fool." Both words translate the Hebrew root, *nabal* (cf. 1 Sam 25). However, Amnon does not listen to her voice (13:14, 16b), because he is driven by lust, nothing more. Once that is satisfied, his "love" is spent. Verse 15 succinctly records this psychological change.

Now Amnon wants rid of her (13:15b-17) but she refuses to be hidden (13:18-19). This crime will not be suppressed; others must respond to it. Absalom's response is twofold. He takes her into his home. His words may seem to dismiss her grief (13:20), but a better translation is, "Do not set your heart on saying anything." He will act for her. Secondly, to Amnon he says nothing, but he bears his sister's shame with a hatred that drives the story on. The other respondent is David. All references to him in the story hint at his love for Amnon: he would do whatever his firstborn asked (13:13). Now he is very angry but does nothing (13:21). Is this extreme indulgence, or is it paralysis as his own failings are mirrored in his son? His inaction only causes the hatred to ferment.

¹⁷but called the youth who was his attendant and said, "Send this girl outside, away from me, and bar the door after her." ¹⁸Now she had on a long tunic, for that is how virgin princesses dressed in olden days. When his attendant put her out and barred the door after her, ¹⁹Tamar put ashes on her head and tore the long tunic in which she was clothed. Then, putting her hands to her head, she went away crying loudly. ²⁰Her brother Absalom said to her: "Has your brother Amnon been with you? Keep still now, my sister; he is your brother. Do not take this so to heart." So Tamar remained, devastated, in the house of her brother Absalom. ²¹King David, when he heard of the whole affair, became very angry. He would not, however, antagonize Amnon, his high-spirited son; he loved him, because he was his firstborn. ²²And Absalom said nothing, good or bad, to Amnon; but Absalom hated Amnon for having humiliated his sister Tamar.

Absalom's Plot. ²³Two years went by. It was sheep-shearing time for Absalom in Baal-hazor near Ephraim, and Absalom invited all the king's sons. ²⁴Absalom went to the king and said: "Your servant has hired the shearers. Please, may the king come with all his servants to your servant." ²⁵But the king said to Absalom, "No, my son, all of us should not go lest we be a burden to you." And though Absalom urged him, he would not go but began to bid him good-bye. ²⁶Absalom then said, "If not you, then please let my brother Amnon come with us." The king asked him, "Why should he go with you?" ²⁷But at Absalom's urging, the king sent Amnon and with him all his other sons. Absalom prepared a banquet fit for a king. ²⁸But Absalom had instructed his attendants: "Now watch! When Amnon is merry with wine and I say to you, 'Kill Amnon,' put him to death. Do not be afraid, for it is I who order you to do it. Be strong and act like warriors."

13:23-39 Absalom's revenge

Absalom bides his time (13:23). A shearing festival (cf. 1 Sam 25) provides the opportunity to act. Verses 24-27a allow the narrator to explore the relationship between David and Absalom. On the surface, all is pleasant consideration (13:24-25), but when Absalom mentions Amnon, David panics (13:26). David is suspicious and needs persuading. Is he conscious of Absalom's unexpressed hatred?

The murder is swift and efficient (13:28a-29). The narrator reports Absalom's instructions to highlight the motive of personal revenge. Then attention focuses on the reaction to this murder. The other brothers panic and flee. The first rumors of a massacre prompt extreme grief. It is ironic that now all tear their garments but no one did so for Tamar (cf. 13:19). Up pops Jonadab to stem the panic by reminding David of Amnon's rape of Tamar (13:32-33). "Now let my lord the king not take so to heart that report" echoes

Death of Amnon. ²⁹When the attendants did to Amnon as Absalom had commanded, all the king's other sons rose up, mounted their mules, and fled. ³⁰While they were still on the road, a report reached David: "Absalom has killed all the king's sons and not one of them is left." ³¹The king stood up, tore his garments, and lay on the ground. All his servants standing by him also tore their garments. ³²But Jonadab, son of David's brother Shimeah, spoke up: "Let not my lord think that all the young men, the king's sons, have been killed! Amnon alone is dead, for Absalom was set on this ever since Amnon humiliated his sister Tamar. ³³Now let my lord the king not take so to heart that report, 'All the king's sons are dead.' Amnon alone is dead." ³⁴Meanwhile, Absalom had taken flight. Then the servant on watch looked out and saw a large group coming down the slope from the direction of Bahurim. He came in and reported this to the king: "I saw some men coming down the mountainside from the direction of Ba-

hurim." ³⁵So Jonadab said to the king: "There! The king's sons have come. It is as your servant said." ³⁶No sooner had he finished speaking than the king's sons came in, weeping aloud. The king, too, and all his servants wept very bitterly. ³⁷But Absalom, who had taken flight, went to Talmai, son of Ammihud, king of Geshur, ³⁸and stayed in Geshur for three years. ³⁹All that time the king continued to mourn his son; but his intention of going out against Absalom abated as he was consoled over the death of Amnon.

14 **The Wise Woman of Tekoa.** ¹Now Joab, son of Zeruiah, knew how the king felt toward Absalom. ²Joab sent to Tekoa and brought from there a wise woman, to whom he said: "Pretend to be in mourning. Put on mourning apparel and do not anoint yourself with oil, that you may appear to be a woman who has long been mourning someone dead. ³Then go to the king and speak to him in this manner." And Joab told her what to say.

Absalom's words to Tamar in verse 20. David is being encouraged to react to Amnon's death as he reacted to the rape, by doing nothing. The arrival of the fleeing princes confirms Jonadab's words (13:34-35), but the grief is not much diminished. David fails to respond appropriately once again.

Meanwhile, Absalom flees (13:34, 37) and is in exile for three years. Revenge took time (13:23), but so also does reconciliation (13:39), all because of David's failure to respond correctly to the crimes of his sons. He has lost his firstborn. Will he now lose the second-born for whom he longs?

14:1-33 Absalom's return

Joab acts to break the stalemate and enable David and Absalom to be reconciled. He prepares a gifted woman from Tekoa (14:2-3) to create a fictional case which, like Nathan's parable, will enable David to see his situation in a new light.

⁴So the woman of Tekoa went to the king and fell to the ground in homage, saying, "Help, O king!" ⁵The king said to her, "What do you want?" She replied: "Alas, I am a widow; my husband is dead. ⁶Your servant had two sons, who quarreled in the field, with no one to part them, and one of them struck his brother and killed him. ⁷Then the whole clan confronted your servant and demanded: 'Give up the one who struck down his brother. We must put him to death for the life of his brother whom he has killed; we must do away with the heir also.' Thus they will quench my remaining hope and leave my husband neither name nor posterity upon the earth." ⁸The king then said to the woman: "Go home. I will issue a command on your behalf." ⁹The woman of Tekoa answered him, "Upon me and my family be the blame, my lord king; the king and his throne are innocent." ¹⁰Then the king said, "If anyone says a word to you, have him brought to me, and he shall not touch you again." ¹¹But she said, "Please, let the king remember the LORD your God, that the avenger of blood may not go too far in destruction and that my son may not be done away with." He replied, "As the LORD lives, not a hair of your son shall fall to the ground."

¹²But the woman continued, "Please let your servant say still another word to my lord the king." He replied, "Speak." ¹³So the woman said: "Why, then, do you think the way you do against the people of God? In pronouncing as he has, the king shows himself guilty, in not bringing back his own banished son. ¹⁴We must indeed die; we are then like water that is poured out on the ground and cannot be gathered up. Yet, though God does not bring back to life, he does devise means so as not to banish anyone from him. ¹⁵And now, if I have presumed to speak to the king of this matter, it is because the people have given me cause to fear. And so your servant thought: 'Let me speak to the king. Perhaps he

---

14:4-20 Absalom's case

The fictional story is simple: her two sons quarrel, one is killed, and the other is under sentence of death. Can David save her surviving son (14:4-7)? David is moved to help her, but the woman extracts an oath that her surviving son will not be harmed (14:8-11). Once David binds himself by oath (cf. 12:5-6), the woman can use the fictional scenario to change David's real situation. Her argumentation is subtle, shifting between real and imaginary cases (14:12-17). The king has responded to a parent's plea. Will he now act as a parent himself? The king keeps his son in exile because he interprets the law to require Absalom's execution (14:13), but such a punitive view ignores how God acts. People die, but God does not banish (14:14). If God can resolve this predicament, so can his people and their king. In her fictional case, the woman considered David wise enough to save her son (14:15-17). Now let him do the same for his own son!

will grant the petition of his servant. [16]For the king must surely listen and rescue his servant from the grasp of one who would destroy both me and my son from the heritage of God.' [17]And your servant says, 'Let the word of my lord the king lead to rest; indeed, my lord the king is like an angel of God, discerning good and evil. The LORD your God be with you.'"

[18]The king answered the woman, "Now do not conceal from me anything I may ask you!" The woman said, "Let my lord the king speak." [19]So the king asked, "Is the hand of Joab with you in all this?" And the woman answered: "As you live, my lord the king, it is just as my lord has said, and not otherwise. It was your servant Joab who instructed me and told your servant all these things she was to say. [20]Your servant Joab did this in order to approach the matter in a roundabout way. But my lord is wise with the wisdom of an angel of God, knowing all things on earth."

Absalom's Return. [21]Then the king said to Joab: "I am granting this request. Go and bring back young Absalom." [22]Falling to the ground in homage and blessing the king, Joab said, "This day your servant knows that I am in good favor with you, my lord king, since the king has granted the request of your servant." [23]Joab then went off to Geshur and brought Absalom to Jerusalem. [24]But the king said, "Let him go off to his own house; he shall not appear before me." So Absalom went off to his house and did not appear before the king.

[25]In all Israel there was no man more praised for his beauty than Absalom, flawless from the sole of his foot to the crown of his head. [26]When he shaved his head—as he used to do at the end of every year, because his hair became too heavy for him—the hair weighed two

In struggling to come to terms with her rhetoric, David guesses that Joab is involved (14:18-19). The woman admits this is so, but stresses the need for a decision (14:20). The fictional tale has enabled David to view his predicament in a new light, and he moves to bring back Absalom.

14:21-33 The verdict

Joab responds gratefully and quickly (14:21-23), but the restoration does not result in reconciliation. Absalom may return to Jerusalem, but David will not meet him (14:24).

The narrator pauses to describe Absalom's beauty. The praise is glowing (14:25-26) but disconcerting. Bathsheba and Tamar were beautiful, but it only caused them trouble. Saul was handsome (1 Sam 9:2) but a failure. The Lord warned against judgment by appearances (1 Sam 16:7). Like his father, Absalom is attractive; he looks as a king should look. Such praise warns of trouble to come. The reference to luxuriant hair (abundant by royal standards!) will be picked up later.

hundred shekels according to the royal standard. ²⁷Absalom had three sons born to him, besides a daughter named Tamar, who was a beautiful woman.

Absalom Is Pardoned. ²⁸Absalom lived in Jerusalem for two years without appearing before the king. ²⁹Then he sent a message asking Joab to send him to the king, but Joab would not come to him. Although he asked him a second time, Joab would not come. ³⁰He therefore instructed his servants: "You see Joab's field that borders mine, where he has barley. Go, set it on fire." And so Absalom's servants set the field on fire. Joab's farmhands came to him with torn garments and told him, "Absalom's servants set your field on fire." ³¹Joab went to Absalom in his house and asked him, "Why have your servants set my field on fire?" ³²Absalom answered Joab: "I sent you a message: Come here, that I may send you to the king to say: 'Why did I come back from Geshur? I would be better off if I were still there!' Now, let me appear before the king. If I am guilty, let him put me to death." ³³Joab went to the king and reported this. The king then called Absalom; he came to him and in homage fell on his face to the ground before the king. Then the king kissed Absalom.

15 **Absalom's Ambition.** ¹After this, Absalom provided himself with chariots, horses, and a retinue of fifty. ²Moreover, Absalom used to rise early and stand alongside the road leading to the gate. If someone had a lawsuit to be decided by the king, Absalom would call to him and say, "From what city are you?" And when he replied, "Your servant is of such and such a tribe of Israel," ³Absalom would say to him, "Your case is good and just, but there is no one to hear you in the king's name." ⁴And he would continue: "If only I could be appointed judge in the land! Then everyone who has a lawsuit to be decided

---

Two years pass and the situation becomes unbearable for Absalom. He seeks Joab's help, but Joab refuses to see him (14:29). He gains Joab's attention with a wanton act of destruction reminiscent of Samson (Judg 15:4-8), another ominous note. Even his speech is rushed and confused (14:32). A meeting is quickly arranged. Absalom's prostration acknowledges the king's authority, but does it express contrition? The king's kiss is according to protocol, but is it reconciliation? Appearances can deceive. Has the long estrangement done irreparable damage to relations?

15:1-12 Absalom's rebellion

A new phase of the narrative begins as Absalom usurps the trappings of a king (15:1). He also seeks to preempt the royal prerogative to administer justice (15:2-6). With promises of favorable judgments, he wins over individuals from the northern tribes. The narrator's concluding remark sums up the irony (15:6b): good judgment from a thief, affection for the disaffected.

might come to me and I would render him justice." ⁵Whenever a man approached him to show homage, he would extend his hand, hold him, and kiss him. ⁶By behaving in this way toward all the Israelites who came to the king for judgment, Absalom was stealing the heart of Israel.

Conspiracy in Hebron. ⁷After a period of four years, Absalom said to the king: "Please let me go to Hebron and fulfill a vow I made to the LORD. ⁸For while living in Geshur in Aram, your servant made this vow: 'If the LORD ever brings me back to Jerusalem, I will worship him in Hebron.'" ⁹The king said to him, "Go in peace," and he went off to Hebron. ¹⁰Then Absalom sent agents throughout the tribes of Israel to say, "When you hear the sound of the horn, say, 'Absalom is king in Hebron!'"

¹¹Two hundred men had accompanied Absalom from Jerusalem. They had been invited and went in all innocence, knowing nothing. ¹²Absalom also sent to Ahithophel the Gilonite, David's counselor, an invitation to come from his town, Giloh, for the sacrifices he was about to offer. So the conspiracy gained strength, and the people with Absalom increased in numbers.

David Flees Jerusalem. ¹³An informant came to David with the report, "The Israelites have given their hearts to Absalom, and they are following him." ¹⁴At this, David said to all his servants who were with him in Jerusalem: "Get up, let us flee, or none of us will escape from Absalom. Leave at once, or he will quickly overtake us, and then bring disaster upon us, and put the city to the sword." ¹⁵The king's servants answered

After cultivating support for four years, Absalom initiates rebellion. The pretext of a vow allows him to go to Hebron, where David was crowned king (2:1-4; 5:1-3). He is as devious as his father, and David is taken in (15:9). Once in Hebron, Absalom sounds the signal for the uprising. The description of the uprising is mixed. It has widespread support in Israel (15:10), yet those from Jerusalem are not involved (15:11). However, at least one counselor, Ahithophel, joins Absalom (15:12). The narrator sums up the ambiguity: this is conspiracy. It may be gathering strength, but this negative evaluation suggests an action lacking in real loyalty.

15:13–16:14 David's flight

A report of the transfer of Israelite affection to Absalom precipitates David's flight from Jerusalem (15:13). This retreat forms the narrative thread linking dialogues between David and those he meets. The real drama lies in these revealing speeches that explore the motivations of the characters.

15:14-16 David and his household

The first dialogue is between David and his household. David's motive for flight is to avoid slaughter. The sword of the Lord's punishment (12:10) looms large in his thinking. His officers' response is immediate and

him, "Whatever our lord the king chooses to do, we are your servants." ¹⁶Then the king set out, accompanied by his entire household, except for ten concubines whom he left behind to care for the palace. ¹⁷As the king left the city, with all his officers accompanying him, they halted opposite the ascent of the Mount of Olives, at a distance, ¹⁸while the whole army marched past him.

David and Ittai. As all the Cherethites and Pelethites, and the six hundred Gittites who had entered his service from that city, were passing in review before the king, ¹⁹the king said to Ittai the Gittite: "Why should you also go with us? Go back and stay with the king, for you are a foreigner and you, too, are an exile from your own country. ²⁰You came only yesterday, and today shall I have you wander off with us wherever I have to go? Return and take your brothers with you, and may the LORD show you kindness and fidelity." ²¹But Ittai answered the king, "As the LORD lives, and as my lord the king lives, your servant shall be wherever my lord the king is, whether for death or for life." ²²So the king said to Ittai, "Go, then, march on." And Ittai the Gittite, with all his men and all the dependents that were with him, marched on. ²³The whole land wept aloud as the last of the soldiers went by, and the king crossed the Wadi Kidron with all the soldiers moving on ahead of him by way of the ascent of the Mount of Olives, toward the wilderness.

David and the Priests. ²⁴Zadok, too, and all the Levites bearing the ark of the covenant of God set down the ark of God until the whole army had finished

---

unswerving. In Hebrew, the verbs "to flee" and "to choose" have the same consonants, and the word play brings out the closeness between master and servants. David leaves ten concubines behind. While he seeks to spare others his punishment, his actions nonetheless prepare for the fulfillment of the oracle (12:11-12).

15:19-22 David and Ittai

As the troops pass in review (15:17-18), the second dialogue occurs with Ittai. Following the general affirmation of devotion, Ittai's is a particular case. He is a non-Israelite, an exile already, and David seeks to spare him further disruption. Ittai's response is a heartfelt oath of devotion (cf. Ruth 1:16). There is a pragmatic dimension to David's solicitude. He invites Ittai to stay behind "with the king" (15:19). This is a test of loyalty and Ittai passes. David may be in flight, but he is consolidating his forces for further action. Even so, such foresight does not minimize the grief of the flight (15:23).

15:24-29 David, Zadok, and Abiathar

David encounters Zadok and Abiathar bringing the ark from Jerusalem. David instructs them to take the ark back. His first statement expresses a

marching out of the city; and Abiathar came up. ²⁵Then the king said to Zadok: "Take the ark of God back to the city. If I find favor with the LORD, he will bring me back and permit me to see it and its lodging place. ²⁶But if he should say, 'I am not pleased with you,' I am ready; let him do to me as he sees fit." ²⁷The king also said to Zadok the priest: "Look, you and Abiathar return to the city in peace, and both your sons with you, your own son Ahimaaz, and Abiathar's son Jonathan. ²⁸Remember, I shall be waiting at the fords near the wilderness until a report from you comes to me." ²⁹So Zadok and Abiathar took the ark of God back to Jerusalem and remained there.

³⁰As David went up the ascent of the Mount of Olives, he wept without ceasing. His head was covered, and he was walking barefoot. All those who were with him also had their heads covered and were weeping as they went. ³¹When David was told, "Ahithophel is among the conspirators with Absalom," he said, "O LORD, turn the counsel of Ahithophel to folly!"

David and Hushai. ³²When David reached the top, where God was worshiped, Hushai the Archite was there to meet him, with garments torn and dirt upon his head. ³³David said to him: "If you come with me, you will be a burden to me; ³⁴but if you return to the city and say to Absalom, 'Let me be your servant, O king; I was formerly your father's servant, but now I will be yours,' you will thwart for me the counsel of Ahithophel. ³⁵You will have the priests Zadok and Abiathar there with you. If you hear anything from the king's house, you shall report it to the priests Zadok and Abiathar, ³⁶who have there with them

---

trusting faith in God (15:25-26). He subjects himself completely to the Lord's will, yet this attitude is combined with political cunning. In his next breath, David sets up a spy ring involving the priestly families (15:27-29). Acceptance of God's will does not rule out human planning, because it is through human action that God carries out his will.

15:32-36 David, Ahithophel, and Hushai

The mourning continues as David's entourage ascends the Mount of Olives (15:30). David learns of Ahithophel's betrayal and prays that his counsel will be thwarted (15:31). Again, petitioning the Lord is paired with human scheming. The next encounter provides the means to thwart Ahithophel: Hushai. A consistent plan is being hatched. David goes into the wilderness with the military, while the rest of his administration is deployed in Jerusalem to safeguard his possessions and to undermine the conspiracy. Hushai's task is the most difficult. He has to pass himself off as a turncoat to enter Absalom's confidence and confuse his counsel (15:34). With Hushai in place, David's deployment is completed before Absalom enters the city (15:37).

their two sons, Zadok's son Ahimaaz and Abiathar's son Jonathan. Through them you shall send on to me whatever you hear." [37]So David's friend Hushai went into the city, Jerusalem, as Absalom was about to enter it.

16 **David and Ziba.** [1]David went a little beyond the top and Ziba, the servant of Meribbaal, was there to meet him with saddled donkeys laden with two hundred loaves of bread, an ephah of cakes of pressed raisins, an ephah of summer fruits, and a skin of wine. [2]The king said to Ziba, "What are you doing with all this?" Ziba replied: "The donkeys are for the king's household to ride on. The bread and summer fruits are for your servants to eat, and the wine to drink when they grow weary in the wilderness." [3]Then the king said, "And where is your lord's son?" Ziba answered the king, "He is staying in Jerusalem, for he said, 'Today the house of Israel will restore to me my father's kingdom.'" [4]The king therefore said to Ziba, "So! Everything Meribbaal had is yours." Then Ziba said: "I pay you homage, my lord the king. May I find favor with you!"

David and Shimei. [5]As King David was approaching Bahurim, there was a man coming out; he was of the same clan as the house of Saul, and his name was Shimei, son of Gera. He kept cursing as he came out, [6]and throwing stones at David and at all King David's officers,

---

16:1-4 David and Ziba

The next encounter is more ambiguous. Ziba arrives with provisions, taken presumably from Meribbaal's estate (cf. 9:9-13). David's interrogation suggests suspicion of this gesture (16:2-3). Ziba claims that Meribbaal has sided with the rebels in the hope of restoring Saul's kingdom (16:3). David accepts this strange claim without question and transfers the family property to Ziba, a revocation of his loyalty to Jonathan in response to an alleged act of disloyalty.

16:5-13 David and Shimei

There follows a hostile encounter with a supporter of Saul. Shimei curses and stones David in the midst of his troops. His curses link the rebellion to David's murderous dealings with Saul's house (16:8). Just as David displaced Saul, so the Lord is displacing David. Guided by the narrator, the reader knows the linkage is inaccurate. The narrator has been at pains to exonerate David of bloodguilt for the house of Saul, yet the perception remains, both for characters in the story and within the historical memory. When the bloodthirsty Abishai wants to kill Shimei, David invokes the Lord's will to stop him (cf.1 Sam 26:8-9). David detects something prophetic in Shimei's words (16:10b). Once again he accepts whatever the Lord plans for him, yet with a prayer that acceptance may lead to mitigation. These

even though all the soldiers, including the royal guard, were on David's right and on his left. ⁷Shimei was saying as he cursed: "Get out! Get out! You man of blood, you scoundrel! ⁸The LORD has paid you back for all the blood shed from the family of Saul, whom you replaced as king, and the LORD has handed over the kingdom to your son Absalom. And now look at you: you suffer ruin because you are a man of blood." ⁹Abishai, son of Zeruiah, said to the king: "Why should this dead dog curse my lord the king? Let me go over and take off his head." ¹⁰But the king replied: "What business is it of mine or of yours, sons of Zeruiah, that he curses? Suppose the LORD has told him to curse David; who then will dare to say, 'Why are you doing this?' " ¹¹Then David said to Abishai and to all his servants: "If my own son, who came forth from my loins, is seeking my life, how much more might this Benjaminite do so! Let him alone and let him curse, for the LORD has told him to. ¹²Perhaps the LORD will look upon my affliction and repay me with good for the curses he is uttering this day." ¹³David and his men continued on the road, while Shimei kept up with them on the hillside, all the while cursing and throwing stones and dirt as he went. ¹⁴The king and all the soldiers with him arrived at the Jordan tired out, and stopped there to rest.

Absalom's Counselors. ¹⁵In the meantime Absalom, with all the Israelites, entered Jerusalem, and Ahithophel was with him. ¹⁶When David's friend Hushai the Archite came to Absalom, he said to him: "Long live the king! Long live the king!" ¹⁷But Absalom asked Hushai: "Is

final comments (16:11-12) speak to a wider audience in the language of faith using the style of psalms of lament: may the Lord see his affliction and come to his rescue. David's journey of affliction has reached its lowest point, the Jordan River, and comes to a halt (16:14).

16:15–17:14 Absalom's counselors

Attention now shifts to Absalom's triumphant entry to Jerusalem (16:15), to tell of the struggle between Absalom's counselors. This struggle will decide the fate of Absalom. The narrative revolves around Ahithophel's advice, which is as respected as a divine oracle (16:23). His counsel is divided in two: the first part is followed successfully to fulfill the oracle of 12:7-12, but the second part is thwarted by Hushai in fulfillment of David's prayer (15:31). Hushai plays a key role, but the attentive reader will be guided by the narrator's concluding comment about the Lord's involvement (17:14b).

Hushai ingratiates himself into Absalom's service (16:16-17). With flattery he overcomes Absalom's suspicions and offers to serve the son as he served the father, or so it seems. It is all doublespeak, but nonetheless effective. Nevertheless, Absalom turns to Ahithophel for advice.

this your devotion to your friend? Why did you not go with your friend?" [18]Hushai replied to Absalom: "On the contrary, I am his whom the LORD and all this people and all Israel have chosen, and with him I will stay. [19]Furthermore, as I was in attendance upon your father, so will I be before you. Whom should I serve, if not his son?"

[20]Then Absalom said to Ahithophel, "Offer your counsel on what we should do." [21]Ahithophel replied to Absalom: "Go to your father's concubines, whom he left behind to take care of the palace. When all Israel hears how odious you have made yourself to your father, all those on your side will take courage." [22]So a tent was pitched on the roof for Absalom, and Absalom went to his father's concubines in view of all Israel.

Counsel of Ahithophel. [23]Now the counsel given by Ahithophel at that time was as though one sought the word of God. Such was all the counsel of Ahithophel both to David and to Absalom.

17 [1]Ahithophel went on to say to Absalom: "Let me choose twelve thousand men and be off in pursuit of David tonight. [2]If I come upon him when he is weary and discouraged, I shall cause him panic, and all the people with him will flee, and I shall strike down the king alone. [3]Then I can bring back the rest of the people to you, as a bride returns to her husband. It is the death of only one man you are seeking; then all

His advice neatly fulfills the Lord's judgment. Absalom has intercourse with David's concubines in full view of the people (16:22; cf. 12:11-12). As in 3:7-8, sexual relations serve as a symbol for political power. Seizure of the concubines is equivalent to seizing the throne. Ahithophel advises a speedy operation to kill David (17:1-3). His wisdom is clear: David is weary, with few supporters, and quick action will reduce bloodshed and animosity later. Yet, amazingly, Absalom seeks another opinion from Hushai (17:5-6).

Hushai begins by playing on their fear of David and his warriors (17:7-10). With extravagant rhetoric, he uses half-truths and lies to undermine Ahithophel's plan. He claims it is too late to catch David without risking a demoralizing defeat. Having magnified the danger, he proposes to maximize the size of the Israelite army, and use overwhelming force in open battle or a siege (17:11-13). Of course, such force takes time to assemble and gives David breathing space to organize. Secondly, Absalom should lead the troops, placing his life at risk. Thus Hushai counters the two main elements of Ahithophel's plan, speed and security.

Rousing rhetoric is effective. All the Israelites support Hushai, whereas older, wiser heads (the elders) back Ahithophel (compare v. 14a with v. 4). However, the deeper reason Absalom heeds Hushai is that the Lord is involved (17:14b). This is one of three places in the Succession Narrative that

the people will be at peace." ⁴This plan sounded good to Absalom and to all the elders of Israel.

Counsel of Hushai. ⁵Then Absalom said, "Now call Hushai the Archite also; let us hear what he too has to say." ⁶When Hushai came to Absalom, Absalom said to him: "This is Ahithophel's plan. Shall we follow his plan? If not, give your own." ⁷Hushai replied to Absalom, "This time Ahithophel has not given good counsel." ⁸And he went on to say: "You know that your father and his men are warriors, and that they are as fierce as a bear in the wild robbed of her cubs. Moreover, since your father is a skilled fighter, he will not spend the night with the army. ⁹Even now he lies hidden in one of the caves or in one of his other places. And if some of our soldiers should fall at the first attack, whoever hears of it will say, 'Absalom's followers have been slaughtered.' ¹⁰Then even the brave man with the heart of a lion—his heart will melt. For all Israel knows that your father is a fighter and those who

are with him are brave. ¹¹This is what I counsel: Let all Israel be assembled, from Dan to Beer-sheba, as numerous as the sands by the sea, and you yourself go with them. ¹²We can then attack him wherever we find him, settling down upon him as dew alights on the ground. None shall survive—neither he nor any of his followers. ¹³And if he retires into a city, all Israel shall bring ropes to that city and we can drag it into the gorge, so that not even a pebble of it can be found." ¹⁴Then Absalom and all the Israelites said, "The counsel of Hushai the Archite is better than the counsel of Ahithophel." For the LORD had commanded that Ahithophel's good counsel should be thwarted, so that he might bring Absalom to ruin.

David Told of the Plan. ¹⁵Then Hushai said to the priests Zadok and Abiathar: "This is the counsel Ahithophel gave Absalom and the elders of Israel, and this is what I counseled. ¹⁶So send a warning to David immediately: 'Do not spend the night at the fords near the

the narrator clearly reports the Lord's involvement (cf. 11:27 and 12:24). These deft touches remind the reader that human affairs, driven and confused by human motivations, are ultimately under divine guidance. That influence is rarely apparent but nevertheless effective. This narrative style challenges modern readers to develop a similar ability to tell their stories in the light of faith.

17:15–18:5 *Preparations for war*

David's scheme was to confuse Absalom's counsel and to gather intelligence. Having done the first, Hushai uses the spy ring to forewarn David of Ahithophel's advice (17:15-16), just in case it is followed. The narrator complicates the plot to increase the excitement of the story (17:17-21). Helped by a quick-witted woman (cf. Josh 2:4-7), the messengers reach David, and the company crosses the Jordan (17:22).

wilderness, but cross over without fail. Otherwise the king and all the people with him will be destroyed.'" [17]Now Jonathan and Ahimaaz were staying at En-rogel. A maidservant was to come with information for them, and they in turn were to go and report to King David. They could not risk being seen entering the city, [18]but an attendant did see them and informed Absalom. They hurried on their way and reached the house of a man in Bahurim who had a cistern in his courtyard. They let themselves down into it, [19]and the woman took the cover and spread it over the mouth of the cistern, strewing crushed grain on the cover so that nothing could be noticed. [20]When Absalom's servants came to the woman at the house, they asked, "Where are Ahimaaz and Jonathan?" The woman replied, "They went by a short while ago toward the water." They searched, but found no one, and so returned to Jerusalem. [21]As soon as they left, Ahimaaz and Jonathan came up out of the cistern and went on to report to King David. They said to him: "Leave! Cross the water at once, for Ahithophel has given such and such counsel in regard to you." [22]So David and all his people moved on and crossed the Jordan. By daybreak, there was no one left who had not crossed.

[23]When Ahithophel saw that his counsel was not acted upon, he saddled his donkey and departed, going to his home in his own city. Then, having left orders concerning his household, he hanged himself. And so he died and was buried in his father's tomb.

[24]Now David had arrived at Mahanaim while Absalom crossed the Jordan

---

Ahithophel took a risk in defecting to Absalom, and his counsel has been rejected. He knows the rebellion is doomed. His suicide preempts the coming destruction (17:23). Amasa takes command of the army (17:24). This is a family affair: father against son, cousin against cousin. Amasa, Joab, and Abishai are all nephews of David, sons of his two sisters, Abigail and Zeruiah (cf. 1 Chr 2:13-17).

David receives ample support from three non-Judahites of importance: the Ammonite prince, Shobi; Machir who had sheltered Meribbaal (cf. 9:4-5); and Barzillai (17:27-29). He is also able to place his forces under three able generals: Joab, Abishai, and Ittai (18:1-2). Even in this moment of difficulty, devotion to David is high and provides him with ample backing. David planned to fight with the troops, but they resist the idea (18:2b). They place a high value on the king's life (18:3), a nice contrast to the risk Absalom has been persuaded to take (cf. 17:11). However, David then complicates issues: "Be gentle with young Absalom for my sake" (18:5). This will be a critical battle for the throne, but now David hampers his generals by commanding gentleness towards the usurper. The narrator notes who heard the command. Everyone knows that David is torn between royal necessity and fatherly love.

accompanied by all the Israelites. [25]Absalom had put Amasa in command of the army in Joab's place. Amasa was the son of an Ishmaelite named Ithra, who had married Abigail, daughter of Jesse and sister of Joab's mother Zeruiah. [26]Israel and Absalom encamped in the land of Gilead.

[27]When David came to Mahanaim, Shobi, son of Nahash from Rabbah of the Ammonites, Machir, son of Ammiel from Lodebar, and Barzillai, the Gileadite from Rogelim, [28]brought beds and covers, basins and pottery, as well as wheat, barley, flour, roasted grain, beans, lentils, [29]honey, and butter and cheese from the flocks and herds, for David and those who were with him to eat; for they said, "The people will be hungry and tired and thirsty in the wilderness."

18 **Preparation for Battle.** [1]After mustering the troops he had with him, David placed officers in command of units of a thousand and units of a hundred. [2]David then divided the troops three ways, a third under Joab, a third under Abishai, son of Zeruiah and brother of Joab, and a third under Ittai the Gittite. The king said to the troops, "I intend to go out with you myself." [3]But they replied: "You must not come out with us. For if we flee, no one will care; even if half of us die, no one will care. But you are worth ten thousand of us. Therefore it is better that we have you to help us from the city." [4]The king said to them, "I will do what you think best." So the king stood by the gate as all the soldiers marched out in units of a hundred and a thousand. [5]But the king gave this command to Joab, Abishai, and Ittai: "Be gentle with young Absalom for my sake." All the soldiers heard as the king gave commands to the various leaders with regard to Absalom.

Defeat of Absalom's Forces. [6]David's army then took the field against Israel, and a battle was fought in the forest near Mahanaim. [7]The forces of Israel were defeated by David's servants, and the

---

18:6–19:1 The death of Absalom

The account of the battle is brief (18:6-8). Given David's command, attention is on Absalom. The odd statement in verse 8b about the consuming thickets may be to lessen internecine guilt (more died by misadventure than were killed by fellow Israelites). It also prepares for Absalom's misadventure. His luxuriant hair (cf. 14:26) catches in branches; his royal mount abandons him; and he hangs "between heaven and earth," in a limbo while others debate his future (18:9). The soldier did not and will not touch him. Joab is furious and does the job himself (18:10-14). The dialogue recalls David's command, which the soldier stubbornly obeys, and thus highlights Joab's disobedience. Joab does not waste time over David's sensibilities, either political (when he killed Abner, cf. 3:24-27) or emotional (in this case). Joab does David's dirty work and secures the throne. With Absalom dispatched, the battle can end (18:16). Absalom is buried unceremoniously, as

casualties there that day were heavy—twenty thousand men. ⁸The battle spread out over that entire region, and the forest consumed more combatants that day than did the sword.

Death of Absalom. ⁹Absalom unexpectedly came up against David's servants. He was mounted on a mule, and, as the mule passed under the branches of a large oak tree, his hair caught fast in the tree. He hung between heaven and earth while the mule under him kept going. ¹⁰Someone saw this and reported to Joab, "I saw Absalom hanging from an oak tree." ¹¹Joab said to the man who told him this: "If you saw him, why did you not strike him to the ground on the spot? Then it would have been my duty to give you fifty pieces of silver and a belt." ¹²But the man replied to Joab: "Even if I already held a thousand pieces of silver in my two hands, I would not lay a hand on the king's son, for in our hearing the king gave you and Abishai and Ittai a command: 'Protect the youth Absalom for my sake.' ¹³Had I been disloyal and killed him, it would all have come out before the king, and you

would stand aloof." ¹⁴Joab replied, "I will not waste time with you in this way." And taking three pikes in hand, he thrust for the heart of Absalom. He was still alive in the tree. ¹⁵When ten of Joab's young armor-bearers closed in on Absalom, and killed him with further blows, ¹⁶Joab then sounded the horn, and the soldiers turned back from the pursuit of the Israelites, because Joab called them to halt. ¹⁷They took Absalom and cast him into a deep pit in the forest, and built up a very large mound of stones over him. And all the Israelites fled to their own tents.

¹⁸During his lifetime Absalom had taken a pillar and set it up for himself in the King's Valley, for he said, "I have no son to perpetuate my name." The pillar which he named for himself is called Absalom's Monument to the present day.

David Told of Absalom's Death. ¹⁹Then Ahimaaz, son of Zadok, said, "Let me run to take the good news to the king that the LORD has set him free from the power of his enemies." ²⁰But Joab said to him: "You are not the man to

a criminal (cf. Josh 7:26; 8:29; 10:27). (The pillar Absalom erected is problematic. The claim that he had no son contradicts 14:27. It is probably a late addition.)

The king must be told the news. The standard pattern of such messages from the front (cf. 1 Sam 4:12-18) is elaborated to increase suspense. Joab refuses to permit the eager Ahimaaz to go because he is aware of the risk (18:19-20). David has killed previous messengers of bad news (cf. 1:15-16). Instead he sends an anonymous Cushite (18:21). However, Joab finally gives way to Ahimaaz's pleading (18:22-23). The narrator is setting up expectations that the son of Zadok may be killed as he races ahead of the Cushite. The narrator shifts to the viewpoint of David, responding over-optimistically to each fragment of the lookout's reports (18:24-27). Suspense mounts as

bring the news today. On some other day you may take the good news, but today you would not be bringing good news, for in fact the king's son is dead." ²¹Then Joab said to a Cushite, "Go, tell the king what you have seen." The Cushite bowed to Joab and ran off. ²²But Ahimaaz, son of Zadok, said to Joab again, "Come what may, permit me also to run after the Cushite." Joab replied: "Why do you want to run, my son? You will receive no reward." ²³But he insisted, "Come what may, I want to run." Joab said to him, "Run." Ahimaaz took the way of the Jordan plain and outran the Cushite.

²⁴Now David was sitting between the two gates, and a lookout mounted to the roof of the gate above the city wall, where he looked out and saw a man running all alone. ²⁵The lookout shouted to inform the king, who said, "If he is alone, he has good news to report." As he kept coming nearer, ²⁶the lookout spied another runner. From his place atop the gate he cried out, "There is another man running by himself." And the king responded, "He, too, is bringing good news." ²⁷Then the lookout said, "I notice that the first one runs like

Ahimaaz, son of Zadok." The king replied, "He is a good man; he comes with good news." ²⁸Then Ahimaaz called out and greeted the king. With face to the ground he paid homage to the king and said, "Blessed be the LORD your God, who has delivered up the men who rebelled against my lord the king." ²⁹But the king asked, "Is young Absalom safe?" And Ahimaaz replied, "I saw a great disturbance when the king's servant Joab sent your servant on, but I do not know what it was." ³⁰The king said, "Step aside and remain in attendance here." So he stepped aside and remained there. ³¹When the Cushite came in, he said, "Let my lord the king receive the good news that this day the LORD has freed you from the power of all who rose up against you." ³²But the king asked the Cushite, "Is young Absalom all right?" The Cushite replied, "May the enemies of my lord the king and all who rebel against you with evil intent be as that young man!"

19 ¹The king was shaken, and went up to the room over the city gate and wept. He said as he wept, "My son Absalom! My son, my son Absalom! If only I had died instead of you, Absalom, my son, my son!"

Ahimaaz arrives and his eloquent proclamation slithers into confusion (18:28-29), because he cannot tell the king of Absalom's death. He is safe, but how will the king learn? The Cushite's report is equally verbose (18:31), again prompting David to ask about the "young Absalom." The Cushite delivers the news in glorious terms (18:32), but the king's reaction breaks all expectations. David breaks down in tears (19:1). His grief is more heart-rending than for Saul and Jonathan (1:17-27), or for his other sons (12:16-17; 13:31, 36). Five times in the inchoate sobbing he calls Absalom "son." Never before has he done so, preferring "young Absalom." If only David had treated Absalom as a son, perhaps he would not be weeping over his death now.

Joab Reproves David. ²Joab was told, "The king is weeping and mourning for Absalom," ³and that day's victory was turned into mourning for the whole army when they heard, "The king is grieving for his son." ⁴The soldiers stole into the city that day like men shamed by flight in battle. ⁵Meanwhile the king covered his face and cried out in a loud voice, "My son Absalom! Absalom! My son, my son!" ⁶So Joab went to the king's residence and said: "Though they saved your life and your sons' and daughters' lives, and the lives of your wives and your concubines, you have put all your servants to shame today ⁷by loving those who hate you and hating those who love you. For you have announced today that officers and servants are nothing to you. Indeed I am now certain that if Absalom were alive today and all of us dead, that would be fine with you. ⁸Now then, get up! Go out and speak kindly to your servants. I swear by the LORD that if you do not go out, not a single man will remain with you overnight, and this will be a far greater disaster for you than any that has come upon you from your youth until now." ⁹So the king got up and sat at the gate. When all the people were told, "The king is sitting at the gate," they came into his presence.

19:2-9a Joab reproves David

David's grief has serious repercussions. The troops valued David's life above their own (18:3), but now he values the traitor more than himself. The death of Absalom turns victory into defeat (19:4). Throughout this unit, "today" is mentioned frequently. This is a critical moment: rebellion is defeated, but will David throw victory away? Joab's actions are the cause of grief, because he killed the son to save the father. Now he must suppress the father's grief for the son (19:6-8). Against this rebel (son), the troops have saved father, sons, daughters, wives. This is the cold truth of political survival. David must choose between the dead Absalom and his living supporters, and he must do so quickly! David obeys Joab and greets the troops (19:9). The correct protocol saves the day, but at what personal cost?

The narrative exonerates David of guilt for Absalom's death and highlights his love for his son. But David's response to his sons' deaths is increasingly unbalanced. He is a paragon of faith in chapter 12; he mourns bitterly when Amnon dies (ch. 13); but now he is unhinged by Absalom's death (ch. 18). The punishment announced in 12:7-14 is bearing a heavy toll on David's character and on his ability to pass the crown to the next generation.

19:9b-44 David returns

The narrative of Absalom's rebellion has an artful symmetry. The contest between counselors (16:15–17:14) is balanced by the contest between the

The Tower of David in present-day Jerusalem.

The Reconciliation. Now the Israelites had fled to their separate tents, [10]but throughout the tribes of Israel all the people were arguing among themselves, saying to one another: "The king delivered us from the grasp of our enemies, and it was he who rescued us from the grasp of the Philistines. Now, he has fled the country before Absalom, [11]but Absalom, whom we anointed over us, has died in battle. Why, then, should you remain silent about restoring the king to his palace?" When the talk of all Israel reached the king, [12]David sent word to the priests Zadok and Abiathar: "Say to the elders of Judah: 'Why should you be last to restore the king to his palace? [13]You are my brothers, you are my bone and flesh. Why should you be last to restore the king?' [14]Also say to Amasa: 'Are you not my bone and flesh? May God do thus to me, and more, if you do not become commander of my army permanently in place of Joab.'" [15]He won the hearts of the Judahites all together, and so they sent a message to the king: "Return, with all your servants."

David and Shimei. [16]So the king returned, and when he reached the Jordan, Judah had come to Gilgal to meet him and to bring him across the Jordan. [17]Shimei, son of Gera, the Benjaminite

---

warriors (17:15–19:9a). The flight from Jerusalem (15:13–16:14) is now balanced by a return to the city (19:9b–20:3). During the flight David encountered three groups: the loyal (Ittai, the priests, and Hushai), the doubtful (Ziba), and the opponents (Shimei). On his return he meets these three groups in reverse order. The rebellion has been presented as a family affair, yet there are hints of wider political divisions. Absalom played on the tension between the northern tribes and the southern monarchy, threatening to turn rebellion into civil war. Nevertheless, he began the rebellion in Hebron, heartland of Judah, and there has been silence on Judah's stance. The king must negotiate these tensions to rebuild support and reunite his kingdom.

19:9b-16 Dealing with division

The northern tribes are divided (19:9b-11), but opinion is swinging towards David. However, it is Judah that worries David more. Using the priests, he prods the Judahite elders to remember clan loyalty (19:12-13), and he makes a bold offer to replace Joab with Amasa, Absalom's general (19:14). This would indicate that support for Absalom was strong in Judah. It also suggests a breach between David and Joab, caused by the death of Absalom. The king's move wins support, but what is Joab's response?

9:17-41 Further dialogues

As David approaches the Jordan, he has three encounters. First, Shimei, who cursed him (16:5-14), comes to beg pardon (19:16-24). Again Abishai

from Bahurim, hurried down with the Judahites to meet King David, [18]accompanied by a thousand men from Benjamin. Ziba, too, the servant of the house of Saul, accompanied by his fifteen sons and twenty servants, hastened to the Jordan before the king. [19]They crossed over the ford to bring the king's household over and to do whatever he wished. When Shimei, son of Gera, crossed the Jordan, he fell down before the king [20]and said to him: "May my lord not hold me guilty; do not remember or take to heart the wrong that your servant did the day my lord the king left Jerusalem. [21]For your servant knows that I have done wrong. But I now am the first of the whole house of Joseph to come down today to meet my lord the king." [22]But Abishai, son of Zeruiah, countered: "Shimei must be put to death for this. He cursed the anointed of the LORD." [23]David replied: "What has come between you and me, sons of Zeruiah, that you would become my adversaries this day? Should anyone die today in Israel? Am I not aware that today I am king over Israel?" [24]Then the king said to Shimei, "You shall not die." And the king gave him his oath.

David and Meribbaal. [25]Meribbaal, son of Saul, also went down to meet the king. He had not cared for his feet nor trimmed his mustache nor washed his clothes from the day the king left until he returned safely. [26]When he came from

wants to kill Shimei (19:22), but with an identical retort (in the Hebrew) David stops him (19:23a; cf. 16:10a). Before, David offered a theological explanation, but now his argument is royal. Joab has succeeded in suppressing the personal under the political, at least where the sons of Zeruiah are involved.

The second encounter involves Meribbaal (19:25-31). His appearance suggests a total lack of self-attention while David was absent (19:25). This is not easy to fabricate. David's question flows from Ziba's allegation (cf. 16:7), and Meribbaal bluntly accuses Ziba of betrayal (19:27). Who is to be believed? Meribbaal throws himself on David's mercy (19:29-30). David cuts him short and makes a quick decision to divide the property (19:31). David's judgment indicates that he cannot decide who is telling the truth. Meribbaal's reply is a dramatic gesture of loyalty, but brings about the final dispossession of the house of Saul.

The encounter with Barzillai is warmer. This wealthy elder, who supported David in exile, is offered a place in Jerusalem (19:32-34). Barzillai politely refuses (19:35-38b): perhaps he wishes to maintain a certain independence from the Jerusalem establishment. Instead, he sends Chimham (his son, according to some ancient versions) to bind the alliance. This final encounter completes the crossing of the Jordan to Gilgal (19:16-41), and the narrator returns to the simmering tension between north and south.

Jerusalem to meet the king, the king asked him, "Why did you not go with me, Meribbaal?" ²⁷He replied: "My lord king, my servant deceived me. For your servant said to him, 'Saddle the donkey for me, that I may ride on it and go with the king'; your servant is lame. ²⁸But he slandered your servant before my lord the king. But my lord the king is like an angel of God. Do whatever seems good to you. ²⁹For though my father's entire house deserved only death from my lord the king, yet you placed your servant among those who eat at your table. What right do I still have to make further appeal to the king?" ³⁰But the king said to him: "Why do you go on talking? I say, 'You and Ziba shall divide the property.'" ³¹Meribbaal answered the king, "Indeed let him take it all, now that my lord the king has returned safely to his house."

David and Barzillai. ³²Barzillai the Gileadite also came down from Rogelim and escorted the king to the Jordan for his crossing, taking leave of him at the Jordan. ³³It was Barzillai, a very old man of eighty, who had provided for the king during his stay in Mahanaim; he was a very great man. ³⁴The king said to Barzillai, "Cross over with me, and I will provide for your old age as my guest in Jerusalem." ³⁵But Barzillai answered the king: "How much longer have I to live, that I should go up to Jerusalem with the king? ³⁶I am now eighty years old. Can I distinguish between good and evil? Can your servant taste what he eats and drinks, or still hear the voices of men and women singers? Why should your servant be any further burden to my lord the king? ³⁷In escorting the king across the Jordan, your servant is doing little enough! Why should the king give me this reward? ³⁸Please let your servant go back to die in my own city by the tomb of my father and mother. Here is your servant Chimham. Let him cross over with my lord the king. Do for him whatever seems good to you." ³⁹Then the king said to him, "Chimham shall cross over with me, and for him I will do whatever seems good to you. And anything else you would like me to do for you, I will do." ⁴⁰Then all the people crossed over the Jordan but the king remained; he kissed Barzillai and bade him farewell as he returned to his own place. ⁴¹Finally the king crossed over to Gilgal, accompanied by Chimham.

Israel and Judah Quarrel. All of the people of Judah and half of the people of Israel had escorted the king across. ⁴²But then all these Israelites began coming to the king and saying, "Why did our brothers the Judahites steal you

---

The Judahites have been present throughout (19:16), but now some Israelites are mentioned (19:41b). Which group will show greater loyalty by escorting David home? Each side stakes its claim. Judah focuses on kinship, while Israel focuses on the office of king (19:42-44). These differences were implicit in David's coronations (2:1-4; 5:1-3), but now they are in the open. In later generations, they will divide the kingdom. Absalom's rebellion failed, but it exposed an inherent weakness in the Davidic monarchy.

away and bring the king and his household across the Jordan, along with all David's men?" ⁴³All the Judahites replied to the men of Israel: "Because the king is our relative. Why are you angry over this? Have we had anything to eat at the king's expense? Or have portions from his table been given to us?" ⁴⁴The Israelites answered the Judahites: "We have ten shares in the king. Also, we are the firstborn rather than you. Why do you slight us? Were we not first to speak of restoring our king?" Then the Judahites in turn spoke even more fiercely than the Israelites.

20 Sheba's Rebellion. ¹Now a scoundrel named Sheba, the son of Bichri, a Benjaminite, happened to be there. He sounded the horn and cried out,

"We have no share in David,
    nor any heritage in the son of
        Jesse.
    Everyone to your tents, O Israel!"

²So all the Israelites left David to follow Sheba, son of Bichri. But the Judahites, from the Jordan to Jerusalem, remained loyal to their king. ³David came to his house in Jerusalem, and the king took the ten concubines whom he had left behind to care for the palace and placed them under guard. He provided for them, but never again saw them. And so

they remained shut away to the day of their death, lifelong widows.

Amasa's Death. ⁴Then the king said to Amasa: "Summon the Judahites for me within three days. Then present yourself here." ⁵Accordingly Amasa set out to summon Judah, but delayed beyond the time set for him. ⁶Then David said to Abishai: "Sheba, son of Bichri, may now do us more harm than Absalom did. Take your lord's servants and pursue him, lest he find fortified cities and take shelter while we look on." ⁷So Joab and the Cherethites and Pelethites and all the warriors marched out behind Abishai from Jerusalem to campaign in pursuit of Sheba, son of Bichri. ⁸They were at the great stone in Gibeon when Amasa met them. Now Joab had a belt over his tunic, from which was slung a sword in its sheath at his thigh; the sword would slide out downwards. ⁹Joab asked Amasa, "Is everything all right, my brother?" and with his right hand held Amasa's beard as if to kiss him. ¹⁰And since Amasa was not on his guard against the sword in Joab's other hand, Joab stabbed him in the abdomen with it, so that his entrails burst forth to the ground, and he died; there was no second thrust. Then Joab and Abishai his brother pursued Sheba, son of Bichri. ¹¹One of Joab's attendants stood by Amasa and said, "Let him who favors

20:1-22 Sheba's revolt

The quarrel endangers David's return. Sheba's cry of rebellion (20:1b) will be repeated when the kingdom divides after Solomon's death (1 Kgs 12:16). David reaches Jerusalem with only the people of Judah loyal to "their king" (20:2). Sheba's rebellion is presented as the conclusion to Absalom's revolt, but it is potentially more dangerous (20:6).

Joab and is for David follow Joab." [12]Amasa lay covered with blood in the middle of the highroad, and the man noticed that all the soldiers were stopping. So he rolled Amasa away from the road to the field and spread a garment over him, because he saw how all who came upon him were stopping. [13]When he had been removed from the road, everyone went on after Joab in pursuit of Sheba, son of Bichri.

Joab Pursues Sheba. [14]Sheba had passed through all the tribes of Israel to Abel Beth-maacah. Then all the Bichrites assembled and they too entered the city after him. [15]So all Joab's troops came and besieged him in Abel Beth-maacah. They built up a mound against the city, so that it stood against the rampart, and were battering the wall to knock it down. [16]Then a wise woman from the city called out, "Listen, listen! Tell Joab, 'Come here, so I can speak with you.'" [17]When Joab had come near her, the woman said, "Are you Joab?" And he replied, "Yes."

She said to him, "Listen to what your servant has to say." He replied, "I am listening." [18]Then she went on to say: "There is a saying from long ago, 'Let them ask if they will in Abel or in Dan whether loyalty is finished [19]or ended in Israel.' You are seeking to batter down a city that is a mother in Israel. Why do you wish to swallow up the heritage of the LORD?" [20]Joab answered, "Not at all, not at all! I do not wish to swallow or batter anything. [21]That is not the case at all. A man from the hill country of Ephraim, whose name is Sheba, son of Bichri, has rebelled against King David. Give him up, just him, and I will withdraw from the city." Then the woman said to Joab, "His head shall be thrown to you across the wall." [22]In her wisdom, the woman went to all the people, and they cut off the head of Sheba, son of Bichri, and threw it out to Joab. He then sounded the horn, and they scattered from the city to their own tents, while Joab returned to Jerusalem to the king.

Clearly, Amasa is a lynchpin in David's relations with Judah (20:4), but his delay places him under suspicion (20:5). Curiously, David turns to Abishai. Has Joab fallen out of favor? Suddenly, Joab appears again (20:7), and he acts with his usual murderous efficiency to regain his position (20:8-10b), with a hidden weapon, a disarming gesture of friendship, and a swift blow. The troops are taken aback, but such doubts are quickly quashed (20:11-13), and Joab is in control again. His campaign takes the usual course of pursuit followed by siege (cf. 10:6-14; 11:1). His brutality is checked by another wise woman (20:16-21). Joab used the wise woman of Tekoa to change the king's mind about Absalom (14:1-20), and this woman now tells Joab what to do about Sheba. In each case, the women strive to avoid bloodguilt and alienation. They appeal to covenant categories to change royal decisions. The woman of Tekoa rescued one man, while this woman saves a city by setting aside one man. The rebellion of Absalom prompted by the first decision is finally laid to rest by the second.

David's Officials. ²³Joab was in command of the whole army of Israel. Benaiah, son of Jehoiada, was in command of the Cherethites and Pelethites. ²⁴Adoram was in charge of the forced labor. Jehoshaphat, son of Ahilud, was the chancellor. ²⁵Shawsha was the scribe. Zadok and Abiathar were priests. ²⁶Ira the Jairite was also David's priest.

V. Appendixes

21 **Gibeonite Vengeance.** ¹In David's time there was a famine for three years, year after year. David sought the presence of the LORD, who said: There is bloodguilt on Saul and his family because he put the Gibeonites to death. ²So the king called the Gibeonites and spoke to them. (Now the Gibeonites were not Israelites, but survivors of the Amorites; and although the Israelites had given them their oath, Saul had sought to kill them off in his zeal for the Israelites and for Judah.) ³David said to the Gibeonites, "What must I do for you and how must I make atonement, that you may bless the heritage of the LORD?" ⁴The Gibeonites answered him, "We have no claim against Saul and his house for silver or gold, nor is it our place to

---

20:23-26 Listing government officials

Joab is back in charge of the army as Absalom's rebellion ends (20:23). Just as 2 Samuel 9–20 was prefaced by a list of David's officials (8:15-18), so it is rounded off by a similar list. There is some rearrangement, but little overall change in government. A new post is added, that of Adoram in charge of forced labor (20:24). Such an addition suggests that David's government is moving towards the ominous pattern of 1 Samuel 8:11-18.

APPENDICES

2 Samuel 21–24

The chapters that follow the long narrative of 2 Samuel 9–20 interrupt the consideration of David's family and the succession. When the continuous Deuteronomistic History was divided into scrolls of relatively equal length, these chapters became the concluding "appendices" of 2 Samuel. This miscellany of independent traditions is arranged in a concentric fashion. In the center are two poems attributed to David (22:1-51; 23:1-7). They are bracketed by two lists of heroes and their exploits (21:15-22; 23:8-39). The miscellany opens and closes with two narratives about public disaster resolved by ritual intercession (21:1-14; 24:1-25).

21:1-14 Gibeonites and a famine

This is a relatively independent tradition with little connection to other stories about David. While placed at the end of the book, some think that

put anyone to death in Israel." Then he said, "I will do for you whatever you propose." ⁵They said to the king, "As for the man who was exterminating us and who intended to destroy us that we might have no place in all the territory of Israel, ⁶let seven men from among his descendants be given to us, that we may execute them before the LORD in Gibeon, on the LORD's mountain." The king replied, "I will give them up." ⁷The king, however, spared Meribbaal, son of Jonathan, son of Saul, because of the LORD's oath that formed a bond between David and Saul's son Jonathan. ⁸But the king took Armoni and Meribbaal, the two sons that Aiah's daughter Rizpah had borne to Saul, and the five sons of Saul's daughter Merob that she had borne to Adriel, son of Barzillai the Meholathite, ⁹and delivered them into the power of the Gibeonites, who then executed them on the mountain before the LORD. The seven fell at the one time; they were put to death during the first days of the harvest—that is, at the beginning of the barley harvest.

¹⁰Then Rizpah, Aiah's daughter, took sackcloth and spread it out for herself on the rock from the beginning of the harvest until rain came down on them from the heavens, fending off the birds of the heavens from settling on them by day, and the wild animals by night. ¹¹When David was informed of what Rizpah, Aiah's daughter, the concubine

---

these events happened prior to David's meeting with Meribbaal (ch. 9). This story reflects a theology which links public disaster to God's anger, which then needs appeasement. Faced with famine, David consults the Lord and learns of the bloodguilt of Saul's house (21:1). He approaches the surviving Gibeonites to arrange expiation of the treaty breach (21:2-3). The Israelites' oath to the Gibeonites alludes to Joshua 9:3-27, but there is no reference to Saul's campaign against them. Their response is cautious. They will not name a price until the king gives his word to carry it out, thus absolving them from any future retaliation. They demand the execution of seven descendants of Saul. Such an execution is both punishment for breach of the treaty and an offering to the Lord to remove the sin of bloodguilt. David agrees, but spares Meribbaal, son of Jonathan, in consideration of his own obligations to Jonathan (21:7).

Rizpah's act of loyalty to the dead spurs David to demonstrate similar loyalty (21:10). Curiously, he focuses on the remains of Saul and Jonathan, disinterring their bones for reburial in the family grave (21:11-12, 14). Almost in passing, the bones of the seven are gathered up (and presumably buried also).

This episode could be read as a positive portrait of David, who is here attentive to the Lord, seeking to remove bloodguilt, showing loyalty to oaths, and honoring Saul's house. Furthermore, the Lord answers his efforts

of Saul, had done, [12]he went and obtained the bones of Saul and of his son Jonathan from the citizens of Jabesh-gilead, who had stolen them away secretly from the public square of Beth-shan, where the Philistines had hanged them at the time they defeated Saul on Gilboa. [13]When he had brought up from there the bones of Saul and of his son Jonathan, the bones of those who had been executed were also gathered up. [14]Then the bones of Saul and of his son Jonathan were buried in the land of Benjamin, at Zela, in the tomb of his father Kish. After all that the king commanded had been carried out, God granted relief to the land.

Exploits in Philistine Wars. [15]There was another battle between the Philistines and Israel. David went down with his servants and fought the Philistines, but David grew tired. [16]Dadu, a descendant of the Rephaim, whose bronze spear weighed three hundred shekels, was about to take him captive. Dadu was girt with a new sword and thought he would kill David, [17]but Abishai, son of Zeruiah, came to help him, and struck and killed the Philistine. Then David's men swore to him, "You must not go out to battle with us again, lest you quench the lamp of Israel."

[18]After this, there was another battle with the Philistines, in Gob. On that occasion Sibbecai the Hushathite struck down Saph, a descendant of the Rephaim. [19]There was another battle with the Philistines, in Gob, and Elhanan, son of Jair from Bethlehem, killed Goliath of Gath, whose spear shaft was like a weaver's beam. [20]There was another battle, at Gath, and there was a giant, who had six fingers on each hand and six toes on each foot—twenty-four in all. He too was descended from the Rephaim. [21]And when he insulted Israel, Jonathan,

---

(21:14b). In contrast, Saul is portrayed in violation of ancient obligations (cf. his breach of the Amalekite ban in 1 Sam 15). However, there is another negative reading. David benefits politically as seven close relatives of Saul are eliminated. Such action would explain Shimei's curse (16:7-8). With so little to go on, both evaluations are valid interpretations of the story.

21:15-27 David's warriors

This collection of exploits by David's warriors dates from the early Philistine wars (5:17-25). The warriors defeat members of the Rephaim, probably an elite military band dedicated to a Philistine god, Rapha. In contrast to the prowess of his servants, David is portrayed as weak and vulnerable (21:15-16). The soldiers then decide that he should not risk himself in battle, a strategy which was reflected in 11:1 and 18:3-4. Their reference to the "lamp of Israel" (21:17) becomes apparent in 22:29. David's relationship with the Lord is a sign of hope and confidence for his followers. First Chronicles 20:5 corrects verse 19 to say that Elhanan killed Goliath's brother, leaving David as Goliath's slayer (1 Sam 17:48-51).

son of David's brother Shimei, struck him down. ²²These four were descended from the Rephaim in Gath, and they fell at the hands of David and his servants.

22 **Song of Thanksgiving.** ¹David proclaimed the words of this song to the LORD when the LORD had rescued him from the grasp of all his enemies and from the grasp of Saul. ²He said:

> O LORD, my rock, my fortress, my
>   deliverer,
>   ³my God, my rock of refuge!
> My shield, my saving horn,
>   my stronghold, my refuge,
>   my savior, from violence you
>   keep me safe.
> ⁴Praised be the LORD, I exclaim!
>   I have been delivered from my
>   enemies.
>
> ⁵The breakers of death surged
>   round about me,
>   the menacing floods terrified me;
> ⁶The cords of Sheol tightened;
>   the snares of death lay in wait
>   for me.
> ⁷In my distress I called out: LORD!
>   I cried out to my God;
> From his temple he heard my voice,
>   my cry reached his ears.

> ⁸The earth rocked and shook;
>   the foundations of the heavens
>   trembled;
>   they shook as his wrath flared up.
> ⁹Smoke rose in his nostrils,
>   a devouring fire from his mouth;
>   it kindled coals into flame.
> ¹⁰He parted the heavens and came
>   down,
>   a dark cloud under his feet.
> ¹¹Mounted on a cherub he flew,
>   borne along on the wings of the
>   wind.
> ¹²He made darkness the cover
>   about him,
>   a mass of water, heavy thunder-
>   heads.
> ¹³From the brightness of his presence
>   coals were kindled to flame.
> ¹⁴The LORD thundered from heaven;
>   the Most High made his voice
>   resound.
> ¹⁵He let fly arrows and scattered
>   them;
>   lightning, and dispersed them.
> ¹⁶Then the bed of the sea appeared;
>   the world's foundations lay bare,
> At the roar of the LORD,
>   at the storming breath of his
>   nostrils.
> ¹⁷He reached down from on high
>   and seized me,
>   drew me out of the deep waters.

22:1-51 Psalm of thanksgiving

The song of chapter 22 is a duplicate of Psalm 18. The poem is part hymn, part thanksgiving. It celebrates the Lord as savior of Israel and of the individual believer, in this case, David. Within the hymnic opening and closing frames (22:2-4 and 22:47-51), there are two panels which celebrate God's deliverance in mythic and historic terms (22:5-20 and 22:33-46 respectively). At the center is a more reflective passage on the poet's relationship to God (22:21-32).

The opening frame establishes the key relationship of psalmist to God. An accumulation of substantives dealing with rescue describes this God

¹⁸He rescued me from my mighty
enemy,
from foes too powerful for me.
¹⁹They attacked me on a day of distress,
but the LORD came to my support.
²⁰He set me free in the open;
he rescued me because he loves
me.

²¹The LORD acknowledged my righteousness;
rewarded my clean hands.
²²For I kept the ways of the LORD;
I was not disloyal to my God.
²³His laws were all before me,
his decrees I did not cast aside.
²⁴I was honest toward him;
I was on guard against sin.
²⁵So the LORD rewarded my righteousness,
the cleanness of my hands in his
sight.
²⁶Toward the faithful you are faithful;
to the honest you are honest;
²⁷Toward the sincere you are sincere;
but to the perverse you are devious.
²⁸Humble people you save,
though on the haughty your
eyes look down.
²⁹You are my lamp, O LORD!

My God brightens the darkness
about me.
³⁰With you I can rush an armed band,
with my God to help I can leap a
wall.
³¹God's way is unerring;
the LORD's promise is tried and
true;
he is a shield for all who trust in
him.
³²Truly, who is God except the LORD?
Who but our God is the rock?
³³This God who girded me with
might,
kept my way unerring,
³⁴Who made my feet swift as a deer's,
set me safe on the heights,
³⁵Who trained my hands for war,
my arms to bend even a bow of
bronze.
³⁶You have given me your protecting
shield,
and your help has made me
great.
³⁷You gave me room to stride;
my feet never stumbled.
³⁸I pursued my enemies and over-
took them;
I did not turn back till I destroyed
them.
³⁹I struck them down, and they did
not rise;

(22:2-4). Moving into the first panel, the need for rescue is made clear using the mythic language of chaos (22:5-6). The psalmist is overwhelmed by death and despair, and does the only thing possible for a person of faith: "I called out: LORD!" (22:7). In response, God "heard my voice." This is the fundamental relationship of Israel's faith experience. The remainder of the panel describes the theophany of deliverance in powerful, majestic language (22:8-20). God's coming overpowers the nothingness of chaos: "he drew me out of the deep waters" (22:17). The imagery is allusive to both creation and exodus. It is elemental yet personal. All this "because he loves me" (22:20).

they fell dead at my feet.
⁴⁰You girded me with strength for
war;
subdued adversaries at my feet.
⁴¹My foes you put to flight before me;
those who hated me I destroyed.
⁴²They cried for help, but no one
saved them,
cried to the LORD but got no
answer.
⁴³I ground them fine as the dust of
the earth;
like mud in the streets I trod them
down.
⁴⁴You rescued me from the strife of
my people;
you made me head over nations.
A people I had not known became
my slaves;
⁴⁵Foreigners cringed before me;
as soon as they heard of me they
obeyed.
⁴⁶Their courage failed;

they came trembling from their
fortresses.
⁴⁷The LORD lives! Blessed be my rock!
Exalted be God, the rock of my
salvation.
⁴⁸O God who granted me vindication,
subdued peoples under me,
⁴⁹and helped me escape from my
enemies,
Truly you have exalted me above
my adversaries,
from the violent you have rescued
me.
⁵⁰Thus I will proclaim you, LORD,
among the nations;
I will sing the praises of your
name.
⁵¹You have given great victories to
your king,
and shown kindness to your
anointed,
to David and his posterity forever.

The gracious condescension of God in verses 8-20 is put to one side in the central reflection (22:21-32). Now God rescues because I deserve it, the psalmist declares (22:21-25). Given David's moral behavior, such a claim is both ironic and inaccurate in a strict theory of distributive justice. But David stands in a vassal-master relationship with God. In 1 Samuel 26:23, he challenged Saul for a failure of *hesed* (loyalty). Loyalty works both ways within a covenantal relationship. David lives in a covenantal relationship with God and has kept that covenant, so he can rely on God to keep loyalty to him (22:26-32). Verse 29 sums up the effect of the relationship: darkness becomes like day for David. The relationship is a "lamp" for David, and through him for the people (cf. 21:17).

Renewed by reflection, the psalmist returns to celebrate deliverance in more historical terms (22:33-46). Taking his cue from verse 29, the confidence of deliverance strengthens the psalmist in the face of his foes (22:30). There is success on the battlefield, but constantly this personal success is attributed to the Lord. The celebration of "I" gives way to thanks to "You." Thus, the poem moves into the final hymnic frame (22:47-51). Once more, God is described with a series of substantives of rescue. The rescue is focused on

23 **The Last Words of David.** ¹These are the last words of David:

The oracle of David, son of Jesse;
   the oracle of the man God raised
      up,
Anointed of the God of Jacob,
   favorite of the Mighty One of
      Israel.
²The spirit of the LORD spoke through
      me;
   his word was on my tongue.
³The God of Israel spoke;
   of me the Rock of Israel said,
"One who rules over humankind
      with justice,
   who rules in the fear of God,
⁴Is like the light at sunrise
on a cloudless morning,
   making the land's vegetation
      glisten after rain."
⁵Is not my house firm before God?
   He has made an eternal covenant
      with me,
   set forth in detail and secured.
Will he not bring to fruition
   all my salvation and my every
      desire?
⁶But the wicked are all like thorns
      to be cast away;
   they cannot be taken up by hand.
⁷One wishing to touch them
   must be armed with iron or the
      shaft of a spear.
They must be utterly consumed
   by fire.

---

the "king . . . anointed . . . David and his posterity" (22:51). The key word is *hesed* ("kindness"). David's success—his very life—is determined by his relationship with the Lord. The Lord is sovereign and when David (or his posterity) forgets that, he fails. The sentiments of the hymn echo Hannah's song (1 Sam 2:1-10). Both celebrate the sovereignty of the Lord and his power to save and protect, and both focus attention on the Lord's anointed as the concrete expression of the Lord's continuing help. Ideologically, kingship is incorporated into the faith of Israel, even if the practical experience of monarchy falls short of the ideal.

23:1-7 Last words of David

The second poem is written in a sapiential style: the opening (23:1a) is similar to the oracle of Balaam (Num 24:3,15) or the sayings of Agar (Prov 30:1). Like 22:51 and 1 Samuel 2:10, verse 1 speaks of God's determination to choose an anointed one as his instrument for wellbeing in Israel. Thus, the monarchy is intimately related to God (23:1-3a) as the concrete manifestation of God's will to establish justice in the world (23:3b-4). Justice is central to social life and is God's gift. God has established the monarchy to mediate that gift into the life of Israel, not just in David's day but forever (23:5). The promise of 2 Samuel 7 is now called an "eternal covenant." In that chapter the key words were "firm" and "forever" (cf. 7:16), but covenant was not used. The language of "eternal covenant" is more often used of creation (cf. Gen 9:16; Isa 54:9-10) and refers to a promise without time

David's Warriors. [8]These are the names of David's warriors. Ishbaal, the son of Hachamoni, chief of the Three. He brandished his spear over eight hundred whom he had slain in a single encounter. [9]Next to him was Eleazar, the son of Dodo the Ahohite, one of the Three warriors with David at Ephes-dammim, when they insulted the Philistines who had massed there for battle. The Israelites had retreated, [10]but he stood there and struck down the Philistines until his hand grew tired from clutching the sword. The LORD brought about a great victory on that day; the army turned back to rejoin Eleazar, but only to strip the slain. [11]Next to him was Shammah, son of Agee the Hararite. The Philistines had assembled at Lehi, where there was a plot of land full of lentils. The people were fleeing before the Philistines, [12]but he took his stand in the middle of the plot, kept it safe, and cut down the Philistines. Thus the LORD brought about a great victory. Such deeds as these the Three warriors performed.

[13]Three of the Thirty chiefs went down to David in the cave of Adullam during the harvest, while a Philistine clan was encamped in the Valley of Rephaim. [14]David was then in the stronghold, and there was a garrison of Philistines in Bethlehem. [15]Now David had a craving and said, "If only someone would give me a drink of water from the cistern by the gate of Bethlehem!" [16]Thereupon the three warriors broke through the encampment of the Philistines, drew water from the cistern by the gate of Bethlehem, and carried it back to David. But he refused to drink it, and instead poured it out to the LORD, [17]saying: "The LORD forbid that I do such a thing! Could I drink the blood of these men who went at the risk of their lives?" So he refused to drink it.

[18]Abishai, the brother of Joab, son of Zeruiah, was the chief of the Thirty; he

---

limits, part of the very fabric of reality. God's promise to David has come to be part of God's created order (cf. Jer 33:17, 20-22). The historical reality of the Davidic dynasty stands in considerable tension with these theological affirmations.

23:8-39 David's warriors

A second catalogue describes two groups. The Three (23:8-12) are champions who fought single-handed against the Philistines and were instrumental in the Lord's victory. The Thirty may be a company of David's bodyguards (23:18-39). The thirty-seven names listed suggest that "The Thirty" is the name of the company whose membership changed over time (note Uriah's inclusion in the list). Some members of the Thirty are singled out for individual exploits (23:18-24), which nevertheless do not elevate them to the level of champions (the Three). Note Joab's absence from both groups. His position is singular among David's men.

brandished his spear over three hundred whom he had slain. He made a name among the Thirty, ¹⁹but was more famous than any of the Thirty, becoming their leader. However, he did not attain to the Three.

²⁰Benaiah, son of Jehoiada, a valiant man of mighty deeds, from Kabzeel, killed the two sons of Ariel of Moab. Also, he went down and killed the lion in the cistern on a snowy day. ²¹He likewise slew an Egyptian, a huge man. The Egyptian carried a spear, but Benaiah came against him with a staff; he wrested the spear from the Egyptian's hand, and killed him with that spear. ²²Such deeds as these Benaiah, the son of Jehoiada, performed; and he made a name among the Thirty warriors ²³but was more famous than any of the Thirty. However, he did not attain to the Three. David put him in charge of his bodyguard. ²⁴Asahel, brother of Joab, was among the Thirty; Elhanan, son of Dodo, from Bethlehem; ²⁵Shammah, from En-harod; Elika, from En-harod; ²⁶Helez, from Beth-pelet; Ira, son of Ikkesh, from Tekoa; ²⁷Abiezer, from Anathoth; Sibbecai, from Husha; ²⁸Zalmon, from Ahoh; Maharai, from Netophah; ²⁹Heled, son of Baanah, from Netophah; Ittai, son of Ribai, from Gibeah of Benjamin; ³⁰Benaiah, from Pirathon; Hiddai, from the valley of Gaash; ³¹Abibaal, from Beth-arabah; Azmaveth, from Bahurim; ³²Eliahba, from Shaalbon; Jashen the Gunite; Jonathan, ³³son of Shammah the Hararite; Ahiam, son of Sharar the Hararite; ³⁴Eliphelet, son of Ahasbai, from Beth-maacah; Eliam, son of Ahithophel, from Gilo; ³⁵Hezrai, from Carmel; Paarai the Arbite; ³⁶Igal, son of Nathan, from Zobah; Bani the Gadite; ³⁷Zelek the Ammonite; Naharai, from Beeroth, the armor-bearer of Joab, son of Zeruiah; ³⁸Ira, from Jattir; Gareb, from Jattir; ³⁹Uriah the Hittite—thirty-seven in all.

24 David's Census; the Plague. ¹The LORD's anger against Israel flared again, and he incited David against them: "Go, take a census of Israel and Judah." ²The king therefore said to Joab and the leaders of the army who were with him, "Tour all the tribes of Israel

---

An interesting vignette (23:13-17) from David's time in the wilderness (1 Sam 22) separates the two lists. It illustrates the devotion of his bodyguards, ready to risk their lives to fulfill a whim of David. David reciprocates by pouring the water on the ground as a libation (23:16-17). The water becomes symbolic of lifeblood, the loyalty between David and his men, and so is holy to the Lord.

24:1-25 Census of the people

This narrative concludes the miscellany of 2 Samuel 21–24 with a second story of ritual appeasement warding off disaster. At one time, the pair of stories may have been linked (note the "again" in v. 1). The opening phrase serves as a title, "The LORD's anger against Israel flared again," rather than a prior cause of the census.

from Dan to Beer-sheba and register the people, that I may know their number." [3]But Joab replied to the king: "May the LORD your God increase the number of people a hundredfold for my lord the king to see it with his own eyes. But why does it please my lord to do a thing of this kind?" [4]However, the king's command prevailed over Joab and the leaders of the army, so they left the king's presence in order to register the people of Israel. [5]Crossing the Jordan, they began near Aroer, south of the city in the wadi, and turned in the direction of Gad toward Jazer. [6]They continued on to Gilead and to the district below Mount Hermon. Then they proceeded to Dan; from there they turned toward Sidon, [7]going to the fortress of Tyre and to all the cities of the Hivites and Canaanites, and ending up in the Negeb of Judah, at Beer-sheba. [8]Thus they toured the whole land, reaching Jerusalem again after nine months and twenty days. [9]Joab then reported the census figures to the king: of men capable of wielding a sword, there were in Israel eight hundred thousand, and in Judah five hundred thousand.

[10]Afterward, however, David regretted having numbered the people. David said to the LORD: "I have sinned grievously in what I have done. Take away, LORD, your servant's guilt, for I have acted very foolishly." [11]When David rose in the morning, the word of the LORD came to the prophet Gad, David's seer, saying: [12]Go, tell David: Thus says the LORD: I am offering you three options; choose one of them, and I will give you that. [13]Gad then went to David to inform him. He asked: "Should three years of famine come upon your land; or three months of fleeing from your enemy while he pursues you; or is it to be three

David orders a census to count those fit for military service (24:9). By doing so, he places the people on standby for war and perhaps subjects them to the purity laws associated with warfare (cf. Deut 23:10-15). Breach of such rules contaminates the land; in the ancient mind, disaster would ensue. Having completed the census, David belatedly recognizes the ritual predicament in which he has placed the people and confesses the sin as his own (24:10). The Hebrew behind "Take away your servant's guilt" means "transfer the guilt" from the people to David (cf. 2 Sam 12:13).

As in 2 Samuel 12, a prophet brings God's answer (24:11-12). Gad was last mentioned in 1 Samuel 22:5. The Lord offers David three choices of disaster for the people (24:12-13), in effect ignoring David's prayer. David ignores the command to pick one (contrary to the narrator's comment in v. 15), opting instead to throw himself on the Lord's mercy (24:14). This is an expression of trust in God similar to 2 Samuel 15:25-26 and 16:12.

The punishment takes the form of pestilence (24:15) carried out by a destroying angel (cf. the "destroyer" of Exodus 12:23). The angel draws

days of plague in your land? Now consider well: what answer am I to give to him who sent me?" [14]David answered Gad: "I am greatly distressed. But let us fall into the hand of God, whose mercy is great, rather than into human hands." [15]Thus David chose the plague. At the time of the wheat harvest it broke out among the people. The LORD sent plague over Israel from morning until the time appointed, and from Dan to Beer-sheba seventy thousand of the people died. [16]But when the angel stretched forth his hand toward Jerusalem to destroy it, the LORD changed his mind about the calamity, and said to the angel causing the destruction among the people: Enough now! Stay your hand. The angel of the LORD was then standing at the threshing floor of Araunah the Jebusite. [17]When David saw the angel who was striking the people, he said to the LORD: "It is I who have sinned; it is I, the shepherd, who have done wrong. But these sheep, what have they done? Strike me and my father's family!"

David Offers Sacrifices. [18]On the same day Gad went to David and said to him, "Go and set up an altar to the LORD on the threshing floor of Araunah the Jebusite." [19]According to Gad's word, David went up as the LORD had commanded. [20]Now Araunah looked down and saw the king and his servants coming toward him while he was threshing wheat. So he went out and bowed down before the king, his face to the ground. [21]Then Araunah asked, "Why does my lord the king come to his servant?" David replied, "To buy the threshing floor from you, to build an altar to the LORD, that the plague may be withdrawn from the people." [22]But Araunah said to David: "Let my lord the king take

near to strike Jerusalem. The narrator offers two simultaneous accounts from different angles: firstly, the Lord relents (cf. 1 Sam 15:11) his action and stops the angel (24:16); secondly, David sees the angel and repents his sin (24:17). The two simultaneous acts of repentance enable each other. Both together create the possibility of a new future.

This new future will build on the relationship between David and the Lord. Its concrete form will be an altar (24:18). The threshing floor belongs to Araunah, one of the original Jebusite inhabitants of Jerusalem. David proceeds to purchase the site in a deal reminiscent of Abraham's purchase of a burial site in Hebron (24:19-24; cf. Gen 23:3-16). Purchase of the land makes it an inalienable possession of the people. First Chronicles 21:26-30 makes the explicit link between this altar and the altar of holocausts in Solomon's temple.

There are some interesting parallels between this narrative and 2 Samuel 11–12. In both cases, David sins. A prophet announces the Lord's condemnation and punishment. David throws himself on the Lord's mercy and

it and offer up what is good in his sight. See, here are the oxen for burnt offerings, and the threshing sledges and the yokes of oxen for wood. ²³All this does Araunah give to the king." Araunah then said to the king, "May the LORD your God accept your offering." ²⁴The king, however, replied to Araunah, "No, I will buy it from you at the proper price, for I cannot sacrifice to the LORD my God burnt offerings that cost me nothing." So David bought the threshing floor and the oxen for fifty silver shekels. ²⁵Then David built an altar to the LORD there, and sacrificed burnt offerings and communion offerings. The LORD granted relief to the land, and the plague was withdrawn from Israel.

---

begs that the sin be transferred. Following punishment, a new future opens up. In chapter 12, it is the birth of Solomon, and in chapter 24 it is the construction of the altar. From David's sins and repentance emerge the two mainstays of dynasty and temple which are central to the continuing history of Israel in the land.

REVIEW AIDS AND DISCUSSION TOPICS

Introductory Topics *(pages 5–7)*

1. Who were the Deuteronomists and how did they compose the Books of Samuel?

2. Describe the genre of the Books of Samuel.

3. What is the relationship between the historical context of Israelite society and the question of leadership?

4. What role do priests and prophets play regarding Israel's political leadership?

1 Sam 1–3 Hannah's Gift *(pages 9–19)*

1. In what ways does the opening of 1 Samuel hearken back to stories in the Book of Judges?

2. To what extent do Hannah's personal need and Israel's predicament illuminate each other (ch. 1)?

3. Discuss how the stories of Samuel, Eli, Hophni, and Phinehas illustrate the theme of reversal in Hannah's song (ch. 2).

4. Reflect on the relationship between God's word and the prophet's word which emerges in chapter 3.

1 Sam 4:1–7:1 The Ark Narratives *(pages 20–25)*

1. Identify the exodus and exile motifs in the ark narratives (chs. 4–5).

2. How does the story of the ark's return illustrate the freedom of God to take the initiative in Israel's history (ch. 6)?

1 Sam 7–15 The Transition to Monarchy *(pages 25–50)*

1. Is it sufficient to describe Samuel's success solely in terms of judgeship (ch. 7)?

2. Does the people's demand for a king contravene the laws of the covenant (Deut 17:14-20; 1 Sam 8)?

3. Compare the mixed reactions to the designation of Saul, by prophetic ecstasy and by lots. What concerns do these raise about his appointment as king (chs. 9–10)?

4. Is Saul more a judge than a king (ch. 11)?

5. How is kingship reconciled within covenant relationships (ch. 12)?

6. To what extent are Saul's problems of his own making, and to what extent is he the victim of others' assessments (chs. 13–14)?

7. What actions of Saul led to his rejection by the Lord? Discuss the paradox of the Lord's repentance in response to Saul's actions (ch. 15).

I Sam 16:1–2 Sam 5:12 The Rise of David *(pages 51–104)*

1. How does God evaluate people? What qualities make David fit for anointing (ch. 16)?

2. What is David's chief motive in confronting Goliath? How does Saul seek to motivate possible champions (ch. 17)?

3. What range of emotions and affections are covered by the term "love" (ch. 18)?

4. How does the narrator portray Jonathan's transformation from king's son to promoter of David's cause? How important is the concept of covenant loyalty in this narrative (chs. 19–20)?

5. David's visit to Ahimelech has fatal consequences. To what extent do the main characters show *hesed* in these events (chs. 21–22)?

6. Compare the two episodes in which Saul falls into David's hands. How did Saul react in each case (chs. 24 and 26)?

7. What does Abigail want? Would she be an ideal wife for David (ch. 25)?

8. Does David's sojourn among the Philistines damage his reputation (ch. 27)?

9. How did Saul die? Which account is to be believed? Does it matter for the overall story (1 Sam 31 and 2 Sam 1)?

10. Who is the power behind Ishbaal's throne and how does he change his loyalty (chs. 2–3)?

11. How does David's coronation over all Israel differ from his coronation over Judah (ch. 5)?

2 Sam 5:13–8:18 The Reign of David *(pages 104–113)*

1. How does the story of Michal end? What has been the outcome of her love, for David's rise, and for herself (ch. 6)?

2. The Lord changes the plans for building a "house": what does this change tell us about the future sign of God's presence among his people (ch. 7)?

2 Sam 9–20 The Family of David *(pages 113–149)*

1. Meribbaal is incapacitated and unable to play an active role, so what is his significance for the story of David (ch. 9)?

2. Describe David's attempts to hide his adultery. What do you think are the motives of the other characters (ch. 11)?

3. How does David's punishment match his crimes? How does the Lord display forgiveness towards David (ch. 12)?

4. To what extent do the crimes of David's sons match his own? How far is David's indulgence of his children to blame for their actions (chs. 13–14)?

5. In what ways does David manifest his faith in the Lord during the flight from Jerusalem (ch. 15–16)?

6. How is David's prayer of 15:31 answered (chs. 16–17)?

7. Evaluate the impact of Joab's actions on David personally and politically (chs. 18–20).

2 Sam 21–24 Appendices *(pages 149–160)*

1. Is David portrayed positively or negatively in the incident of the Gibeonite bloodguilt (ch. 21)?

2. Does David's claim to be deserving of God's protection contradict the wider portrayal of God's gracious salvation (ch. 22)?

3. Why does David buy the threshing floor of Araunah? What does it later become (ch. 24)?

INDEX OF CITATIONS FROM THE
CATECHISM OF THE CATHOLIC CHURCH

The arabic number(s) following the citation refer(s) to the paragraph number(s) in the *Catechism of the Catholic Church*. The asterisk following a paragraph number indicates that the citation has been paraphrased.

1 Samuel		2 Samuel	
1	489*	7	709*
1:9-18	2578*	7:14	238,* 441*
3:9-10	2578	7:18-29	2579*
9:16	436*	7:28	215, 2465*
10:1	436*	12:1-4	2538*
12:23	2578	12:4	2538*
16:1	436*	12:7-15	1736*
16:12-13	436*		
16:13	695*		
28:19	633*		

Israel Settled in Canaan

····· APPROXIMATE BOUNDARY OF
       ISRAEL'S TRIBES
  ○   CITIES OF REFUGE

0 ————————————————— 30 Miles
0 ————————————————— 30 Kilometers

Sidon

Damascus

Mt. Lebanon

Mt. Hermon

Tyre

Dan
(Laish)

ARAM

Kedesh

ASHER

NAPHTALI

Hazor

Acco

Achshaph

Sea of
Chinnereth

Golan

Ashtaroth

Mt.
Carmel

ZEBULUN

Shimron

Mt.
Tabor

ISSACHAR

Edrei

The Great
Sea

Dor

Megiddo

Shunem

Ramoth-gilead

Wadi Kishon

Mt.
Gilboa

Beth-
shean

MANASSEH

Taanach

MANASSEH

Thebez

Zaphon

Mt. Ebal

Mt. Gerizim

Shechem

River Jordan

River
Jabbok

GAD

Joppa

Shiloh

EPHRAIM

Bethel

Rabbah

DAN

Gezer

BENJAMIN

Gibeah

Jericho

Bezer

AMMON

Ashdod

Ekron

Jerusalem

Mt. Pisgah

Mt. Nebo

Ashkelon

PHILISTINES

Beth-
shemesh

Bethlehem

REUBEN

Gath

Gaza

Hebron

The Salt Sea

Dibon

Debir

JUDAH

Ziklag

River
Arnon

Beer-
sheba

Brook
Besor

SIMEON

MOAB

The Negeb

Brook Zered

EDOM

LUCIDITY INFORMATION DESIGN, LLC

N

United Monarchy of Israel

- - - MAXIMUM EXTENT OF THE UNITED MONARCHY
AREAS OF INFLUENCE
CONQUERED AREAS
■ SITES FORTIFIED BY SOLOMON
ASHER ISRAELITE TRIBES
MOAB NON-ISRAELITE GROUPS

0 _____ 30 Miles
0 _____ 30 Kilometers

Sidon

Damascus

SIDONIANS

Mt. Lebanon

Mt. Hermon

Tyre

SYRIA (ARAM)

Abel-beth-maccah

Dan

ASHER

NAPHTALI

Hazor ■

Acco

Ashtaroth

Chinnereth

Sea of Chinnereth

Helam

Cabul

ZEBULUN

Mt. Carmel ▲

Mt. Tabor ▲

Jokneam

ISSACHAR

MANASSEH

Dor

Megiddo ■

Jezreel

Wadi Kishon

Ramoth-gilead

Taanach

Mt. Gilboa ▲

Beth-shean

Rogelim

The Great Sea

Hepher?

ISRAEL

Abel-menolah

MANASSEH

Samaria

Tirzah

Mt. Ebal ▲

Mahanaim

Mt. Gerizim ▲ Shechem

River Jabbok

Zarethan?

River Jordan

Joppa

Shiloh

GAD

EPHRAIM

Beth-horon ■

Bethel

Rabbah

Baalath? ■

BENJAMIN

Jericho

AMMON

Gezer ■

Gibeah

Ashdod

Ekron ■

✦ Jerusalem

Mt. Pisgah ▲

Gath? ■

Beth-shemesh

Mt. Nebo ▲

Ashkelon

PHILISTINES

Bethlehem

Gaza

Hebron

Dibon

Gerar

Carmel

The Salt Sea

Ziklag?

JUDAH

Beer-sheba

Arad

River Arnon

SIMEON

MOAB

Brook Besor

Kir-hareseth

The Negeb

Zoar

Brook Zered

Tamar ■

EDOM

N

LUCIDITY INFORMATION DESIGN, LLC